D0937423

Native American Catholic Studies Reader

Native American Catholic Studies Reader: History and Theology

David J. Endres, Editor

The Catholic University of America Press
Washington, DC

Copyright © 2022
The Catholic University of America Press
All rights reserved

The paper used in this publication meets the minimum requirements of American National Standards for Information Science—Permanence of Paper for Printed Library materials, ANSI Z39.48-1984.

∞

Cataloging-in-Publication Data available from the Library of Congress
ISBN: 978-0-8132-3589-9 | eISBN: 978-0-8132-3590-5

Contents

Native American Lives

Foreword

N O CULTURES CAN BE SAID to have been Christian at their start. Therefore, the history of indigenous peoples in the Americas is the story of adaptation, conversion, and change. My own tribe, the western Lakota (Sioux), accepted Catholicism and Christianity as an outgrowth of traditional spirituality. Catholicism's acceptance and growth can be seen as a form of natural development of and by the people. This development has not always been linear, however. There are fits and starts, beginnings and interruptions. A disruption, particularly impacting young native people, occurred during the 1960s when many were unsure what to believe: traditional Lakota religious practices or Catholicism or a combination of both?

This *Native American Catholic Studies Reader* offers non-Indian perspectives on the development of Catholicism among indigenous peoples. In exploring these dynamics, it provides a discussion that is critical today, especially for the benefit of those who may not be steeped in the tradition of their ancestors. The confusion among indigenous peoples is related to the loss of native language, often because Indian youth attended boarding schools and received a non-native education without being taught traditional native history, culture, and spirituality. The Lakota young people, for instance, who went to boarding schools often did not participate in Lakota Catholic activities and became distant from the Catholic practice of the community. Since faith practices were tied to the Lakota language, if they forgot their native language, they could no longer understand what was happening nor fully participate in Catholic activities.

Non-Indian scholars who have studied the phenomenon of native people accepting and adapting to Catholicism offer a vital perspective for native scholars who seek to understand the possible synthesis of the two belief systems. To synthesize the two, an understanding and appreciation of both are needed. To put both together, one needs to understand native spirituality and its belief system and Catholic understandings and practices.

Growing up in a traditional Lakota family and community, I do not remember efforts toward synthesizing the two belief systems. Unlike other languages that have been used to convey the faith, Lakota is not a written language. What is learned in Lakota is transmitted orally. Therefore, knowledge of traditional Lakota culture and spirituality is passed on by word from one generation to the next. Communication is enhanced by actions as many of the Lakota ceremonies are vigorously acted out. The living memory that these actions convey is lost for those who do not participate in traditional native ceremonies and activities. Perhaps the strong reaction against certain forms of education and their relationship to Christianity is because the schools successfully assimilated the native students. Many native youth missed the cultural learning that was necessary in their formative years.

The works presented here illustrate a broad picture of native evangelization and adaptation, showing the creative ways in which Christianity was passed on to native peoples. Some approaches were very effective, such as using native ceremonial practices and incorporating them into Catholic practice, teaching Christianity through the native languages, and showing pictures illustrating Catholic truths.

Many of the developments described in this volume are reflective of the old saying, "When I finally begin to understand what they are trying to teach me, everything changes." These changes can be experienced as both negative and positive. For native peoples, the speed at which the world changes seems only to accelerate, and they spend most of the time trying to play catch-up. Amidst so much change, the foundations of native peoples' lives are culture and spirituality. They keep native lives livable.

The constancy of the Catholic Church has helped native peoples navigate change, making the transition from Lakota beliefs to Catholic beliefs. The teachings of the Catholic Church are complex and not always understood. Not all native peoples accept them. For those that do, they must navigate a path of synthesis. At what point in their lives do native people become truly Catholic? The way of transformation is not always clear. Perhaps raising some native people to sainthood, who could serve as an example of this synthesis, may help.

For those interested in the relationship of Catholicism to Native Americans, the research presented in the *Native American Catholic Studies Reader* illustrates various perspectives that help us recognize that adaptation, conversion, and change are essential experiences of native peoples and Christian believers.

Ben Black Bear, Jr.

Introduction

THE STORY OF CATHOLICISM in the United States is often told beginning with the arrival of English colonists to Maryland. But before there was an immigrant American Church, there was a Native Church. By the seventeenth century, Catholic missionaries were active in the Great Lakes, South, and Southwest, including missions to Native Americans. Though the Native-Christian relationship could be marked by tension, coercion, and even violence, the Christian faith took root among Native Americans. For those who accepted it and bequeathed it to future generations, it became not an imposition but a natural expression of Native identity. Today, there are more than half a million Native American Catholics, representing one-fifth of indigenous people in the United States. More than 300 U.S. Catholic congregations predominately serve Native Americans, with many more worshipping in congregations that are not primarily indigenous.

Historians have noted the historical presence of Native Catholics, especially in the Great Plains, Southwest, and West, but in the last fifty years, Catholic scholars have intensified their study of indigenous Catholicism. These histories have highlighted the interaction of missionaries and tribal leaders, the relationship of traditional Native cosmology and religiosity to Christianity, and the role of geography and tribal consciousness in accepting and maintaining a Native-Catholic identity. Most recently, scholars have shifted attention to the more negative aspects of the Native-Christian exchange, including the destruction of Native culture and the difficult history of government- and Church-run boarding schools.

This *Native American Catholic Studies Reader* offers a curated collection of readings on the Native American Catholic experience. The *Reader* is divided into three sections: education and evangelization, tradition and transition, and Native American lives. It concludes with a selected bibliography. These readings highlight this emergent field and suggest further avenues for research and publication.

Assembled from several sources, this volume's articles include essays that first appeared in the *U.S. Catholic Historian.* Long-time editor Christopher J. Kauffman (1936–2018) brought scholarly attention to ethnic and racial minorities and oversaw the publication of two thematic issues devoted to Native American Catholics.[1] Other essays contained herein were initially printed in the *Catholic Historical Review.*

This volume's first section offers three studies of Native American education and evangelization. In the lead essay, Christopher Vecsey examines how missionaries communicated Christianity through print and image and the ways Native peoples responded to and claimed ownership of these means of expression. Next, Mark G. Thiel analyzes a visual method of communicating the faith: catechetical ladders. The late Gerald McKevitt, S.J., provides a case study of European Jesuits' efforts to spread the faith in the Pacific Northwest.

The second section of the *Reader* explores the theme of tradition and transition, examining the versatility of Native Catholic practice. In an essay on "Native Americans on the Path to the Catholic Church," Ross Enochs analyzes the ways that Native American culture and belief structures could either impede or encourage acceptance of Catholicism. The late Carl F. Starkloff, S.J., a well-known sociologist, narrates the struggles and tensions of Native Catholics since the 1960s. Based on fieldwork in Eastern Montana, Mark Clatterbuck explores the impact of the Catholic charismatic renewal on Native practice.

Finally, the third section examines Native American lives. The first Native American saint, Kateri Tekakwitha, and her successful "Americanization" is the subject of Allan Greer's study. Conor J. Donnan writes about the surprising relationship between Irish and Native Americans. In the final essay, Damian Costello considers Nicholas Black Elk, whose cause for sainthood has been introduced, arguing that Catholic sacramental theology and Native ontology share commonalities.

---

1   See *U.S. Catholic Historian* 16, no. 2 (Spring 1998) and 27, no. 1 (Winter 2009).

These assembled essays form a panoply of Native American Catholic scholarship. They collectively argue that even if tension marked some interactions between indigenous peoples and Catholicism, the faith of Native Catholics was expressed not as a foreign identity but as an inculturated one. Their faith became a means of communicating and celebrating language, family, and tribe. As Native peoples were among the first to hear and respond to the Gospel in the Western hemisphere, this volume explores the distinct history of Native Catholics as the American Church's eldest members.

David J. Endres
Editor, *U.S. Catholic Historian*

Contributor Biographies

Mark Clatterbuck

Mark Clatterbuck is associate professor and chair of the Religion Department and co-director of the Native American and Indigenous Studies Program at Montclair State University in Montclair, New Jersey. He has conducted extensive field research among Native Americans in Montana. He is the author of two books: *Demons, Saints, and Patriots: Catholic Visions of Native America* (2009) and *Crow Jesus: Personal Stories of Native Religious Belonging* (2017). His third book, now underway, explores spiritually-grounded environmental activism led by Indigenous communities.

Damian Costello

Damian Costello is director of postgraduate studies at NAIITS: An Indigenous Learning Community. His study of the intersection of Catholic theology, missionization, and indigenous spirituality have been informed by five years of ethnographic field work on the Navajo Nation. He is the author of *Black Elk: Colonialism and Lakota Catholicism* (2005).

Conor J. Donnan

Conor J. Donnan is a doctoral candidate in history at the University of Pennsylvania and an adjunct professor at Hood College in Frederick, Maryland. His research reconstructs the interactions of Irish Catholics and Native Americans against the backdrop of American imperial expansion, industrialization, and questions of citizenship in the trans-Mississippi West from 1840 to 1930.

Ross Enochs

Ross Enochs is assistant professor and chair of the Department of Philosophy and Religious Studies at Marist College in Poughkeepsie, New York. His scholarly publications include *The Jesuit*

Mission to the Lakota Sioux: Pastoral Theology and Ministry, 1886–1945 (1996) and a chapter, "Black Elk and the Jesuits," in *The Black Elk Reader* (2000).

Allan Greer

Allan Greer, professor of history and Canada Research Chair in Colonial North America at McGill University in Montreal, Canada, is author of *Mohawk Saint: Catherine Tekakwitha and the Jesuits* (2005), *La Nouvelle-France et le monde* (2009), *Property and Dispossession: Natives, Empires and Land in Early Modern North America* (2018), among other publications. He was the recipient of a Guggenheim Foundation Fellowship and a Killam Research Fellowship and has been a visiting scholar at Cambridge University, the John Carter Brown Library, and the Institut d'études avancées de Paris.

Gerald McKevitt, S.J.

Father Gerald McKevitt, S.J. (1939–2015) served as archivist and professor of history at Santa Clara University. He wrote extensively on Jesuits in the American West, including their missionary work among Native Americans.

Carl F. Starkloff, S.J.

Father Carl F. Starkloff, S.J. (1933–2008) served as a professor at Regis College in the Toronto School of Theology. He focused his studies on Native Americans and religion, especially the role of syncretism and inculturation. His works included *The People of the Center: American Indian Religion and Christianity* (1974) and *A Theology of the In-between: The Value of Syncretic Process* (2002).

Mark G. Thiel

Mark G. Thiel is archivist emeritus at Marquette University, Milwaukee, Wisconsin. He administered its Native Catholic collections and has coauthored or edited several books: *Guide to Catholic Indian Mission and School Records in Midwest Repositories* (1984), *The Crossing of Two Roads: Being Catholic and Native in the United States*

(2003) (with Christopher Vecsey and Marie Therese Archambault), and *Native Footsteps: Along the Path of Saint Kateri Tekakwitha* (2012) (with Christopher Vecsey).

Christopher Vecsey

Christopher Vecsey is the Harry Emerson Fosdick Professor of the Humanities, Native American Studies, and Religion at Colgate University. He is the author of several books about American Indian Catholics, including *On the Padres' Trail* (1996), *The Paths of Kateri's Kin* (1997), and *Where the Two Roads Meet* (1999). Most recently, he has co-edited *Native Footsteps: Along the Path of Saint Kateri Tekakwitha* (2012) (with Mark G. Thiel).

The Good News in Print and Image: Catholic Evangeliteracy in Native America

CHRISTOPHER VECSEY*

I N COMPARATIVE STUDY of New World colonialism and the culture of writing, I am interested in how Christian missionaries—especially Roman Catholics—employed writing in their evangelism, and how the Indians of the Americas have responded—primarily within the regions now controlled by the United States. How important was literacy in the evangelical process and how important in the indigenous reply?

One might say that the "colonial" epoch ended in 1776, or perhaps in 1821, or one might perceive its persistence to the present for these colonialized peoples. There is a colonizing continuum between past and present; therefore, I am looking at five centuries of "evangeliteracy"—a word I have coined to indicate that the spreading of the word and the writing of the word have often gone hand in hand.

The Book and the Land

Today a sharp dichotomy is made between "cultures of the book" (evolved from "religions of the Book") and "Native American understandings of land"[1]; indeed, one critic calls Western culture in

---

* Passages in this article appear in the author's works: *On the Padres' Trail* (Notre Dame, IN: University of Notre Dame Press, 1996), *The Paths of Kateri's Kin* (Notre Dame, IN: University of Notre Dame Press, 1997), and *Where the Two Roads Meet* (Notre Dame, IN: University of Notre Dame Press, 1999). Used here with permission of University of Notre Dame Press. This selection was previously published in *U.S. Catholic Historian* 27, no. 1 (Winter 2009): 1–19.

1   Philip P. Arnold, "Black Elk and Book Culture," *Journal of the American Academy of Religion* 67, no. 1 (1999): 86–87.

America one big "paper chase."[2] In 1969 Lakota theologian Vine Deloria, Jr., provided rhetorical flourish to this distinction: "It has been said of missionaries that when they arrived they had only the Book and we had the land; now we have the Book and they have the land."[3]

Walter D. Mignolo has examined "the complicity between language and religion"[4] in the New World. He writes of the colonizing process regarding Indian languages through alphabetic writing: reducing them to written, latinized translations and grammars. As Christian missioners subjected Indian communities to reductions—centralizing them for the process of indoctrination and control—they also reduced Indian languages to alphabetic hegemony, according to Mignolo. To the religious colonizers of New Spain, like Pedro de Gante, Bernardo de Sahagún, or Diego de Landa, the basic difference between themselves and Indians was that the latter were unlettered; the indigenes employed images in their lives, but not the alphabetic, encyclopedic exactitude of written expression.

The same could be said of Protestants, as well as Catholics. The Reformation, after all, was a media revolution as well as an ecclesiastical one. Martin Luther and his followers buttressed their preaching with pamphlet propaganda and they translated the Bible into the vernacular languages of Europe and beyond. Europe was becoming a culture of books, just as the New World was discovered. Until 1500, about 27,000 texts had been printed on the continent—about ten million items. In the next century, as Protestants and Catholics vied for spiritual supremacy, the number of titles grew fivefold, amounting to 500 million printed books by the beginning of the seventeenth century (although it should be noted that many were heavily illustrated). Protestants in New England, even more than Catholics in New Spain, regarded writing as an essential ingre-

---

2   Philip P. Arnold, "Paper Ties to Land: Indigenous and Colonial Material Orientations to the Valley of Mexico," *History of Religions* 35, no. 1 (1995): 58.

3   Vine Deloria, Jr., *Custer Died for Your Sins: An Indian Manifesto* (New York: Macmillan, 1969), 101.

4   Walter D. Mignolo, *The Darker Side of the Renaissance: Literacy, Territoriality, and Colonization*, 2nd ed. (Ann Arbor, MI: University of Michigan Press, 2003), 31.

dient in missionary effort, absolutely necessary for godliness and civility among the Native converts.[5]

Modern, Western theorists like Jack Goody[6] and Walter Ong[7] have emphasized the dichotomy between literate and non-literate peoples: the key to defining "modern"—supposedly logical, scientific, abstract, skeptical, historical—and "traditional"—putatively pre-logical, primitive, savage, mythopoeic—ways of thinking in contrast to one another. More recent critics[8] have thrown doubt on these theoretical models, and I am not compelled by the stark distinctions Goody and Ong delineate.

Visual and Literary Evangelism

For, as we shall see, Catholic evangelical culture in the Americas was highly visual—relying largely on images—and participatory—emphasizing sacramental liturgy like baptisms, processions, dramas, recitations of rosaries, and the like. At the same time the Indians of the Americas had their own forms of writing and record keeping, not all of them imagic. Amidst the alphabets, syllabaries, and pictograms[9] of the world's writing systems—the grammatology of Mesopotamian cuneiform, Egyptian hieroglyphs, Semitic epigraphic scripts, Asian calligraphy, Greek alphabet, musical notations, etc.[10]—we find Mayan and other Mesoamerican scripts—as many as a dozen different kinds. Gary Urton's attempt to decipher Andean khipus for their narrative threads beyond accounting and

---

5 Hilary E. Wyss, *Writing Indians: Literacy, Christianity, and Native Community in Early America* (Amherst: University of Massachusetts Press, 2000), 7–8.

6 Jack Goody, *The Domestication of the Savage Mind* (New York: Cambridge University Press, 1977), and Jack Goody, ed., *Literacy in Traditional Societies* (New York: Cambridge University Press, 1968).

7 Walter J. Ong, *Orality and Literacy: The Technologizing of the World* (London: Methuen, 1982).

8 Marilyn Cooper, *Writing as Social Action* (Portsmouth, NH: Heinemann, 1989), and Sylvia Scribner and Michael Cole, *The Psychology of Literacy* (Cambridge, MA: Harvard University Press, 1981).

9 Akira Nakanishi, *Writing Systems of the World: Alphabets, Syllabaries, Pictograms* (Rutland, VT: C.E. Tuttle, 1990).

10 Peter T. Daniels and William Bright, eds., *The World's Writing Systems* (New York: Oxford University Press, 1996).

recounting, i.e., beyond mathematics and mnemonics,[11] suggests writing in South as well as Mesoamerican civilizations. In the boondocks of Native North America one can see the various types of picture-writing,[12] including birchbark scrolls of the Ojibways, wampum belts among the Iroquois,[13] Siouian winter counts, etc.

Gordon Brotherston has gathered various imagic texts of the New World in a book, illustrating aboriginal Native worldview.[14] Spaniards noted not only Mayan writing, but also Nahuatl books and calendars. The Indians of Mexico had developed technologies to produce paper, although it was employed primarily for ceremonial banners and costumes; whereas colonists used paper for intellectual purposes: printed books, legal documents, land titles, and the like. Janet Catherine Berlo has shown that Indian verbal and visual arts were combined[15]; however, Arthur G. Miller argues how little writing there was in the Americas, even among the Mayans, when compared with European literacy, and how "purposeful" was the Indians' use of "visual imagery," taking on the "burden of writing" in the New World. Pre-Hispanic America was, relatively speaking, "a civilization of few written words."[16]

---

11 Gary Urton, *Signs of the Inka Khipu: Binary Coding in the Andean Knotted-string Records* (Austin: University of Texas Press, 2003), and Jeffrey Quilter and Gary Urton, *Narrative Threads: Accounting and Recounting in Andean Khipu* (Austin: University of Texas Press, 2002).

12 Garrick Mallery, *Picture-writing of the American Indians*, Bureau of American Ethnology Annual Report 10 (Washington, DC: Government Printing Office, 1893).

13 Tehanetorens, *Wampum Belts* (Onchiota, NY: Six Nations Indian Museum, 1972).

14 Gordon Brotherston, ed., *Image of the New World: The American Continent Portrayed in Native Texts* (London: Thames and Hudson, 1979).

15 Janet Catherine Berlo, ed., *Text and Image in Pre-Columbian Art: Essay on the Interrelationship of the Verbal and Visual Arts*, International Congress of Americanists Proceedings 44 (Oxford: British Archeological Reports, 1983).

16 Arthur G. Miller, "Image and Text in Pre-Hispanic Art: Apples and Oranges," in *Text and Image in Pre-Columbian Art: Essay on the Interrelationship of the Verbal and Visual Arts*, ed. by Janet Catherine Berlo, International Congress of Americanists Proceedings 44 (Oxford: British Archeological Reports, 1983), 45, 42.

Whatever we can say of the indigenous peoples of the Americas, the Christian missionaries came with writing, and used it as a technology helpful to their purposes. Literacy, territoriality, and colonization were partners in Christian expansion. According to Walter D. Mignolo, when Bernardo de Sahagún tried to supersede Nahuatl in the creation of his own Florentine Codex—recording Nahuatl rituals while aiming to destroy them—and when Diego de Landa put Mayan books to the torch in the Yucatan churchyard, the Catholic clerics were engaged in a cultural war, a contest of literacies, not just a struggle between writing and orality.

Over the past five centuries Native Americans have felt the influences of Christianity and millions of them have come to identify themselves as Christians. Among the 40 million self-identifying Indian peoples in the hemisphere (over two million in the United States, a million in Canada), the majority are Christians, including 350,000 Catholic Indians in the U.S. and a quarter million in Canada. In three volumes I analyzed the history of Native Catholicism in North America, assaying the various causes for Indian adoption of Catholic forms and the various adaptations between Catholic and Native cultures, including conversion, compartmentalization, and syncretism. In this essay I ask what role writing played in Catholic proselytism and what was writing's effect on the course of Indian Catholic participation.

Should writing be added to guns, germs and steel,[17] as technologies of European conquest? Surely as a means of communicating over long distance and of keeping administrative records, writing solidified the power of missionaries and their imperial allies. The evangelists were able to accumulate knowledge, to coordinate policy, to pass down successful techniques from generation to generation. In the nineteenth century, e.g., the Jesuit Pierre-Jean de Smet used a handbook of Paraguayan reductions from the seventeenth in order to create a wilderness kingdom of God in the Rocky Mountains, as he recorded in his voluminous letters.[18] (His fellow,

---

17   Jared Diamond, *Guns, Germs, and Steel: The Fates of Human Societies* (New York: W. W. Norton, 1997).

18   Hiram Martin Chittenden and Alfred Talbot Richardson, eds., *Life, Letters, and Travels of Father Pierre-Jean de Smet, S.J., 1801–1873*, 4 vols. (New York: Francis P. Harper, 1905).

Nicolas Point, S.J., kept his own Rocky Mountain mission records in exquisite paintings!)[19]

The origins of writing in Mesopotamia began with bureaucratic lists, and this Old World technology came to the Americas with evangelization. The missionaries kept excellent records—of baptisms, marriages, deaths, etc.—and in the process the Church became the Indians' historian, in some cases providing them with documented identity for longitudinal study. The Houma Indians of Louisiana, for instance, have been able to trace their lineages through the copious records of the Diocese of Houma-Thibodaux.[20] Even when certain peoples were extinguished—by disease, warfare, slavery, and acculturation—their memory was passed on in Catholic archives, like those in California. When members of a nearly defunct Californian tribe discovered an ancestor's name in the mission record books, they commented, "Did he but know it, that writing is his death-warrant?"[21]

Through writing, Catholic missionaries got to tell their own story, creating a cumulative tradition of representation—of themselves and of Indians. From Columbus in 1492, who said that the Caribbean islanders he met "would easily be made Christians"[22]; to Fray Alonso Benavides, who in 1630 wrote a glowing summary of Franciscan "pious tasks"[23] among the Pueblo Indians of New Mexico; to Fray Francisco Palóu, who gathered Junípero Serra's written effects in order to create a biography, which "has been the basic text employed by writers in producing the books,

---

19   Nicolas Point, S.J., *Wilderness Kingdom, Indian Life in the Rocky Mountains: 1840–1847*, trans. Joseph P. Donnelly, S.J. (New York: Holt, Rinehart & Winston, 1967).

20   Donald J. Hebert, *South Louisiana Records: Church and Civil Records of Lafourche-Terrebonne Parishes*, 12 vols. (Cecilia, LA: Donald J. Hebert, 1978–1985).

21   Charles Francis Saunders and J. Smeaton Chase, *The California Padres and Their Missions* (Boston: Houghton Mifflin, 1915), 334.

22   Christopher Columbus, *The Journal of Christopher Columbus*, trans. by Cecil Jane (New York: Bramhall House, 1960), 24.

23   Frederick Webb Hodge, George P. Hammond, and Agapito Rey, eds. and trans., *Fray Alonso de Benavides' Revised Memorial of 1634* (Albuquerque: University of New Mexico Press, 1945), 100.

articles, brochures, pageants and orations about Serra that in almost endless succession have appeared down to our day."[24] Right down to the *transumptum* for Serra's candidacy toward sainthood, the missionaries have produced documents of legitimization for their cause.

No ruling narratives of Catholic missions have been more famous than the *Jesuit Relations*[25] of New France: periodic reports from the field for regional superiors, who collated and edited the letters for viewing by Church superiors, but also for the educated classes of Europe. The *Relations* served as devotional literature and fundraising propaganda, with hagiographical accounts of converts such as the famous Mohawk Kateri Tekakwitha. Claude Chauchetière, S.J., memorialized her not only in words, but also in a painting, still hanging at the Caughnawaga church where she lived and died in the late seventeenth century.

The *Jesuit Relations* have served scholars for generations in piecing together the interactions among missionaries and Indians in New France. Numerous record groups are now accessible through Marquette University's "Guide to Catholic Records about Native Americans in the United States."[26]

Of course, these archives include some Indian viewpoints; however, missionaries maintain their hegemony, even when (or especially when) representing Indian responses to proselytism. Sahagún's fictionalized colloquies between sixteenth-century Franciscans and Nahuatl priests; debates with a Montagnais holy man in the seventeenth century; disputations with Canadian Ojibways, recorded by Jesuits in the 1840s—all of them had the ring of ventriloquy. Even when Indians got their seeming say, the missionaries remained the authors of the texts.

---

24 Maynard J. Geiger, O.F.M., *Palóu's Life of Fray Junípero Serra* (Washington, DC: Academy of American Franciscan History, 1955), ix.

25 Reuben Gold Thwaites, ed., *The Jesuit Relations and Allied Documents*, 73 vols. (Cleveland: Burrows Brothers, 1896–1901).

26 Marquette University, Department of Special Collections and University Archives, "Guide to Catholic Records about Native Americans in the United States," https://www.marquette.edu/library/archives/NativeGuide/.

The most sustained and most thoroughly documented dialogue between missionaries and Indians, the medicine men and clergy meetings organized by William F. Stolzman, S.J., on the Lakota Rosebud Reservations in the 1970s, constituted a breakthrough, because it was tape-recorded and largely transcribed. Nonetheless, the transcriptions omitted all statements in Lakota language. In writing, thus, only English speakers got their sound bites.

The publication of *Black Elk Speaks* in 1932[27] enraged the Jesuits at Pine Ridge Reservation, and they made the Lakota holy man and Catholic catechist, Nicholas Black Elk, sign two disavowals of the book, which seemed to glorify his pagan past and suggested his partial apostasy from Catholicism. To backslide in print created a scandal requiring drastic action: two written recantations, each with his shaky signature (he was functionally illiterate in English), to be kept in the permanent Jesuit archive, symbols of their power over his faith. Nothing more exemplified the Catholic missionary attempt to control its historical records.

Catholic evangelism relied on writing to keep its accounts, to tell its story, and also to proclaim its public power. In 1493, one year after Columbus' landfall, Pope Alexander VI produced the famous bull, *Inter caetera*, which claimed the right of "discovery" by Christian sovereigns. A subsequent bull divided the New World between Portugal and Spain, providing them with the power to initiate empires for the purpose of expanding Christian institutions and faith among the Natives of the New World. These proclamations carried legal weight against other European powers, and against the Indians and their own territorial autonomy.

Twenty years later the Spanish jurist, Palacio Rubios, penned "the Requirement,"[28] a document to be read aloud in Spanish by each "discoverer" upon encountering the American indigenes in their lands. The Requirement recounted biblical history and the papal succession from St. Peter, "Lord and Superior of all the men

---

27 John G. Neihardt, *Black Elk Speaks* (New York: William Morrow, 1932).

28 John H. Parry and Robert G. Keith, eds., *New Iberian World: A Documentary History of the Discovery and Settlement of Latin America to the Early 17th Century* (New York: Times Books, 1984), 289–290.

in the world," to "One of these Pontiffs, who . . . made donation of these isles and Tierra-firme" to the Spanish sovereigns: "So their Highnesses are kings and lords of these islands and land of Tierra-firme by virtue of this donation."

The Requirement then came to the crux of the matter:

> We ask and require . . . that you consider what we have said to you, and that you take the time that shall be necessary to understand and deliberate upon it, and that you acknowledge the Church as the Ruler and Superior of the whole world, and the high priest called Pope, and in his name the King and Queen . . . as superiors and lords and kings, . . . and that you consent and give place that these religious fathers should declare and preach to you the aforesaid.

> If you do so, you will do well, . . . and we . . . shall receive you in all love and charity, and shall leave you and your wives, and your children, and your lands, free without servitude.

The Requirement promised that conversion was to be voluntary, following religious instruction; however, should the Indians prevent the preaching of the Christian faith, or make delay in deciding,

> With the help of God, we shall powerfully enter into your country, and shall make war against you in all ways and manners that we can, and shall subject you to the yoke and obedience of the Church and of their Highnesses; we shall take you and your wives and your children, and shall make slaves of them, and as such shall sell and dispose of them as their Highnesses may command; and we shall take away your goods, and shall do you all the mischief and damage that we can, as to vassals who do not obey, and refuse to receive their lord and resist and contradict him; and we protest that the deaths and losses which shall accrue from this are your fault. . . .

The Spaniards employed this written document throughout the sixteenth century, thereby setting a militant theological tone—not unlike that of Islamic *jihad*—for the spread of Christianity in the Americas.

Indeed, the first centuries of Spanish Catholic expansion to the Americas were less about "mission" (going out to convince the

Natives, leaving open a choice of acceptance or refusal) than they were about proclaiming, instructing, and baptizing, under legal authority of the Crown, itself under the aegis of the Church. The written word served these latter purposes.

At the same time, the public proclamations of "discovery" and "requirement" were part of the ritualized drama of establishment, like planting crosses and displaying rosaries and iconic images, as Coronado did among the Pueblos in 1540. Coronado's companion, Fray de Padilla, noted that,

> In the places where we erected crosses, we taught the natives to venerate them, and they offered them their powders and feathers, some even the blankets they were wearing. They did it with such eagerness that some climbed on the backs of others in order to reach the arms of the crosses to put plumes and roses on them. Others brought ladders, and while some held them others climbed up to tie strings in order to fasten the roses and feathers.[29]

Juan de Oñate read the Requirement and displayed Catholic paraphernalia at Acoma Pueblo and elsewhere in 1598. He and his soldiers staged a reenactment of Cortés' conquest of Mexico, carrying a banner of Our Lady and dancing a pageant of Spanish military might, *Los Moros y Cristianós*, in order to impress the Indians. Thus he initiated what he called "the conversion of the souls of these Indians, the exaltation of the Holy Catholic Church, and the preaching of the Holy Gospel."[30]

Almost two hundred years later, in 1769, Governor Don Gaspar de Portola and Father Juan Crespi planted crosses along the coast of Alta California, and Father Francis Norbert Blanchet did the same on Whidbey Island in the Puget Sound in 1840. The ritual power of the cross was at least as powerful as any words on a page. Even a defiant enemy of Euroamerican expansion like the Lakota

---

29 Allison Bird, *Heart of the Dragonfly: Historical Development of the Cross Necklaces of the Pueblo and Navajo Peoples* (Albuquerque: Avanju, 1992), 2.

30 John L. Kessell, *Kiva, Cross, and Crown: The Pecos Indians and New Mexico, 1540–1840* (Washington, DC: National Park Service, U.S. Department of the Interior, 1979), 78–79.

warrior, Sitting Bull, was known in the late nineteenth century to wear a crucifix given to him by Father de Smet.

The Authority of the Word

Beyond proclamation, Catholic evangelizers employed writing in the creation of doctrinal and catechetical texts, devices to help subjugate Indians' wills to God's will through education, and instruments of strategy in explicating the sinfulness to be overcome by churchly grace. Codification also took place in ritual dramas and displays, which Indians like the Yaquis of Mexico (and now of Arizona) took as their own, especially during Holy Week commemorations, with their *maestros* keeping written notations in their sacerdotal guidebooks. For the Catholic priests, however, *doctrinas* and *confesionarios* comprised the instructional literature for enculturation and introspection among the Natives.

The central doctrines of late medieval Christianity focused upon a single, all-powerful God who gives eternal rewards or punishments to humans, depending on their service or offense to Him. This one God consists of a trinity of persons—Father, Son, and Holy Spirit—each fully divine and fully effective in the activities of creation, salvation, and judgment. Human sinfulness, epitomized by Adam and Eve's proud disobedience to God's command, is atoned for by the sacrificial suffering, blood, and death of Jesus in order to redeem humans from their alienation from God on earth, and even an eternity of alienation in hell. Most Catholics of the colonial period believed membership in the Church created by Christ was necessary for salvation. The Catholic Church was the visible means by which God provided the grace necessary for humans to overcome their sinfulness and perhaps to attain heaven. Baptism was the sacramental initiation into the Church; penance was available for the forgiveness of individual sins; and the Eucharist provided direct rapport between humans and God.

The Church's liturgical calendar designated seasons (Advent, Christmas, Lent, Easter, Pentecost), marking the salvific events of Jesus' life and individual days celebrating the Christian saints, whose lives served as models of heroic virtue and whose powers could be tapped in order to intercede to God and to aid particular enterprises, such as warfare. Mary, the mother of Jesus, was the greatest of the saints, as intercessor and helper. Rites of passage—baptism, matrimony, extreme unction before death—marked a person's life as sacred. Creeds and other prayers reminded Catholics daily of the doctrinal content of the Church's faith. Sacramentals, such as the praying of the Rosary or the Stations of the Cross, helped persons to meditate upon God and practice sanctioned modes of devotionalism.

The Church itself was sacramental—an outward institution created by Christ to give grace to humans—and its hierarchical and geographical organization (its bishops, priests, dioceses, parishes, religious orders, and sodalities, all under the authority of the pope and his clergy) claimed authority to teach doctrines and morals; to nurture the faithful and punish wrongdoers; to validate and censure political rulers. Church authorities held rightful power deriving from God Himself; to exercise that power, they said, was to insure order in this world and salvation in the next. In a world in which the devil was a theological fact, an embodiment of evil who fought mightily against Jesus, the authority of the Church was considered a bulwark in a cosmic struggle.

Missionaries focused instruction upon American Indian youths—especially the sons of the Native aristocracy—as a means of building a future Church, but also of influencing the adults. The publication of the papal bull *Sublimis deus* in 1537 underscored the necessity of instructing rational, ensouled Indians in Christian doctrine. Neophytes were to declare themselves against traditional Indian religion, and through the instruction grounded in the *doctrinas* and *confesionarios*, they were to memorize the rudiments of Christian catechetical knowledge and to examine their conscience. "Sometimes," it is said regarding Mexican Indians, "they made their confessions in writing, which . . . had been done in their confession to the pagan goddess."[31]

In contemplating the human condition, innate sinfulness was the major message of these written texts. Two examples of these

---

31   Charles S. Braden, *Religious Aspects of the Conquest of Mexico* (Durham, NC: Duke University Press, 1930), 233.

writings—one produced in Florida in 1613, the other in Alta California in 1798—make that clear. Fray Francisco Pareja's 1613 *confesionario*,[32] a booklet written in Timucua and Spanish, guided the priests to root out the ceremonies, omens, and religious beliefs of the Timucua Indians. The aim was to turn the Indians from their aboriginal orientation (guided by dreams, auguries, taboos, and the like) toward the Christian God. In the missionary worldview the supernaturals to which the Indians entrusted their lives were devils, pictured in the *confesionario* woodcuts carrying off a naked Native or trying to keep a neophyte from making confession. These images were used as a vivid reminder of the devilish spirits, in order to hasten the acceptance of Christianity and to prevent backsliding. The *confesionario* promulgated a Christian ethic, emphasizing sins of sexuality, and also abortions, untruths, thievery, witchcraft, as well as various superstitions.

Fray Juan Cortés' *doctrina* and *confesionario* of 1798 aimed to inculcate the same lessons among the Chumash Indians, reminding the neophytes of the importance of a good confession:

> If you die in sin, your soul goes to Hell to suffer forever from every ill and every infirmity, much hunger, much thirst, much coldness, eternal darkness, and you will be there burning like a tile in the furnace, suffering such as I am unable to describe. But if you are good and have no sin, you will go to heaven with God for eternity, where all the good things and all the sweet things and all the beautiful things are. There, best of all, you will see God, Jesus Christ, Blessed Mary. . . .[33]

The priests hoped that by reciting such *doctrinas* and reflecting upon such *confesionarios*, the California Indians would enter the Christian worldview and way of life.

---

32   Jerald T. Milanich and William C. Sturtevant, eds., *Francisco Pareja's 1613 Confesionario: A Documentary Source for Timucuan Ethnography* (Tallahassee: Division of Archives, History, and Records Management, Florida Department of State, 1972).

33   Harry Kelsey, *The Doctrina and Confesionario of Juan Cortés* (Altadena, CA: Howling Coyote Press, 1979), 118.

Pictorial Catechesis

If we emphasize the place of writing in codifying Christian doctrine for the colonial edification of America's Natives, we should not neglect the pictorial catechisms used everywhere from the Quechuas[34] to the Micmacs, and beyond. In North America the Recollect Chrétien Le Clercq developed a hieroglyphic system for teaching prayers and catechism to the Micmacs. He wrote these glyphs on paper and the Indians treated them with great devotion—as they would their aboriginal mnemonic parchments—by placing them in bark cases with wampum beads and porcupine quills. Le Clercq wrote that the Indians "scruple to throw them into the fire. When they are torn or spoiled, they bring the fragments to me. They are more religious, a hundred-fold, than the Iconoclasts, who, through a sacrilegious impurity, broke the most sacred images."[35] Through these scrolls, and later through an alphabet developed by another priest, the Micmacs became accustomed to voicing Catholic ideas—like the Lord's Prayer[36]—in their own language.

The Jesuits of New France made use of pictography—in the dirt, on bark, and on paper—to express the tenets of Christian faith to the Indians. They also used pieces of wood to indicate lessons, giving these sticks and their catechetical meanings to prayer chiefs to employ among Indians in the absence of clerics. In 1646 Jerome Lalemant, S.J., called these devices "books."[37] Father Jean Pierron, S.J. and other priests made use of paintings, engravings, and tableaux to make palpable the decisive events of the last judgment and the eternal fates of heaven and hell. These illustrations made it clear, at least in the Jesuits' minds, how momentous a decision it was for Indians to choose or reject baptism and Christian identity. Music and games

---

34   Barbara H. Jaye and William P. Mitchell, eds., *Picturing Faith: A Facsimile Edition of the Pictographic Quechua Catechism in the Huntington Free Library* (Bronx: Huntington Free Library, 1999).

35   Chrétien Le Clercq, *New Relation of Gaspesia, with the Customs and Religion of the Gaspesian Indians*, trans. and ed. by William F. Ganong (Toronto: Champlain Society, 1910), 133.

36   Chrétien Le Clercq, *First Establishment of the Faith in New France*, trans. by John Gilmary Shea (New York: John G. Shea, 1881), opposite 16.

37   Thwaites, *Jesuit Relations*, 18: 151.

also had catechetical purposes in the Jesuit missions, and the priests of New France described the Indian converts in their confessionals, recalling their sins with mnemonic aids—pieces of stick, drawings on bark or skin, calendrical etchings, and even rosaries. Thus, writing was important but no more significant a tool than various types of imagery, in advancing the Christian faith.

When Catholic evangelism reached the Indians of Oregon Country in the nineteenth century, Father Francis Norbert Blanchet designed for their "untutored minds"[38] a teaching device with marks indicating Christian ideas, e.g., a cross symbolizing the crucifixion. Like priests before him for several centuries, Blanchet created a mnemonic device for catechetical purposes, which the Indians called in Chinook Jargon the Sahale (Heaven) or Soul Stick. From these first carvings Father Blanchet soon concocted what he called a ladder, like that seen by the patriarch Jacob in his biblical dream, from which the Lord spoke. It was a pictorial catechism, a chart of ink on paper with linen backing. The priests and the Indians hung these charts from trees as the reference points for instruction. The ladder made it possible to expand upon the rudimentary message of the Sahale Stick, and in 1842 Blanchet began to manufacture many copies of his diagram.

The Catholic ladder marked Christian history with bars (centuries) and dots (years), from Adam through Christ to 1842, from the beginning of time to the present day. It pictured biblical scenes: Adam and Eve in the garden, the Tower of Babel, Noah's ark, Sodom and Gomorrah, the commandments at Mount Sinai, Solomon's Temple, and so on. The appearance of the star of Bethlehem introduced redemptive history, followed by representations of the Virgin Mary and Jesus, His life, death, resurrection, and ascension. The Holy Roman Catholic Church appeared with its sacraments, commandments, and prayers, as well as its creeds. St. Peter's Basilica represented Catholicism at the core. A branch veering from a central path showed the heretics, from Martin Luther and John Calvin to King Henry VIII, leaving the true Church. Other markings represented the doctrines of Catholic theology.

---

38   Francis Norbert Blanchet, *The Key to the Catholic Ladder* (New York: T.W. Strong, 1859), 1.

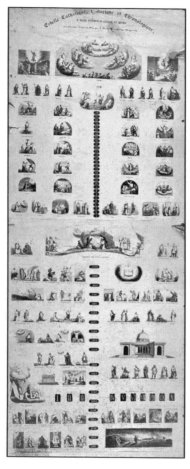

The Catholic Ladder by Father Francis Blanchet, ca. 1856 (Courtesy of Department of Special Collections and University Archives, Marquette University Libraries).

In the decades that followed, Father Albert Lacombe, an Oblate missionary among the Blackfoot in western Canada, produced a colorful elaboration of Blanchet's ladder,[39] organized around two paths, ascending in parallel lines, one toward heavenly reward and the other to eternal damnation, thus illustrating the crucial choice

---

39   Albert Lacombe, *Pictorial Catechism* (Montreal: C.O. Beauchemin, & Fils, 1896).

Indians must make to determine their fate. Lacombe's Ladder received papal approval and remained in use well into the twentieth century—as did Blanchet's original ladder.

Acculturation, Conversion, and Conquest

Whether employing writing or images, Catholic missionaries had in mind to overturn Indian ways of life. Whatever the technological innovations, the larger goal was to acculturate Indians from their known world and to superimpose a new framework for understanding all manner of things. By superposition—imposing Catholic structures atop traditional Indian edifices; by dazzling displays of generosity, ceremonialism, and military force; by establishing institutional structures of stability and control, missionaries aimed to place themselves at the center of Indian life. They hoped, in the long run at least, for a "total renewal"[40] of Indian life according to a Christian model: conversion, which meant turning away from Native tradition as well as turning to Catholic life.

Toward this end, writing was but one aspect of innovation. When Spanish evangelists entered the Indian world in order to transform it, they introduced all manner of new material culture: domesticated animals and agricultural bounty. They taught occupations, and tutored Indians in music and Christian hymnody. In that context they also established schools and taught Latin, Spanish, reading, writing, math, along with Christian doctrine.

In the formative missions of Alta California, the Franciscans operated total institutions of conquest. The Indians there planted, weeded, harvested, and milled the fields and tended the kitchen gardens. They herded sheep and cared for the livestock; they tended orchards and vineyards. In addition, they constructed and maintained aqueducts, dams, and reservoirs. The neophytes made pottery and also bricks and tiles, from which mission buildings were fabricated, and they hauled and fashioned wood, laid adobe walls, and layered masonry. During each day they engaged in a

---

40   Robert Ricard, *The Spiritual Conquest of Mexico* (Berkeley: University of California Press, 1966), 284.

round of trades: making shoes, saddles, hats, clothes, candles, soap, wine, and olive oil. They tanned hides and melted tallow for mission revenues. They also spun wool, sheared sheep, wove cloth, and blacksmithed. Indian artists decorated the walls of churches, and Indian musicians performed in orchestras and choirs, playing instruments made in the mission workshops. Reading and writing did not take up many of the neophytes' hours.

If we look to literacy as a factor in Indian conversion to Catholicism, it smalls even more on the horizon when we consider the effects of contagious diseases brought along by the European invaders and incubated disastrously in the mission hotbeds. We know that Indians died by the millions, with the concomitant result of multiple losses: of Native stability, autonomy, and religious faith. The powers of writing and imaging were little, in comparison to these sea changes that opened their hearts for conversion.

Nonetheless, Catholic missionaries understood the importance of language in their quotidian work. Even in New France—often perceived as an exemplar of Jesuit accommodation to Indian culture—the transforming of Indian languages was a primary task. Father Paul Le Jeune, S.J., reminded his fellow Jesuits that "faith ... enters by the ear,"[41] and that Algonkian and Iroquoian languages were inadequate to express the profundities of Catholic doctrine. The Society of Jesus contained skilled and determined linguists, who employed their Latin-based grammatical training in order to recast Indian speech into Christian expression. Their hope was to grasp the Indian tongues with a device of Latin grammar, and then to translate Christian ideas into the Indian languages, using latinized forms. By thus "conquering"[42] Indian languages, the Jesuits desired to prevail over the Indians' paganism and bring them to Christian worldview and worship. Linguistics, carried out through writing and speech, was for the priests an engine of spiritual war-

---

41   Kenneth M. Morrison, "Discourse and the Accommodation of Values: Toward a Revision of Mission History," *Journal of the American Academy of Religion* 53, no. 3 (September 1985): 368.

42   Victor Egon Hanzeli, *Missionary Linguistics in New France: A Study of Seventeenth- and Eighteenth-Century Descriptions of American Indian Languages* (The Hague: Mouton, 1969), 45.

fare, and they became so adept at translation that by 1665 they requested from France a printing press with which they could produce in written form the Indian languages and Christian translations for New France. The Jesuits thus transmuted complex Christian concepts into Indian languages, by introducing new French terms, by constructing composites of Indian and French terms, and by using Indian words, all with the stamp of Latin grammar.

Indian languages had to be clarified through Latin, just as the pagan lands of the New World had to be purified by planted crosses. But purification was not so simple an assignment. As Louise Burkhart has shown so well, the translation of Christian terminology into Indian consciousness was a "slippery dialogue,"[43] in which meanings were hard to fix with any certainty. In my work,[44] I have investigated the complexity of translation, examining Father J.B. Boulet's 1879 version of the Lord's Prayer in Snohomish. Lushootseed linguist Vi Hilbert provided the insights, as she shifted the text between her Native tongue and English, demonstrating the cultural confusion within the prayer, as written by Boulet, whose goal, after all, was to move the Natives to a new cultural life, oriented to Jesus and the Church, without perpetuating their traditional worldview. Rendering religiousness in print was part of an attempt by Catholic missionaries to cause metamorphosis among the indigenes.

Native Employment of Literacy

What was the effect of literacy on Indians? Did they resist it? No, indeed, they adopted whatever technologies that seemed appropriate to them. One can thus find Yaqui *maestros*, who—in the absence of their expelled Jesuit instructors—took on the task of reading missals and breviaries and keeping devotional records, liturgies, calendars, and song texts in handwritten books which they themselves have transcribed over the centuries. The *maestros* are still sufficient in Latin and Spanish in order to lead standard prayers—the *Ave Maria*, the *Pater Noster*, the *Credo*, the *Salve*, the

---

43   Louise M. Burkhart, *The Slippery Earth: Nahua-Christian Moral Dialogue in Sixteenth-Century Mexico* (Tucson: University of Arizona Press, 1989).

44   Vecsey, *The Paths of Kateri's Kin*, 322–326.

Confiteor, and others. Other Indians, like the Micmacs and the Crees, adopted missionary syllables (the latter created by the Protestant missionary, James Evans, in the nineteenth century) without reticence. Mohawks have preserved their language partially through the recitation of Catholic hymn texts recorded in books. Mohawk is a recognized liturgical language in Catholic tradition, benefiting both Church and tribe.

Some Indians have learned to mimic the writing of sacred scripts without adopting the articles of Christian faith. Indeed, some Nativists, like the Delaware prophet, Neolin, in the eighteenth century, created their own pictorial Bibles whose message was to resist white encroachment in every form. The Midewiwin religion of the Ojibwa Indians—a formalization of their traditional religious beliefs and rituals combined with portions of Catholicism gained from the French—made use of birchbark scrolls which were consulted like biblical writings. One can see, then, that "the influence of European literacy by no means indicated a tacit approval of white culture in general or even literacy in particular."[45]

We might say that, for some Indians, "literacy was seen as having functional, not spiritual, value."[46] On the other hand, for some christianized Indians, writing was intimately connected to their new-formed faith. Andrew Blackbird, an Ottawa whose brother died on the eve of ordination to the Catholic priesthood, formulated twenty-one precepts of Ottawa lore, rules which syncretized Native and Christian moral concepts. They included diverse commandments, e.g., against stealing from one's neighbor, or coveting his goods, mocking or mimicking the thunderers, or eating with women during their menstruation.[47] Blackbird wrote these directives in a book of his own making, to help his fellows attain heaven.

---

45   Ronald Niezen, *Spirit Wars: Native North American Religions in the Age of Nation Building* (Berkeley: University of California Press, 2000), 207.

46   Niezen, *Spirit Wars*, 207.

47   Andrew J. Blackbird, *History of the Ottawa and Chippewa Indians of Michigan, and Grammar of Their Language* (Ypsilanti, MI: Ypsilantian Job Printing House, 1887), 103–105.

By the nineteenth century, Catholic Indians of North America, especially those men and women training for priesthood and sister-hood, were producing their own written documents. In *The Crossing of Two Roads: Being Catholic and Native in the United States*,[48] one can find the fruits of evangeliteracy: petitions, reminiscences, diaries, manifestos, missives written by literate Indians to priests, prelates, bureaucrats, the pope (Pius XII, in 1952), even to Santa Claus (in 1937). Although he could not write, the Lakota chief Red Cloud had a letter composed in 1877, asking for Catholic priests and sisters, "so that they could teach our people how to write and read."[49] In the 1930s, impoverished Lakotas penned letters to Catholic boarding school officials, requesting admission for their starving children, in the hope of gaining for them a literate education.

Probably the earliest literary work by a California Indian, "Con-versión de los San Luiseños de Alta California,"[50] was composed—at least in part—by a Catholic Indian youth named Pablo Tac while attending seminary in Rome in 1835. Within a decade, the destruction of the California missions in what is now the Diocese of San Diego was nigh complete in the throes of Mexican independence, secularization, and colonial greed for ecclesial and indigenous property. As the mis-sions collapsed around Tac's Luiseño people, they were seen, "clinging to pitiful scraps of paper which they claimed gave them title to their lands."[51] The next half century, following the American takeover of California, was a disaster for the Mission Indians. An eyewitness in 1903 saw the sorry eviction of Cupeño Indians. One Cupeño woman threw books and other material into a fire: "She explained that now they hated the white people and their religion and their books,"[52] which offered them no help in maintaining their tribal territory.

---

48   Marie Therese Archambault, O.S.F., Mark G. Thiel, and Christopher Vecsey, eds., *The Crossing of Two Roads: Being Catholic and Native in the United States* (Maryknoll, NY: Orbis, 2003).

49   Archambault, Thiel, and Vecsey, eds., *The Crossing of Two Roads*, 118.

50   Pablo Tac, *Indian Life and Customs at Mission San Luis Rey*, eds. and trans. by Minna Hewes and Gordon Hewes (San Luis Rey, CA: Old Mission, 1958).

51   Edith Buckland Webb, *Indian Life at the Old Missions* (Lincoln: Univer-sity of Nebraska Press, 1982), 300.

52   George Wharton James, *Picturesque Pala* (Pasadena, CA: Radiant Life Press, 1916), 51.

In the past century, the descendants of the Mission Indians have maintained a love-hate relationship with the Catholic Church. Today, one of the greatest sources of rankling among Catholic Luiseños is the loss of aboriginal culture brought about through Church evangelism. The Indians of the Diocese of San Diego had their religions "suppressed," according to one Luiseño Indian I interviewed in 1992: "We were very well evangelized."[53] Another Luiseõ reported that "ninety percent of the traditions are gone."[54] In their resentment, they said of their non-Indian pastor that he was more interested in his financial "books" than in his parishioners, and they took umbrage at his legalistic, "by-the-book"[55] approach to Native ministry.

So, today some Catholic Indians rue the book-based religion to which they find themselves attached. But were their ancestors initially attracted to Christianity in part because of its association with literacy and other forms of technology? Some Jesuits of New France thought so. Even as they were referred to as clerks of the fur trade, they also tried to play the role of magicians, performing amazing acts—employing magnets, magnifying glasses, almanacs, and the like—in order to draw the aura of the supernatural upon themselves, while claiming the power of their God over disease, drought, hunting, harvest, and war.

The Hurons may have shown amazement at a clock they encountered in the Jesuits' residence. The timepiece's mechanical motions and sounds caused them to think of it as a living person, "the Captain of the day,"[56] and the priests expressed a smug superiority to naïve Natives who could not fathom clockwork machinery. At the same time, however, the Hurons were as astonished by the Frenchmen's behavior—the foreigners obeyed the commands of their automatic "Captain" when it directed them to wake, eat, or pray—as they were by the machine itself. The wonder of the clock did not lead the Hurons automatically to conversion.

---

53   Vecsey, *On the Padres' Trail*, 322.
54   Vecsey, *On the Padres' Trail*, 322.
55   Vecsey, *On the Padres' Trail*, 343.
56   Thwaites, *Jesuit Relations*, 8: 111.

Nor did their amazement when the Jesuits were able to communicate with one another by reading the jots on bits of paper. It did seem like magic, like soul travel, like conjuring, that one priest could know the mind of another at great distance, simply by consulting these devices. Literacy earned the priests a reputation as wonder-workers—but also as sorcerers. If Christianity was the means by which these extraordinary feats were possible, perhaps the Indians would want a piece of the action; however, they might also wish to keep their distance from such potent dangers.

I have said that Indians came to Christianity, not primarily because of literacy, but rather because of the crises of health, land, community, autonomy, and subsistence, which swept over their existence. Spiritual conquest was a subset of the more general conquest of colonialism. They were also attracted at times to the powerful message of Christian doctrine, the splendor of its ritualism, the character and convictions of its evangelists, Protestant and Catholic alike.

Still, one should witness the testimony of a convert as he portrayed the attraction of Christianity to him. Little Pine, an Ojibwa of the nineteenth century, recalled a trip he made to Toronto:

> When I entered the place where the speaking paper (newspaper) is made, and saw the great machines by which it is done, and by which the papers are folded, I thought, "Ah, that is how it is with the English nation, every day they get more wise, every day they find out something new. The Great Spirit blesses them and teaches them all these things because they are Christians, and follow the true religion. Would that my people were enlightened and blessed in the same way!"[57]

For many Indians, conversion—for all its ambiguity—was a means toward Native agency, a way to share in the power and status of whites, which the Indians associated both with literacy and Christianity. To them the religion was a means of gaining wealth, power, and knowledge, and they wanted to share in those goods.

---

57 Edward F. Wilson, *Missionary Work among the Ojebway Indians* (London: Society for Promoting Christian Knowledge, 1886), 82.

Whatever the attraction of writing to Indians as part of the conversion process, by the twentieth century, many Catholic Indians had learned the ways of the written word to suit their various purposes. A Jesuit who had lived among the Mohawks for many years once told me how demanding they could be, when they needed something of him. "Priest! Write this down!,"[58] they barked, when they wanted him to fabricate records to please one bureaucracy or other. When Pueblo Indians were faced with episcopal proclamations and legal maneuvering in the Archdiocese of Santa Fe, including threats to shut down sacramental services unless the Pueblos gave in to Church demands—e.g., in Santo Domingo in 1935 or Isleta in 1965—Indian officials were reluctant to sign formal agreements and produced their own written ordinances.

My impression regarding contemporary American Indians is that they take more interest in the ceremonial procession, the image, the banner of Catholicism, than they do the written word when participating in their faith. Catholic Passamaquoddy in Maine revere their rosary beads and use them at funerals and other services. "They like prayer beads better than books," states one Passamaquoddy Catholic, "and in church you pray with books."[59]

When Indians are intent upon setting themselves apart from Christianity (Protestant or Catholic, as a symbol of Euroamerican colonialism), they often represent the written word as a failure of Western culture. Chief Seattle's famous speech of 1855 has become a classic statement of Indian rebuke for the ways of the white man:

> Your religion was written on tablets of stone by the iron finger of an angry God lest you forget. . . . The red man could never comprehend nor remember it. . . . Our religion is the tradition of our ancestors, . . . [t]he dreams of our old men, given to them in the solemn hours of the night by the great spirit and the visions of our leaders[,] and it is written in the hearts of our people.[60]

---

58   Vecsey, *The Paths of Kateri's Kin*, 126.
59   Vecsey, *The Paths of Kateri's Kin*, 165.
60   Vecsey, *The Paths of Kateri's Kin*, 350.

A Muskogee medicine man, Phillip Deere, once warned me against writing down words. (Obviously, I have paid his advice no mind.) He said that when you write down words, you freeze them, kill them, put them to sleep. For Deere, a word is important only when it is attached to a person whom you know and trust, someone to whom you are attached through kinship, shared work, and common place. On a page, as in the Bible, a word is untrustworthy and can be interpreted variously, without recourse to intent. Face-to-face, when you hear a person's words, and you see his or her mien, when the words' immediate contexts and applications are apparent, only then do they hold meanings for you, the recipient of the words. Your grandfather's advice is true and useful, Deere said, only if you remember it and reiterate it for yourself and perhaps for others.

Furthermore, Indians like Phillip Deere have encountered the written word in two main ways: in the Christian scriptures and in governmental treaties. In his view, neither has given Natives much reason to trust the integrity of writing. Christians have rarely lived up to the promises of their biblical ideals, and the United States has rarely honored its legal obligations. Thus, for Deere, the written word is not reliable.

Still, Indians use writing today in their arguments against the hegemony of Christianity, and the West more generally. Since the Columbian Quincentenary, members of the Indigenous Law Institute—including Shawnee/Lenape Steven Newcomb and Lakota Birgil Kills Straight, along with Onondaga faithkeeper Oren Lyons—have petitioned the papacy to rescind the 1493 bull, *Inter caetera*, and its successors. According to the text of the typewritten memorandum,

> These bulls provided the foundation of the theft of Indigenous lands throughout the world that continues up to this day. These bulls subjugated innocent and unsuspecting Native peoples and subjected them to more than five hundred years of slavery, genocide, and a less than human identity. These bulls established a process of land taking based upon the racist Christian "doctrine of discovery" that reached around the world. These bulls provided the foundation for Christian hegemony around the world. This doctrine became part of the Law of Nations and still provides the basis for discriminatory law against Indigenous peoples of the world. . . . We continue to

suffer from what could be called an international conspiracy of nations, now become nation-states, to continue to perpetuate this racist doctrine promulgated by the Roman Catholic Church.[61]

When Europeans arrived in the Americas, they proclaimed the "good news" of biblical Christianity. In word and deed, in print and image, they told American Indians what they knew and what to do. For all their righteous faculties, however, the invaders did not merit a monologue. In the early seventeenth century, a Christian Quechuan chronicler, Felipe Guáman Poma de Ayala, narrated the monumental history of his people in writing and drawing, as a critique of Spanish rule.

In North America, many Indian communities have produced their own chronicles, none more famous than *The Cherokee Phoenix*, first published in 1828, the product of Sequoyah's syllabary, Cherokee nationalism, and Protestant instruction. The *Phoenix* is still in print, one among hundreds of contemporary tribal newspapers. When Episcopalian-trained Vine Deloria, Jr., declared, "We Talk, You Listen"[62] in 1970, he may have been feeling the oats of American Indian Movement militancy. Yet, he stood in a tradition of Indians, having received Christian formation, ready to speak back to evangeliteracy, and to put it in writing.

---

61   Steven Newcomb, Birgil Kills Straight, and Oren Lyons, "Letter to Pope Benedict XVI," September 21, 2005. In author's possession.

62   Vine Deloria, Jr., *We Talk, You Listen: New Tribes, New Turf* (New York: Macmillan, 1970).

Catholic Ladders and
Native American Evangelization

MARK G. THIEL*

SAINTS PETER, PAUL, and Augustine successfully proclaimed the Christian God to the Greco-Roman world. They did this by presenting concise and tangible glimpses of their God as an active agent who guided humanity to salvation throughout history. They described a monotheistic and Trinitarian God and focused on the essential Christian belief in Jesus. By building on the people's existing concepts, symbols, and language, the earliest missionaries overcame cultural and linguistic barriers and introduced Gentile audiences to the new concept of the Messiah. They also avoided complex moral and theological concepts and made no assumptions about a people's existing religious ideas.[1]

Many missionaries were pragmatists. To communicate Christian teachings across languages, missionaries invented and borrowed instructional aids. One such device, the Catholic ladder, resembled a ladder and was a thematic sequence of symbols or pictures for instructing candidates on how to achieve heaven. Read bottom to top, it was carved into wood or printed on paper. The

---

* An earlier version of this essay was published in *U.S. Catholic Historian* 27, no. 1 (Winter 2009): 49–70.

1 In North America, the preaching methods of the first Jesuits and later those of Father François Blanchet, among other missionaries to Native Americans, closely followed the preaching methods of the apostles Peter and Paul. Their differences pertained largely to the cultural and historical backgrounds of their respective audiences. But in all instances, they presented the revelation of the Judeo-Christian God in chronological fashion, beginning with the Old Testament. In *De Catechizandis Rudibus* [The Catechizing of the Uninstructed], Saint Augustine echoed Peter and Paul. He stated that when instructing non-Christians, catechists must present revelation as a general and comprehensive story with the focus on the foreshadowing of Christ in the Old Testament and the belief that Jesus is the Christ in the New Testament.

Catholic ladder had many predecessors. In the Mexican State of Oaxaca during the sixteenth through eighteenth centuries, native converts and catechists and Spanish clergy relied on hieroglyphic traditions to convey Christian prayers, beliefs, and conduct,[2] and in New France during the seventeenth and eighteenth centuries, the Jesuits developed catechetical techniques with images and mnemonic devices that subsequent clergy also employed.

In New France, the Jesuits were the first evangelizers of Native Americans. Because many natives were anxious to trade with the French, they were hospitable to the Jesuits who maximized the opportunity to convert them with new strategies invented through experimentation. To convey the Christian message, the Jesuits clarified and simplified it in ways analogous to the Greco-Roman evangelizers, which necessitated extensive study of native languages. As needed, the Jesuits facilitated oral and visual learning by drawing impromptu pictures in the soil, on bark, and on paper, and regularly distributing pictures, rosaries, religious medals, and card games as instructional aids. Many of the pictures conveyed concepts of heaven, hell, and the Last Judgment with sharp contrasts between good and bad ways of conduct with outcomes of the saved and the condemned. Typically, heaven featured tranquil scenes of angels and the Virgin Mary whereas hell swarmed with snakes.[3]

In 1637 near Québec, the Jesuit Paul Le Jeune reported on his instructing of Makheabichtichiou, a Montagnais Indian leader. Le Jeune had presented him with a chronological summary of Christian salvation, which Makheabichtichiou reviewed by sketching the principal points in order. Le Jeune noted that, "[He] . . . took a pencil and marked upon the ground the different periods in their order, 'Here is he who made all, he begins in this place to create the Angels and the world; there he created the first man and the first

---

2   William P. McDonald, comp., "A Mazahua Picture Catechism (c. 1791)," *Christian Catechetical Texts* (Lewiston, NY: Edwin Mellen Press, 2011), 913–916.

3   Reuben Gold Thwaites, ed., *The Jesuit Relations and Allied Documents; Travels and Explorations of the Jesuit Missionaries in New France, 1610–1791; the Original French, Latin, and Italian Texts; with English Translations and Notes* (Cleveland: Burrows Brothers, 1896–1901); 2:53, 11:151–159.

woman; see how the race of men, increasing, divides, and offends God; here is the deluge, here are the Prophets,'—in short, he came up to our own time. . . ."

Makheabichtichiou's concise but matter-of-fact summary reflected the prevailing egalitarian nature of Native American societies in the Northeast. But Le Jeune, who was the Jesuit superior of Québec and a convert himself, sought a compelling way to persuade candidates to choose Christian teachings over their existing beliefs. At the time, the Jesuits experienced great difficulty in persuading their native neophytes. So, they were anxious to find effective approaches, and Le Jeune looked elsewhere and declined to build on Makheabichtichiou's model.[4]

Nonetheless, while the Jesuits failed to develop compelling native-centric conversion messages, their native collaboration resulted in some innovative elements that ultimately were included in Catholic ladders. In 1646, the Jesuit Jérôme Lalemant described a system of instructional sticks with color-coded and mnemonic symbols. "Black" denoted native beliefs, white symbolized daily Christian prayers, and red symbolized observances for Sundays and holy days. Jesuit-sanctioned symbols included rope dangles to denote deficiencies in need of correction and certain native designs denoted approved conduct and ways to thank God. During the 1670s, another Jesuit reported displaying a sequence of three large vivid pictures depicting the Last Judgment, heaven, and hell at his Ojibwa mission in present-day Wisconsin.[5]

From 1769 to the 1830s, native evangelization ebbed, as the Jesuit order had been disbanded, and few diocesan priests were available to replace them. Nonetheless, the available priests continued to evangelize with Jesuit-tested models while frontier laity, comprised of mixed-race natives and fur trade employees, taught Christian basics to their Native American friends and relatives.[6]

---

4   Thwaites, *Jesuit Relations,* 7: 101; 11:151–159, 177.

5   Thwaites, *Jesuit Relations,* 18: 151; 29: 45–46, 137, 141; 56: 135.

6   Christopher Vecsey, *The Paths of Kateri's Kin* (Notre Dame, IN: University of Notre Dame Press, 1997), 241, 292; Christian Feest, *Indianer: Ureinwohner Nordamerikas* (Schallaburg: Schallaburg Kulturbetriebsges, 2008), 85.

During the years after the War of 1812, Kenekuk, the Kickapoo prophet, preached a new native religious movement to his band, which had been ravaged by smallpox and whiskey. They resided first in adjacent portions of Illinois, Indiana, and Wisconsin, and then on the Kickapoo Reservation in Kansas, where some neighboring Potawatomi Indians joined them. This movement used Christian-inspired beliefs and prayers including hand-held pictographic sticks with prayer messages comparable to the earlier Jesuit devices. One stick, from Indiana in 1830, was made of maple wood and measured twelve by two inches. Its pictographs were arranged vertically in rows that represented heaven at the top and hell at the bottom. Also included were three sets of the same five symbols repeated along the shaft as mnemonics for memorized prayers or stories. The sides were painted red and green respectively and the verso remained blank.[7]

Meanwhile, the dramatic influx of European immigrants necessitated the recruitment of priests to serve in the United States. Individual dioceses recruited them in Europe, some of whom became missionaries to Native Americans. In 1833, the Second Baltimore Council, a gathering of American bishops, recommended that the newly restored Society of Jesus (Jesuits) should again evangelize the native peoples in the United States. Soon, the Jesuit ranks rebounded, and once again, they were actively engaged in native ministry.

From 1840 to 1848, Jesuits and the Sisters of the Society of the Sacred Heart instructed Potawatomi children and adults at the Sugar Creek Mission in Kansas. This effort continued the evangelization begun earlier in their former homeland in Michigan, Indiana, and Wisconsin. With paper and India ink at the mission, the Potawatomi made ladder-like pictographic charts that showed the way to heaven. They used native designs which were displayed and

---

7   Charles Chandler, Richard K. Pope, and Susan M. Pope, "Kickapoo," *Handbook of North American Indians: Northeast* (Washington, DC: Smithsonian Institution, 1978), 15: 663. Included are illustrations of a Kenekuk prayer stick and a Kickapoo Indian praying with the aid of one; the latter was reproduced from a painting by George Catlin; see George Catlin, Ah-tón-we-tuk (Cock Turkey) with prayer stick (1831), Catholic Ladder Pictorial Catechisms, Marquette University Special Collections and Archives, Milwaukee, Wisconsin (MUA).

read vertically from bottom to top, comparable to the prayer sticks used by followers of the early Jesuits and Kenekuk.[8]

Blanchet's Ladder

In 1838, François Xavier Norbert Blanchet[9] and Modeste Demers, two Québec diocesan priests, responded to requests for missionaries from Hudson Bay Company (HBC) employees in the Oregon Country.[10] During the next several years, they evangelized the French-Canadians, Métis, and Native American tribes of the Columbia River valley, the shores of Puget Sound, and the interior of Southern British Columbia, a region where decades before the fur trade had transformed native life. Horses, guns, and European diseases were commonplace and native religious traditions were threatened. Several of the approximately 2,000 HBC employees became embedded in local tribes, and in so doing, they mastered their languages, married their women, and taught Bible stories and

---

8   Vecsey, *The Paths of Kateri's Kin*, 244–245; Paul O. Myhre, "Potawatomi Transformation: Potawatomi Responses to Catholic and Baptist Mission Strategy and Competition, 1822–1872" (Ph.D. dissertation, Saint Louis University, 1999), 298–299. Myhre includes a ladder-like drawing reportedly from Sugar Creek Mission, Kansas, and now held by the Kansas Historical Society. In October 2008, a search by a KHS archivist failed to locate the drawing or any related records. Christian Feest, "The Prophet Stick: Detective Stories from the Museum World," in *Forschungsberichte: Amerika* 5, no. 31 (2019): 1–47, includes a discussion of Midwest Native American religious movements and associated mnemonic devices that were influenced by Christian missionaries during the eighteenth and nineteenth centuries.

9   Blanchet began his pastoral ministry in 1821, first in Canada's Maritimes with Micmac Indians and new European immigrants, and then near Montréal in Cedres, Québec, with Iroquois Indians and French-Canadians. Using proven methods, Blanchet taught prayers with pictographic aids and learned to evangelize diverse people in several languages, which provided valuable experiences for evangelizing Oregon Country. Kris A. White and Janice Saint Laurent, "Mysterious Journey: The Catholic Ladder of 1840," *Oregon Historical Quarterly* 97 (1997): 70–90.

10   Until 1848, Oregon Country comprised present-day British Columbia, Idaho, Oregon, Western Montana (west of the Cascade Mountains), and Washington under joint United States and British jurisdiction. The Diocese of Québec provided ecclesiastical jurisdiction until 1843, when the Vicariate Apostolate of Oregon Territory was erected, and Blanchet was appointed its vicar.

basic Christian prayers. They included French-Canadians in the Willamette Valley and Christian Iroquois among the Flathead Indians on the Plateau. In 1823, HBC ruled that all residents of its forts—Native Americans and non-natives alike—were required to attend Sunday services. Furthermore, changing local conditions precipitated the emergence of the Prophet's Dance, a ceremony with Christian elements that began among the Flathead and spread throughout much of Oregon Country.[11]

The next spring, from March 17 to May 1, 1839, Blanchet held a mission event, primarily for French-Canadians, downriver from Fort Vancouver on the Columbia. He had expected few Native Americans to attend because he had not begun to actively evangelize them. Nonetheless, several contingents came from the Coast Salish tribes. Among them was an exhausted delegation of twelve from Puget Sound, who had traveled for five days by canoe and on foot.[12]

On the first day, Blanchet preached through translators about the "God of the Incarnation and the Redemption." He recognized immediately that his efforts were ineffectual and that he had to revamp his preaching if he was to retain the attention of the large Native American presence. He knew that his problem was more than just traversing the region's linguistic diversity.[13] Like Le Jeune

---

11   Christopher L. Miller, *Prophetic Worlds: Indians and Whites on the Columbia Plateau* (Seattle, WA: University of Washington Press, 2003), 37–46, 52–53, 57–58.

12   This was Blanchet's second mission event, which was comparable to the first mission one held in January–February 1839, at Willamette, Oregon, that reportedly went well. It focused on the needs of French-Canadian settlers and included translated instructions for Native Americans in Colville, Flathead, and Chinook Jargon, the lingua franca of the Northwest Pacific coast from Canada to Alaska. Because local Native Americans had a relatively long and close association with French-Canadians, presumably they had grasped some basics of Christian belief. Clarence B. Bagley, ed., *Early Catholic Missions in Old Oregon* (Seattle: Lowman & Hanford, 1932), 1: 61–62, 64, 69.

13   In Blanchet's day, the Northwest Pacific coast was one of the most linguistically diverse regions on earth, which led to the development of Chinook Jargon. It worked well for trade negotiations. But its limited vocabulary and structure was not suited for teaching religious concepts, which were too abstract. Cameron Addis, "The Whitman Massacre: Religion and Manifest

two hundred years earlier, Blanchet saw that the natives did not understand the Christian need for salvation. But contrary to Le Jeune, Blanchet saw the importance of presenting Christian beliefs matter-of-factly.

The next day, using a white square rule, a sharp knife, and a translator, Blanchet began anew.[14] In chronological order and in plain language without complex theology, he focused on the essential Christian themes for achieving heaven. In so doing, he may have been inspired by Jacob's Ladder, one of the Bible's best-known symbolic pathways between heaven and earth.[15] Blanchet explained creation, the fall of the angels, Adam and the promise of a savior, Christ's life and crucifixion, and the mission of the apostles. He began at the bottom and progressed to top; he cut two series of hash-marks the width of the rule and two series of small points bisecting

---

Destiny on the Columbia Plateau, 1809–1858," *Journal of the Early Republic* 25, no. 2 (Summer 2005): 237; R. James Holton, *Chinook Jargon: The Hidden Language of the Pacific Northwest* (San Leandro, CA: Wawa Press, 2004).

14　While the precise dimensions of the original Sahale sticks are unknown, it is believed that the square rule, from which Blanchet made his first Sahale stick, was a carpentry tool between two and five feet in length. Besides using the square rule, Blanchet used other resources from Fort Vancouver, such as the sharp knife and interpreter, which suggests that the square rule was common at the fort, such as a two-foot carpenters' rule or the standard three-foot English yard. Others noted the ease of use of a forty-eight by two by two-inch replica in front of an audience, which suggested that it may represent the size of Blanchet's original. This replica by a Saanich Indian is held by the Victoria Diocesan Archives in British Columbia. Another clue is the Sahale stick copy made by Tslalakum, Blanchet's first catechist, which he wrapped in the skin of a sea lion or "peau de loup marin." If the wrap comprised a skin from an adult sea lion, it likely measured between seven to eleven feet (2.1 to 3.3 meters) in length, which would have easily held a three to five-foot Sahale stick. John Darling, *The Carpenters Rule made easie: or, the Art of measuring Superficies and Solids* (London: Three Flower-de-luces in Little Britain, 1694), 1; Philip M. Hanley, *History of the Catholic Ladder* (Fairfield, WA: Ye Galleon Press, 1993), 19, 22–23.

15　See Genesis 28: 10–17; John 1: 51. Jacob dreamt of a ladder that was set upon the earth and its top reached to heaven with angels ascending and descending on it. Jesus used its symbolism while describing his intercessory role to his disciple, Nathanael: ". . . hereafter you shall see heaven open, and the angels of God ascending and descending upon the Son of Man."

its width at the center. Forty hash-marks represented the forty centuries before Christ; thirty-three points and a cross represented the thirty-three years of Christ's life and crucifixion; and eighteen hash-marks plus thirty-nine points represented the subsequent eighteen centuries plus thirty-nine years to 1839.[16]

Blanchet's audience watched and listened intently and respectfully. These people were visual and oral learners and woodworkers familiar with specially designed staffs, planks, and totem poles.[17] Furthermore, Tslalakum, the Swinomish chief of a Puget Sound delegation, requested clarity on some points and he requested that Blanchet add special signs to denote Noah's Ark and the deluge, the Ten Words or Commandments, and Blanchet's arrival to instruct them. This exchange too, became part of the gestational process that led to the birth of the Sahale stick—meaning "stick from above (or God)."[18]

The Sahale stick became an immediate success. It enabled neophytes, who were visual and oral learners, to memorize summaries of the Bible's principal events in a mere eight days, and to over-

---

16   Bagley, *Early Catholic Missions in Old Oregon*, 1: 69–70; Hanley, *History of the Catholic Ladder*, 19–20.

17   Bill Holm, "Art," *Handbook of North American Indians: Northwest Coast* (Washington, DC: Smithsonian Institution, 1990), 17: 620–622; Roy I. Wilson, *The Catholic Ladder and Native American Legends: A Comparative Study* (Bremerton, WA: Roy I. Wilson, 1996), 11–12. Through the fur trade, native artists acquired steel tools for the first time, and they developed totemic monuments from cedar poles as a new art form to memorialize lineage histories and ancestral legends. Wilson, a Methodist minister and Coast Salish Indian, theorized that local totem poles inspired the Sahale stick. Both were read from bottom to top.

18   Hanley, *History of the Catholic Ladder*, 186, and Wilson, *The Catholic Ladder and Native American Legends*, 11–12. "Sahale stick" translates "stick from above" in Chinook Jargon; other terms used include "Jesus stick" and "soul stick." While never conducive to extensive reproduction, oversized Sahale stick replicas have served well as historical monuments. Parishioners erected one such monument at St. James the Greater Proto-Cathedral, Vancouver, Washington, 2017. See "The Making of the Sahale Stick (Catholic Ladder)," Proto-Cathedral Historical Society, Vancouver, Washington, February 10, 2017, https://protocathedralhistoricalsociety.wordpress.com/2017/02/10/the-making-of-the-sahale-stick-catholic-ladder/.

come the language and cultural diversity among them. Blanchet appointed Tslalakum his first catechist and gave him a Sahale stick with procedural instructions on teaching others. During the next two months, Blanchet made and distributed copies to several new catechists. In turn, these catechists, from Oregon to British Columbia, made and distributed more copies, some of which were still cherished over seventy years later.[19]

Meanwhile, Blanchet realized that the Sahale stick did not lend itself to visual improvements, flexible use, and fast reproduction. Using locally available materials, he developed a chart or scroll for evangelizing groups. He brushed India ink onto durable yellow wrapping paper, and he backed it with white linen affixed with paste. Blanchet's first paper ladder reportedly measured seventy-two by eighteen inches. He replaced the stick's hash-marks and points with a vertical timeline of bars and dots, and at the mid-point, he replaced the single cross for the crucifixion with a mound and three crosses. He also added several new but simple pictures on both sides of the timeline. Most notable from bottom to top, were: six circles for the six days of creation, a boat for Noah's Ark, a tower for the Tower of Babel, an open book for the Ten Words or Commandments of the Old Testament, a church building for the Catholic Church, another open book for the Gospel of the New Testament, and a withered branch for the Protestant Reformation.[20]

That summer Blanchet introduced the Catholic ladder to native crowds, first on the Columbia River in July and August, and then at Fort Nisqually on Puget Sound in August and September. During the daylight hours, he instructed outdoors by hanging it vertically from a tent pole or tree branch and pointing to specific symbols with a stick. During the evenings, chiefs and head men continued

---

19   Francis Norbert Blanchet, *The Key to the Catholic Ladder* (New York: T.W. Strong, 1859), 1; Charles M. Buchanan, "The Catholic Ladder," *The Indian Sentinel* 1, no. 7 (January 1918): 22; Paul Gard, "Letters from Indian Missionaries: I. Tulalip Indian Mission," *The Indian Sentinel* (1913): 39; Hanley, *History of the Catholic Ladder*, 128–131.

20   Blanchet, *The Key to the Catholic Ladder*, 1; Hanley, *History of the Catholic Ladder*, 36–45.

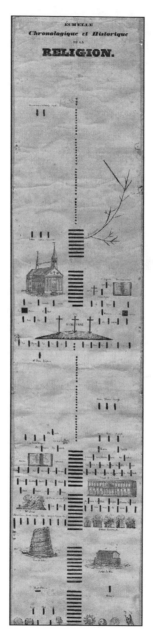

A portion of the Catholic Ladder by Father François Blanchet, 1839
(Courtesy of Department of Special Collections and University
Archives, Marquette University Libraries).

to instruct by campfire. But while they attracted native crowds, satisfying their doubts on the need for redemption remained the greater challenge.

The 1840s were a decade of expansion for Catholic missions and Blanchet's ladder. In Oregon Country and elsewhere, it was in demand wherever missions were in their formative stage on the U.S. and Canadian frontiers. When Blanchet conducted his itinerant mission events, he found himself making several ladders at night by candlelight. Soon requests for copies became daily occurrences and entailed significant time commitments to honor and special copies were made up to ten feet in length for use by larger audiences.[21]

In February 1842, Blanchet initiated arrangements to publish his ladder through Archbishop Joseph Signay of Québec. In November, he sent the finalized and corrected manuscript with an explanation for all symbols, which included new innovations such as the tree and serpent from the Garden of Eden suggested two years before by Jesuit priest Pierre-Jean De Smet. Blanchet wrote that he needed large and small copies. In the following April, Signay sent word that he would be sending Blanchet 2,000 ladder copies by canoe and sea, and that others would be sent to the missions on the Red River, in present-day Minnesota and North Dakota, and to the missions in western Canada. Titled *Echelle Chronologique et Historique de la Religion*, it was published on coarse grained paper and measured approximately thirty-four by seven inches. It also appeared within the 1843 annual report of the diocesan Society for the Propagation of the Faith.[22]

Revisions of Blanchet's ladder began immediately in Québec City and the Willamette Valley. The next year, it is believed that Aubin, a Québec diocesan priest, made the first revisions approved

---

21   Bagley, *Early Catholic Missions in Old Oregon*, 1:77–81; Hanley, *History of the Catholic Ladder*, 33–34; Jarold Ramsey, "The Bible in Western Indian Mythology," *The Journal of American Folklore* 90 (1977): 358, 446–447.

22   Hanley, *History of the Catholic Ladder*, 39, 46–49; Francis Norbert Blanchet, *Echelle Chronologique et Historique de la Religion* (1839–1843, 1856), Catholic Ladder Pictorial Catechisms, MUA; Blanchet, *Catholic Ladder. . .* (ca. 1840), Oregon History Project, https://www.oregonhistoryproject.org/.

by Blanchet. He rearranged slightly the order of symbols and added a few new ones such as hell, heretics, and schisms. At St. Paul's Mission in the Willamette Valley, the newly arrived Sisters of Notre Dame de Namur[23] produced specialty manuscript copies, such as a pocket-sized version with a wooden spindle at one end and a protective cowhide sheath on the other, and a Sister Aloysia created intricately hand-drawn copies in color.[24]

De Smet's Ladder

Meanwhile in 1843, De Smet published his ladder in two formats as the *Indian Symbolical Catechism*. He retained Blanchet's technique of bars and dots and added his own modifications, most notable of which was the Judeo-Christian tradition of two ways or roads with the good Way of Life and the evil Way of Death.[25] He depicted the good road beginning at the Garden of Eden and leading straight to Jesus Christ, the Catholic Church, and redemption in heaven and the bad road leading to the great schisms, the "pretended" Protestant Reformation, and the Devil and hell.[26]

---

23   The Sisters of Notre Dame de Namur ministered at St. Paul's Mission in the Willamette Valley, 1844–1853.

24   Hanley, *History of the Catholic Ladder*, 57–60, 204–211; Mary Dominica McNamee, *Willamette Interlude* (Palo Alto, CA: Pacific Books, 1959), insert between 110–111, 147, 284; White and Laurent, "Mysterious Journey," 72–74, 82–84.

25   Alistair Stewart-Sykes, ed., *On the Two Ways: Life or Death, Light or Darkness: Foundational Texts in the Tradition* (Yonkers, NY: St. Vladimir's Seminary Press, 2011), 13–14, 18. In Jewish ethical teaching, the prophets beginning with Moses set forth the commandments of God in clear and unambiguous terms that they would receive a blessing if they followed God's commandments and a curse if they did not. The two ways formed an ethical discourse of life or death, light or darkness, which early on became part of Christian discourse as well. The second-century text *The Didache* (also known as the *Doctrine of the Twelve Apostles*) begins, "There are two Ways, one of life and one of death, and there is much difference between the two Ways."

26   Hanley, *History of the Catholic Ladder*, 120, 237; Pierre-Jean De Smet, *Letters and Sketches: With a Narrative of a Year's Residence among the Indian Tribes of the Rocky Mountains* (Philadelphia: M. Fithian, 1843), 245–246, 252–253; Pierre-Jean De Smet, *Indian Symbolic Catechism* (1843), Catholic Ladder Pictorial Catechisms, MUA.

As a book tip-out, De Smet's ladder was published with an instructor's manual in his *Letters and Sketches with a Narrative of a Year's Residence among the Indian Tribes of the Rocky Mountains*. It was printed in black ink and measured twenty-four by seven inches with the manual including sixty numbered captions that correlated with numbered images on the chart. Fifteen captions also added special "instructions" for the instructor to impart on the listeners and one included a general note to the instructor. As a stand-alone chart, De Smet's ladder was printed first in black ink and measured twenty-five by ten inches and then the following year it was printed in color with the same measurements as the earlier tip-out. Both variations were lithographed in Europe and the United States.[27]

De Smet's ladder quickly helped to fill the demand for Catholic ladders across the U.S. and Canadian West. Many Catholic missionaries knew about Blanchet's version, but it was not yet readily available. Consequently, when necessary, some resorted to excising De Smet's tip-out ladder from *Letters and Sketches*. Early on at Saint Mary's Mission in Western Montana, then part of Oregon Country, De Smet's ladder served as a crucial aid for evangelizing the Flathead Indians.[28]

Protestant Ladders

Protestant missionaries also took note of De Smet's ladder, which confirmed its rapid distribution. Everywhere they complained strenuously about his term, "pretend Reformation," which he used in the key to his ladder within *Letters and Sketches*.[29] In

---

27   De Smet, *Letters and Sketches,* 245–252; Hanley, *History of the Catholic Ladder,* 94–96.

28   Jacqueline Peterson with Laura Peers, *Sacred Encounters: Father De Smet and the Indians of the Rocky Mountain West* (Norman: De Smet Project with University of Oklahoma Press, 1993), 108–109. The illustrations include paintings by Nicholas Point, S.J., depicting Flathead Indians at Saint Mary's Mission studying Christianity with De Smet's ladder and other pictures. In one, children are gathered around a ladder on a wall with their focus drawn to a specific item with a pointer stick.

29   Philip M. Hanley, "Father Lacombe's Ladder," *Éstudes Oblates* 32 (1973): 91; Hanley, *History of the Catholic Ladder,* 8, 120, 237.

Oregon Country, but not elsewhere, four Protestant missionaries responded by creating ladder catechisms, which they used for the remainder of their ministries. At least two versions vilified the Catholic Church.[30]

Methodist missionary David Lee, of Willamette Valley in present-day Oregon, created his ladder by April 1840. He made several copies for use by his assistants and their native helpers, but none of them survived and existing descriptions are vague. His ladder presumably presented a concise and straightforward summary of Methodist belief, somewhat analogous to Blanchet's first ladder. Its size likely ranged between fifty-eight to sixty-eight by seven to twenty-two inches, which are the dimensions of Blanchet's first ladder and those made by other Protestant missionaries. Lee and his associates used their ladder throughout the Columbia and Willamette valleys, and when Blanchet visited Chief Katamus' Clackamas Indian village at Wapato Lake, he saw Katamus place his Catholic ladder and Lee's side-by-side for careful comparison with his people concluding that Lee's did not come from Jesus.[31]

Presbyterian missionaries Henry H. and Eliza Spalding of near Lapwai in present-day Idaho created their ladder after Lee, between late 1840 and 1846. Henry Spalding had an affinity for graphic design and his wife Eliza had some artistic abilities. Theirs was the first to use color and to feature two roads with pictures—a broad and easy Catholic way with alleged abusive practices leading to hell and a narrow, difficult, and virtuous Protestant way leading to heaven. Eliza Spalding drew and painted the pictures on paper with black ink

---

30 Bagley, *Early Catholic Missions in Old Oregon*, 2: 36–37, 50–51; Hanley, *History of the Catholic Ladder*, 107–109, 219; Melinda Jette, "Protestant Ladder," Oregon Historical Society, 2003, https://www.oregonhistoryproject. org/articles/historical-records/protestant-ladder/pdf/; Ramsey, "The Bible in Western Indian Mythology," 444–445; De Smet, *Letters and Sketches*, 245. The Methodist Episcopal Board and the American Board of Commissioners for Foreign Missions (ABCFM) sponsored the Protestant missions in Oregon Country with the ABCFM affiliating with the Congregationalist, Dutch Reformed, and Presbyterian churches. Missionaries from the two agencies operated several missions from 1834–1847.

31 Hanley, *History of the Catholic Ladder*, 92, 113, 217, 219–220.

and colored berry dyes and natural pigments, which provided green, red, blue, brown, and yellow. She made several copies that their followers used in Idaho and nearby areas of adjacent states. Henry Spalding relied almost entirely on their ladder for his preaching, and they reported that native preachers who used it attracted larger native crowds than those who used Blanchet's.[32] The Jesuit priest Joseph A. Cataldo acknowledged that the Spaldings' ladder achieved some conversions and added that Henry Spalding ". . . succeeded in poisoning their native minds against the Catholic religion."[33]

Presbyterian missionary Marcus Whitman led a small, but loyal, congregation among the Cayuse Indians near Fort Walla Walla in present-day Washington. He also provided medical care. Whitman readily showed his dislike of the Catholic Church and he believed that Native Americans versed in the Catholic ladder were no longer interested in the Protestant way.[34] At Fort Walla Walla on September 23, 1847, he met Blanchet for the first time and told him about his plan to cover a Catholic ladder with blood to show past Catholic persecution of Protestants.[35] Meanwhile, a macabre chain of events unfolded: the Cayuse Indians had become very suspicious of the flood of Oregon Trail emigrants who stopped for aid at the Whitman Mission[36]; a measles epidemic struck the Cayuse tribe and Whitman's medicines failed to prevent half of the tribe from perishing; Cayuse custom then gave the families of the deceased the right to take the life of a failed healer; and on November 29, several Cayuse Indians participated in taking Spalding's life and that of his wife Eliza.[37] Later with the Cayuse chiefs, Blanchet held an inquest in which a chief's

---

32   Clifford M. Drury, *The Diaries and Letters of Henry H. Spalding and Asa Bowen Smith relating to the Nez Perce Mission, 1838–1842* (Glendale, CA: Arthur H. Clark, 1958), 170–171, 233; Hanley, *History of the Catholic Ladder*, 113, 121; Melinda Jette and Nellie B. Pipes, "The Protestant Ladder," *Oregon Historical Quarterly* 37 (1936): 239; Henry H. Spalding and Eliza Spalding, *Protestant Ladder*, 1845, Oregon History Project, https://www.oregonhistoryproject.org/.

33   Miller, *Prophetic Worlds*, 95.

34   Miller, *Prophetic Worlds,* 95.

35   Bagley, *Early Catholic Missions in Old Oregon*, 1: 188.

36   Addis, "The Whitman Massacre," 240.

37   Whitman Mission National Historical Site, https://www.nps.gov/whmi/learn/.

son presented Whitman's blood-stained Catholic ladder and repeated Whitman's words when he had shown it to them about a week or two before his murder. "You see this blood! It is to show you . . . because you have the priests among you. The country is going to be counted in blood! You will have nothing now but blood!"[38]

Ladder catechisms in Oregon Country proved effective for both Catholic[39] and Protestant missionaries. But the simultaneous use of competing ladders sowed confusion among native converts and contradicted the Christian teaching that all people are God's children. Among the Coast Salish tribes, the ladders also inspired the Prophet Dance and the Shaker Church, which created comparable documents known as the "Prophet's Maps."[40]

In about 1846, the Sisters of Notre Dame de Namur prepared a revised Blanchet ladder that was lithographed in Namur, Belgium. Apparently dissatisfied, Blanchet scrapped this edition without explanation and no copies are known to exist. He had it destroyed, it is believed, for reasons inherent within the publication. Judging from the edition that followed, it is possible that the Spaldings' extensive use of detailed graphic imagery may have heightened Blanchet's sensitivities and affected his decision.[41] Between August

---

38 Bagley, *Early Catholic Missions in Old Oregon*, 1: 201–203.

39 In 1845, Blanchet estimated that 6,000 Northwest natives were Catholic.

40 Bagley, *Early Catholic Missions in Old Oregon*, 2:47–48; Robert I. Burns, "Roman Catholic Missions in the Northwest," *Handbook of North American Indians: Indian-White Relations* (Washington, DC: Smithsonian Institution, 1998), 4: 498; Deward E. Walker and Helen H. Schuster, "Religious Movements," *Handbook of North American Indians: Plateau* (Washington, DC: Smithsonian Institution, 1998), 12: 510. Colville Shakerism contains many Roman Catholic elements and ninety percent of the first Colville Shakers had been Roman Catholics.

41 Hanley, *History of the Catholic Ladder*, 61–62, 65, 211–212. The Spaldings' ladder was created no later than 1846 since Blanchet was in Western Europe, September 28, 1845 to February 22, 1847. If Blanchet lacked prior news about it, no doubt his priests would have learned about it soon after its creation and forwarded word to him immediately. A letter from Oregon would have taken six months to reach Belgium, which may have been in time to affect his decision about the Namur edition.

1846 and some time the following year,[42] Blanchet arranged for Typographic de Firmin Didot in Paris to publish the next edition titled, *Echelle Catholique, Historique, et Chronologique ou maniere d'expliquar la catechism aux sauvages, Inventee dans l'Oregon en 1839 par M. Blanchet Archeveque d'Oregon City.* Essentially it was a compendium of detailed Biblical pictures with captions aligned along a timeline of short bars and it superseded the previous editions of simple drawings with sequences of bars and dots. It was printed as four sheets measuring twenty-eight by twenty-two inches pasted together to form a scroll measuring 112 by 22 inches. Judging from where worn copies have been found at missions, this ladder was used in British Columbia, Washington, Oregon, and Idaho.[43]

In 1848, under Blanchet's leadership, the first Council of the Ecclesiastical Province of Oregon decreed the use of the Catholic ladder throughout the dioceses of the province for instruction of both Native Americans and non-natives.[44] Oblate priest Eugène-Casimir Chirouse, who had effectively used the ladder, had a custom-made ladder carved out of cedar boards. He used it concurrently with a palette of resources that included statues, pictures, singing prayers and hymns, reading apostolic works, and telling native stories.[45]

---

42 Hanley, *History of the Catholic Ladder,* 65. Blanchet was named Archbishop of Oregon City in 1846, which is noted on the ladder published in Paris, dating its publication to sometime after August 6, 1846.

43 Hanley, *History of the Catholic Ladder,* 64–66, 71, 212–215; Blanchet, *Echelle Chronologique. . .* (Paris, 1846–1847), MUA, Oregon Historical Society, and Yale University. Blanchet also sent a copy to Propaganda Fide, Rome, in 1850. But Hanley, with the help of the Propaganda Fide archivist, was unable to find the copy.

44 First Oregon Provincial Council, *Acta,* 1848. The Ecclesiastical Province of Oregon encompassed all dioceses in present-day Oregon, Idaho, Washington State, and British Columbia under the metropolitan see of Oregon City. British Columbia was separated in 1850.

45 Charles M. Buchanan, "Reverend Eugene Casimir Chirouse, O.M.I., Apostle of the Indians of Puget Sound," *The Indian Sentinel* 1, no. 7 (January 1918): 10–13; Gard, "Letters from Indian Missionaries," 34–35. Chirouse evangelized the native communities of the Puget Sound plus the Cayuse and Yakima Indians, 1847–1878, and natives of Northern British Columbia, 1878–1892.

Beginning in 1856, Catholic missions worldwide began to use Catholic ladders. In that year, Blanchet solicited donations for his diocese in South America and while in Valparaiso, Chile, he arranged for Libas to lithograph his latest ladder version, which provided his most extensive summary of Catholic doctrine to date. It included the familiar bars and dots for centuries and years, extensive explanations in Spanish, but far fewer Biblical pictures than the Paris ladder.[46]

Blanchet's New York ladder appears to have been his final edition. It was lithographed in 1859–1860 in New York City with the title, *Catholic Ladder a Chronological and Historical Chart of the Christian Religion and Doctrine*. Essentially, it was an English-language version of the Spanish ladder with much of the same material plus a few additions. It measured fifty by twenty-five inches with folds so that it made a small booklet measuring three by five inches with a front cover titled "Catholic Ladder." Accompanying it was a companion booklet, *The Key to the Catholic Ladder, Containing a Sketch of the Christian Religion and Universal History Useful to All* published by T.W. Strong of New York in 1859. Ironically, book distributor C. Leblanc reported that the catechism, which intended to overcome language barriers, was itself beset by them: ". . . the French don't read English and the Irish are poor."[47]

Lacombe's Ladder

During the summer of 1865, in Alberta, Canada, the Oblate priest Albert Lacombe[48] discussed some Christian beliefs with two

---

46   Hanley, *History of the Catholic Ladder*, 73–74, 80, 215–216; Blanchet, *Echelle Chronologique* (1856), Catholic Ladder Pictorial Catechisms, MUA, and Oregon Historical Society.

47   Hanley, *History of the Catholic Ladder*, 83, 216–217; Blanchet, *Catholic Ladder*. . . (New York, 1859–1860), MUA, Oregon Historical Society, Portland Archdiocesan Archives (Oregon), and Oregon Province Archives in the Jesuit Archives and Research Center (JARC), St. Louis, Missouri.

48   Lacombe (1827–1916) was born in Saint-Sulpice, Canada, to parents of Métis, Cree, and Saulteaux ancestry who were involved in the fur trade. He was ordained in 1849 and joined the Oblates in 1856. No doubt he was acquainted with Blanchet's ladder. The accounts about it in the annual mission

Blackfoot Indian men, and he augmented his explanations with pictures drawn in the sand. Immediately, he saw that the pictures enhanced their understanding. So, Lacombe improved his visual approach the next day while discussing the Bible with a group of catechumens. With charcoal he sketched more figures onto a buffalo hide laced between two upright poles, which then inspired him to create his own ladder.

Upon returning to his base at Saint Albert, Lacombe took paper and ink, and over the course of eight years, he transformed the Catholic ladder into a small masterpiece of pedagogy. It presented Catholic dogma, morality, and history as clear and uncomplicated concepts that resembled the climbing pole used by some native shamans to climb to heaven and return to earth.[49] First published in 1872, Lacombe's ladder took the "two roads" concept to a higher level. It retained Blanchet's bars and dots from creation to the life of Jesus and to judgment for all; it featured two paths—one of good with the Old Testament, three virtues, and the seven Catholic sacraments, and one of evil with idolatry, paganism, and seven capital sins; and it added numbered points[50] for the convenient identification of its multitude of pictures. Constructed as a rolled scroll, his ladder measured sixty-eight by eleven inches with canvas backing and a small stick support inserted at the top end. The first edition was lithographed double-wide[51] and cut in half lengthwise with the two halves pasted together end-to-end to create a scroll.[52]

---

reports of the Society for the Propagation of the Faith in Québec were avidly read by all Canadian missionaries, and Lacombe had served mission areas where its use was known, including the Métis and Ojibwa of the Red River settlements in the Manitoba-Ontario-North Dakota-Minnesota border region and among the Cree in Alberta.

49   Hanley, *History of the Catholic Ladder*, 121; Raymond Huel, *Proclaiming the Gospel to the Indians and Métis* (Edmonton: University of Alberta Press, 1996), 326–327.

50   Lacombe's first edition included fifty-nine points and the 1895 edition included eighteen. Hanley, "Father Lacombe's Ladder," 94–99.

51   Double-wide refers to the printing of content onto two columns per sheet.

52   Hanley, "Father Lacombe's Ladder," 92–97; Hanley, *History of the Catholic Ladder*, 117–118, 234–235; Huel, *Proclaiming the Gospel*, 94, 96.

A portion of the Catholic Ladder by Father Albert Lacombe, O.M.I., from *Tableau-catéchisme*, 1874 (Courtesy of Department of Special Collections and University Archives, Marquette University Libraries).

Once added, the vivid graphics remained unchanged in all subsequent editions. Unique to the long-running editions published by C.O. Beauchemin and Sons of Montréal was the use of English and French captions, and varying dramatically among all of them, were its dimensions and sizes.[53]

Under the title, *Tableau-catéchsime* or *Pictorial Catechism*, Lacombe's chart achieved global distribution. A recommendation by Pope Pius IX prompted the printing of several thousand copies for missions worldwide, which was followed by a recommendation from the Oblate superior general that caused the printing of another 10,000 copies in Paris and Montréal in 1874. Letaille in Paris also published 16,000 copies that year. From 1895 through at least the 1920s, Beauchemin published substantial runs. After 1930, the Jesuits' Catholic Press of Ranchi, India, published copies as did the Institute of Missiology at the University of Ottawa in the late twentieth century.[54]

Lacombe's ladder achieved unprecedented distribution from Lake Superior to the Pacific in Canada[55] and the northern two tiers of states in the United States.[56] The Benedictine priest Martin

---

53 Lacombe, *Pictorial Catechism* (Montréal: C.O. Beauchemin et fils, 1873–1874, 1895–1896), Catholic Ladder Pictorial Catechisms, MUA. Beauchemin and Ranchi Press published single-wide ladders measuring seventy by twelve inches and thirty-six by eleven inches, respectively, and the Oblates and Beauchemin published double-wide ones measuring fifty-nine by twenty-four inches and thirty-nine by twenty-four inches, respectively. In the late twentieth century, the University of Ottawa Institute of Missiology published a double-wide ladder measuring thirty-nine by twenty-six inches and individual users made letter-size photocopies, some measuring as small as ten by six inches. Hanley, *History of the Catholic Ladder*, 121, 234–235; "Wilfred Schoenberg Travel Diary," 1 (1946): 95, JARC.

54 Hanley, *History of the Catholic Ladder*, 121; Michael F. Steltenkamp, *Black Elk: Holy Man of the Oglala* (Norman: University of Oklahoma Press, 1993), 100; White and Laurent, "Mysterious Journey," 87. Steltenkamp and other Jesuits noted that some copies of Lacombe's ladder used in the South Dakota missions came from the Ranchi (India) Catholic Press, which was founded in 1930.

55 Hanley, *History of the Catholic Ladder,* 118.

56 Louis Goll, *Jesuit Missions among the Sioux* (St. Francis, SD: St. Francis Mission, 1940), 29; Hanley, *History of the Catholic Ladder*, 235; "Wilfred

Marty, who became the first bishop of North and South Dakota and later the first bishop of St. Cloud, Minnesota, promoted Lacombe's ladder unceasingly among Native American converts and fellow missionaries.[57] In turn, it eliminated the missionaries' frequent difficulties in explaining Christianity and it rapidly empowered native catechists who were trained to use it in their own language. Using traditional native oral ways of learning, their homes became centers of Christian education without regular involvement by non-native clergy and religious whose understanding of native language and culture was often lacking. Catechists would visit their neighbors; friends would soon follow; ". . . and within an hour quite a few would smoke the pipe."[58]

Orthodox Ladders

In Alaska, Catholic missionaries presumably introduced Catholic ladders when they entered the territory in 1878. It is also possible that native Catholics from tribes in British Columbia introduced them earlier through potlatches and related socio-economic exchanges with native tribes in Alaska.[59] While the Jesuits in Alaska

---

Schoenberg Travel Diary," 1: (1946) 95, JARC. Single-wide copies of Lacombe's 1874 ladder were found at Saint Paul's Mission on the Fort Belknap Reservation, Montana, and in the possession of two nearby Assiniboine Indian catechists, Paul and Felicitas Two Kill. Hanley, *History of the Catholic Ladder*, 235, incorrectly cites from the "Wilfred Schoenberg Travel Diary," 95, that these ladders were acquired near Saint Ignatius Mission on the Flathead Reservation, Montana.

57   P. Florentin Digmann, St. Francis, South Dakota to Charles S. Lusk, Bureau of Catholic Indian Missions (BCIM), Washington, D.C., June 12, 1912, BCIM Records, series 1-1, box 78, folder 15, MUA; Marie Therese Archambault, Mark G. Thiel, and Christopher Vecsey, eds., *The Crossing of Two Roads: Being Catholic and Native in the United States* (Maryknoll, NY: Orbis Books, 2003), 119–120, for a narrative description of Lacombe's Two Roads by Jesuit Henry Grotegeers. Marty served as Vicar Apostolic of Dakota/Bishop of Sioux Falls, North and South Dakota, 1879-1895, and Bishop of St. Cloud, Minnesota, 1895–1896.

58   Goll, *Jesuit Missions among the Sioux*, 29, 35–36.

59   Diocesan priests from British Columbia, Oblates, Jesuits, and Sisters of Saint Ann served in nineteenth century Alaska and came from areas familiar with Catholic ladders by Lacombe and others.

were not known to use Lacombe's ladder, they did use comparable pictorial charts. One Jesuit, Bellarmine Lafortune, evangelized the Behring Strait Eskimo for over forty years, beginning in the early twentieth century. He used handmade charts and large colored ones published by La Maison de la Bonne Presse of Paris.[60] Nonetheless, the development of Orthodox[61] counterparts infers the presence of Catholic ladders, which no doubt provided the necessary inspiration.

Among the Tlingit Indians in the panhandle region, totem pole sculpting flourished and increasing numbers converted to Orthodoxy in response to U.S. government and missionary pressures to become "civilized." At the time, one native artist sculpted an unprecedented pole reminiscent of the Sahale stick. This monumental catechetical aid proclaimed the Christian message by combining Christian and native symbols and artistic conventions.[62]

Simeon Nishnyakov, Archpriest of Moscow, authored the Orthodox pictorial chart, which measures nineteen by sixteen inches and was lithographed in Moscow in 1892. Unlike the Catholic and Protestant ladders, it lacked graphic pathways or roads to heaven and acrimony towards the Catholic Church. Rather, it arranged symbols of Christian beliefs and revelation with simplicity and symmetry in the form of a cross.

It presented the decisive elements of Christian belief in the center: the Lord's Table of the Last Supper, the Cross of the crucifixion with the Orthodox three-bars, and the scales of the Last Judg-

---

60   Louis Renner and Dorothy Jean Ray, *Pioneer Missionary to the Behring Strait Eskimos: Bellarmine Lafortune, S.J.* (Portland, OR: Binford & Mort for the Alaska Historical Commission, 1979), 130.

61   Russian Orthodox evangelization began in 1794. By 1867, when the United States purchased Alaska, the Orthodox counted 12,000 Native American Christians.

62   Holm, "Art," *Handbook of North American Indians*, 17: 604, 615; Sergei Kan, "The Russian Orthodox Church in Alaska," *Handbook of North American Indians: Indian-White Relations* (Washington, DC: Smithsonian Institution, 1998), 4: 513–514, 518. Most poles were created before the United States had purchased Alaska in 1867 and most conversions to Orthodoxy happened afterwards. Declining numbers of poles were created throughout the nineteenth century, but Orthodox displays of Romanoff family imagery continued.

ment. To the right and left, respectively, were depictions of Moses and the Jewish people of the Old Covenant and Saint Peter and the Early Church of the New Covenant. Above were depictions of the Trinity and heaven with the angels and saints—the hope for all Christian believers—and below the Devil and hell with the damned. Fifteen examples of damned persons, thieves, idolaters, drunkards, etc., were depicted across the bottom. Hell was embellished with immense yellowish flames engulfing the damned whereas elsewhere most other figures were embellished in greenish tones. The imagery draws the viewer's gaze from the center to the bottom and then the top with the representation of a monstrous snake representing sin, which reaches up and out of hell with a menacing reach. Twenty numbered sins, heresy, sodomy, adultery, etc., were inscribed along the length of its body. Starting in the left-side margin and continuing in the right-side one, the texts begin with Matthew 25:32-46 and continue with a commentary about the miserable condition of sinners and God's mercy towards faithful Christians. The verso featured nine Biblical verses in archaic Russian in the left-side column and Cyrillic phonetic translations of a Native American language, possibly Yupic Eskimo, in the right-side column. Ephesians 5:18; Luke 21:34; and 1 Thessalonians 6 were the first three selections.[63] The chart was used primarily to evangelize in northern Eskimo communities, which continued throughout the twentieth century.[64]

Lacombe's ladder also provided the tinder for a final salvo in the long-running war between church and state regarding schools for native youth in the United States. Echoing past Protestant criticisms, a May 1912 convention of the Episcopal Diocese of Washington, D.C., charged that Catholic teachers at U.S. government schools covered the walls with the "Two Roads," which was offensive because it showed that all but Catholics were damned. Their

---

63   Simeon Nishnyakov, [illegible title] (Moscow: Literary Partnership of Y.D. Sytin, 1892), translated by Tantyana Lide and George Khristish, October 2008. The chart was found at the Tununak Orthodox rectory, Nelson Island, Alaska, and transferred to the Oregon Province Archives, JARC; untitled Orthodox chart (Moscow, 1892), Catholic Ladder Pictorial Catechisms, MUA.

64   Kateri Mitchell, email to author, October 22, 2008. Kateri Mitchell (Mohawk) of the Sisters of St. Anne served at a mission school in Alaska and then as Executive Director of the Tekakwitha Conference, 1998–2017.

conclusions were based solely on the accusations of one Reverend Aaron B. Clark, an Episcopal missionary on the Rosebud Reservation in South Dakota. A subsequent investigation by the Bureau of Catholic Indian Missions (BCIM) yielded no evidence of the "Two Roads" or similar religious pictures displayed at the government schools, and the Catholic Bureau's secretary Charles S. Lusk defended Catholic teachings and practice further by stating he firmly believed that the chart was never interpreted by Catholic missionaries as alleged by Clark and the Episcopal convention because such teaching was contrary to Catholic doctrine.[65]

Utilizing and Exporting Lacombe's Ladder

Meanwhile near Philadelphia, Mississippi, the Choctaw Indian community was growing, and so too, were the local Catholic parishes that served them.[66] In 1916, Father William H. Ketcham,[67] the Catholic Bureau director, shipped to them the new catechism in Choctaw he coauthored with Choctaw catechists in Oklahoma, and he also included copies of Lacombe's ladder. No doubt Ketcham had learned of its utility through his travels to missions on the Northern Plains. Thereafter, he and the missionaries in Mississippi expressed confidence that the ladders, too, would be helpful in teaching religion.[68]

---

65 Randolph H. McKimm to Lusk, May 15, 1912; McKimm to Lusk, May 25, 1912, BCIM Records, series 1-1, box 79, folder 5; Lusk to Superintendents of Indian Schools, June 8, 1912; William H. Ketcham to William Hughes, June 12, 1912; McKimm to Lusk, June 25, 1912; Lusk to McKimm, June 27, 1912, Lusk to McKimm, June 27, 1912, BCIM Records, series 1-1, box 79, folder 6, MUA; Francis Paul Prucha, *The Churches and the Indian Schools, 1888–1912* (Lincoln: University of Nebraska Press, 1979), 201–202.

66 The Jesuits evangelized the Choctaw Indians, 1702–late 1700s. In 1883, Catholic efforts resumed at Holy Rosary Mission, near Philadelphia, Mississippi, which became a viable congregation by the 1890s. Vecsey, *The Paths of Kateri's Kin*, 200.

67 Ketcham (1868–1921) was a diocesan priest and missionary among the Choctaw Indians of Oklahoma. He became BCIM director in 1901 and continued to support Choctaw concerns in Mississippi and Oklahoma.

68 Ketcham to P.J. Ahern, Philadelphia, Mississippi, August 21, 1916; P.J. Hendil, Saint Joseph's Church, Meridian, Mississippi, to William H. Ketcham, August 26, 1916; Ketcham to P.J. Ahern, August 21, 1916, BCIM

two Of all the many native catechists who evangelized with Lacombe's Two Roads ladder, Nicholas Black Elk is clearly the one whose life is best documented. Black Elk, an Oglala Lakota Indian from the Pine Ridge Reservation in South Dakota, was an exceptional native religious thinker and public speaker who was steeped in Lakota heritage and life experiences as a warrior, traditional holy man, and Wild West show dancer. Thereafter as an ardent and skillful catechist who studied the Bible, he was called to evangelize on several Indian reservations from Montana to Nebraska, he baptized over 400 Native Americans, and he taught with the Two Roads, which reverberated throughout his teachings.[69]

Records, series 1-1, box 102, folder 6, MUA. Ketcham's introduction of Lacombe's ladder in Mississippi represents the author's only discovered use of Catholic ladders in the South where Choctaw people then had little or no English proficiency. Apparently, Benedictions (Oklahoma) and Franciscans in comparable circumstances (Arizona, California, Michigan, New Mexico, and Wisconsin) did not use them.

69 Black Elk, *Black Elk Speaks,* ed. by John G. Neihardt, with introduction by Philip J. Deloria and annotations by Raymond J. DeMallie (Lincoln: University of Nebraska Press and Bison Books, 2014). Neihardt selected and edited Black Elk's translated interviews for aesthetics, clarity, and readability by English speakers, which he published in 1932. He included Black Elk's childhood and great vision, and his life as a warrior, traditional healer, and Wild West show dancer. But he ended the story abruptly in 1890 at the Wounded Knee Massacre in South Dakota while Black Elk was still a young man, and he omitted Black Elk's interviews as a catechist and family man. This annotated edition of *Black Elk Speaks* adds extensive contextual interpretation by DeMallie from his lifelong study of Black Elk's life and his Lakota language, culture, and history. Black Elk had observed Christianity closely since the 1880s, was baptized in 1904, and was appointed as a catechist in 1907. Thereafter he called others to Christ with examples from Scripture and his own life in a way analogous to Saint Paul. In so doing, Black Elk wrote three letters published in Dakota in *Iapi Oaye = Word Carrier,* 1885–1889, and at least sixteen letters published in Lakota in *Šina Sapa Wocekiye Taeyanpaha = The Catholic Voice,* 1907–1916, undated. The Nicholas Black Elk Collection, MUA, holds multiple translations of Black Elk's published letters. Selected excerpts appear in Archambault, Thiel, and Vecsey, *The Crossing of Two Roads,* 134–140. Cf. Michael F. Steltenkamp, *Nicholas Black Elk: Medicine Man, Missionary, Mystic* (Norman: University of Oklahoma Press, 2009).

Likewise, the Two Roads contains striking similarities with many images Black Elk described from the great vision of his youth in *Black Elk Speaks,* his autobiography. Although the vision happened years before his baptism, he came to identify its "Red Road" as the way of Jesus and the "Black Road" as the way of evil doing. Walking the sacred Red Road was its main action, the understanding of which evolved with his understanding of salvation history and the Great Mystery. Its closing prayer to God—Wakan Tanka—also alluded to Lacombe's ladder: "The good road and the road of difficulties you have made to cross; and where they cross, the place is holy." His daughter Lucy believed that her father saw parallels and connections between their native beliefs and Christianity.[70]

While Lacombe's ladder spread worldwide, new forces began to curtail use of Catholic ladders. In 1881, the second bishops' conference of the Oregon Ecclesiastical Province banned their use, which the previous council had endorsed. With the ascendancy of literacy, the bishops believed that specialized catechisms for certain Catholics were no longer necessary, and that standard textbooks such as the *Baltimore Catechism* were superior. No doubt the bishops were unaware that wherever Catholic ladder use continued, it typically was done in tandem with other resources deemed appropriate by local religious educators. By the 1920s, in the Oregon Province and elsewhere in the United States, native literacy and the use of standard catechisms in English and native languages prevailed and Biblical lectures with new lanternslide "picture machines" became commonplace. Nonetheless, Catholic ladders, with their visual and oral instructional approach, remained popular among many Native American Catholics wherever they had been introduced previously.[71]

---

70   Black Elk, *Black Elk Speaks,* 34–61; Damian Costello, *Black Elk: Colonialism and Lakota Catholicism* (Maryknoll, NY: Orbis Books, 2005), 97, 105–106; Steltenkamp, *Black Elk: Holy Man of the Oglala,* 95, 102; Lacombe, *Pictorial Catechism,* Catholic Ladder Pictorial Catechisms, MUA. Thunder beings, a daybreak star, flying men, friendly wings, and an evil blue man living in flames are other images described by Black Elk in his great vision that correspond with ones in Lacombe's ladder.

71   *The Indian Sentinel* 2, no. 12 (October 1922): 541.

While the bishops' ban no doubt dampened the use of ladders in the Oregon Province, some Native American families saved copies as mementos, especially if their ancestors were catechists who had been instrumental in spearheading its debut. About fifty years later, with the ban still in force but long forgotten, women religious successfully reintroduced Catholic ladders with old copies provided by these families. In 1929, the sisters at Saint Mary's Mission School, at Omak on the Colville Reservation in Washington, successfully resurrected the use of Blanchet's ladder. It provided elementary religious instruction that paved the way for higher-level study with other resources. In 1937, Spokane Dominicans introduced the ladder at weekly Sunday school classes held at the U.S. Government Indian School in Tulalip, Washington. Each week's lesson was based on the ladder, which began with a student explaining one of its pictures, such as the Ten Commandments. In turn, that student called upon another to explain a different aspect of the picture, such as another commandment.[72]

Today's modern era is an ambiguous time. Many Americans in popular culture have favored Native American values and spirituality over Christian beliefs and Catholic influence has declined in Indian Country, especially among the youth. Since the Second Vatican Council, the Church has renounced conformity to its standard Latin interpretation in favor of a universal Church comprised of local churches embracing their cultural interaction and lived experience of the Gospel. In 1982, the Tekakwitha Conference, a Native American Catholic association, and the United States Catholic Conference Department of Education, co-sponsored a catechetical conversation. Participants acknowledged the bicultural struggles of past catechists such as Black Elk; they noted the crucial importance of modern catechetical materials developed with native participation; and they articulated the goal that like Black Elk, native cate-

---

72   Mary Jean Dorcy, "The Catholic Ladder," *The Indian Sentinel* 21, no. 5 (May 1941): 67–68; Catechism class (1941), Catholic Ladder Pictorial Catechisms, MUA; Mary Fitzgibbons, "Okinagan (sic) Indians Fervent," *The Indian Sentinel*, Saint Mary's Mission (Washington) Edition 10, no. 1 (1929–1930): cxii; Hanley, *History of the Catholic Ladder*, 125–126. From 1850 to 1951, the Ecclesiastical Province of Oregon comprised the dioceses in Oregon, Washington, and Idaho. Dorcy's illustration shows that classes used a Blanchet ladder.

chists proclaim the Gospel message according to their life experiences with oral traditions, stories, and tribal relationships.[73] Meanwhile, religious leaders and educators in native parishes and schools have sought new teaching resources while a few have rediscovered the old as well.[74] Since the 2017 opening of Black Elk's canonization cause and the subsequent broadcast of his life story, *Walking the Good Red Road: Nicholas Black Elk's Journey to Sainthood*, several U.S. and Canadian educators and devotees have rediscovered Lacombe's ladder, and one native catechist has sought to recreate Black Elk's narrative interpretation of the Two Roads.[75]

---

73   Huel, *Proclaiming the Gospel*, 284; U.S. Catholic Conference, Department of Education, *Faith and Culture: A Multicultural Catechetical Resource* (Washington, DC: U.S. Catholic Conference, 1987), 3–4. See, especially, three selections in *Faith and Culture*: Michael Galvan, "Native American Catechesis and the Ministry of the Word," 15–21, Genevieve Cuny, "Leadership and Professional Development in Light of the Native American Experience," 53–64, and Kateri Mitchell, "Program Development and Native American Catechesis," 81–90.

74   Emails/interviews of native parish leaders by author, September-October 2008, and Vecsey, *The Paths of Kateri's Kin*, 315, 348. In 2008, some churches reported that Catholic ladders remained on walls, which served as relics of the past and not as contemporary instructional aids. Nonetheless, several pastors and religious educators in native parishes and schools expressed a desire to attempt the use of Catholic ladders for teaching Biblical themes because they were not satisfied with their current results, and it seemed that they would better fit the preferred learning styles of their students. In 2008, John Roselle III, a high school teacher at Red Cloud Indian School, Pine Ridge Reservation, South Dakota, reported success with his students making their own Catholic ladders to demonstrate their reflections on and interpretations of the Bible.

75   Judith Ann Zielinski, writer/producer, *Walking the Good Red Road: Nicholas Black Elk's Journey to Sainthood* (South Bend, IN: NewGroup Media, 2020), 1-hour video. Of the 250 ABC-TV network stations, 188 broadcasted *Walking the Good Red Road*, May 17–July 5, 2020, which prompted a renewed interest in the 1874 Lacombe ladder as an historical document and supplemental catechetical aid. ABC-TV Clearances Report, May 18, 2020. Since then, downloadable copies have been available from the website of the Diocese of Rapid City, South Dakota, along with other materials pertaining to Black Elk's cause. Digital copies of Lacombe's 1874 Catholic ladder and other related materials are available from MUA, which experienced an uptick in requests following the documentary's broadcast. Subsequently, a deacon on the Pine Ridge Reservation, South Dakota, has reported on his efforts to recreate Black Elk's interpretive narrative of Lacombe's ladder.

The Contemporary Ladders of Goutier, Ballard, and Lavoie

With the intent of putting religious education back in the hands of parents and catechists, Bishop Paul J. O'Byrne of Calgary, Alberta,[76] commissioned a modern version of Lacombe's ladder to support the prevailing visual and oral ways of learning familiar in native communities. In 1984, the Oblate priest Maurice Goutier, with assistance from the Blackfoot artist Standing Tall or Niitsit Aipoiyi, responded by creating *Come to Me . . . I am the Way*. This multi-color ladder retained the essence of Lacombe's version while adding several new distinctive features. Published in Calgary and measuring thirty-eight by nineteen inches, its overriding symbol is the sacred circle of life and its corollary, a smaller circle within that represents the Indian shield and the shield of Christ. Other symbols represent the Bible, Christ's life and redemption, the sacraments, the sweat lodge, good ways, and bad ways. It tells the Catholic faith story with Blackfoot symbols, including a Sun Dance pole, sweat lodge, Peyote altar, and the Virgin of Guadalupe. But also retained were images depicting the Protestant Reformation leading to damnation. In the companion narrative, Goutier admonished readers that his ladder was sketchy and not fully developed. So, he invited readers to develop their own narrative according to their own needs.[77]

Come to Me achieved success in Canada and went through multiple printings despite criticism that its retention of "pre-Vatican II images rejecting the Protestant Reformation and non-Christian religions was outdated."[78] Nonetheless, strong interest continued for depicting salvation history pictorially with bicultural symbols from

---

76 O'Byrne served as Calgary's bishop, 1968–1998, soon after the Second Vatican Council (1962–1965) had addressed Catholic Church relations with the modern world.

77 Maurice Goutier, *Come to Me . . . I am the Way* [leaflet] (Calgary, Alberta, undated [1984?]), 3-4. Goutier was an Oblate priest ordained in 1956. He ministered to Sarcee Indians at Calgary area native parishes and schools, 1960s–1970s.

78 Goutier, *Come to Me . . . I am the Way*, 1–12; Rodney Lorenz interview, July 5, 2008. Laminated charts were available before 2000 whereas those available since feature a new durable finish. Lorenz was a vendor who sold the Goutier ladder at the Tekakwitha Conference in Edmonton, Alberta, July 2–6, 2008.

Native American and Judeo-Christian traditions. In British Columbia, Oblate priest Brian Ballard collaborated with a native artist who transformed the Two Roads into a singular spiral "Spirit Trail" that captured post-Vatican II theology and the cyclical rhythm of the four directions. Ballard introduced this new catechetical format and added a supplemental video recording for baptism preparation before his death in 2001.[79]

Goutier then encouraged Oblate priest Sylvain Lavoie to create a contemporary pictorial catechism, which he did while serving the native peoples of northern Saskatchewan. In so doing, Lavoie followed Ballard's lead by arranging lessons in circular progression and he added the "Medicine Wheel" concept of the Cree people. This resulted in the *"Spirit Trail" Leader's Guide* and the *"Spirit Trail" Commentary*, which present twenty-five Bible-based lessons for groups. Each one contains prayer and Scripture readings with bulleted highlights, a "Sharing Circle" for discussions on insights and questions, and suggestions for fellowship. The first ten sessions present Old Testament topics from Creation, the Covenant, and Moses to the Promised Land whereas the last fifteen present New Testament topics from Jesus' life, the Church, and the Sacraments to Eternity. Also, the leader's guide briefly explains Native American, Hebrew, and Christian worldviews and the commentary offers added theological insights for each session, which the leader may add as appropriate. Since 2005, Lavoie paused the Spirit Trail project indefinitely while serving as archbishop of Keewatin-La Pas, encompassing northern Saskatchewan, Manitoba, and Ontario.[80]

---

79   Roman Catholic Diocese of Prince George (British Columbia), https://www.pgdiocese.bc.ca/; Sylvain Lavoie, *The "Spirit Trail" Leader's Guide* (St. Albert, Alberta: 2013), 2. Brian Ballard (1950–2001), an Oblate priest based in Nanaimo, British Columbia, ministered for twenty-three years among Carrier and Sekani Indians in the Prince George Diocese.

80   Lavoie, *The "Spirit Trail" Leader's Guide*, 16 pp, illus., prepublication draft, and Sylvain Lavoie, *The "Spirit Trail" Commentary* (St. Albert, Alberta, undated), unpaginated (17 pp.), prepublication draft. Sylvain Lavoie, emails to author, August 26 and September 6, 2021. Catholic-Hierarchy, https://www.catholic-hierarchy.org/, and Oblates of Mary Immaculate Canada, https://www.omi.ca/. Sylvain Lavoie (1947–), an Oblate and archbishop emeritus, ministered among native peoples of northern Saskatchewan and Manitoba, 1974–2012, and served as coadjutor and archbishop of Keewatin-La Pas, 2005–2012.

Conclusion

Centuries ago in North America, Catholic missionary priests studied native languages to engage the people and present Bible fundamentals and prayers. They extended their efforts with native catechists, Biblical images, and hand-made mnemonic aids. But overall, their effectiveness was limited. During the nineteenth and twentieth centuries, pictorial Catholic ladders became complex learning aids that revolutionized native catechesis. Finetuned through dialogue between missionaries and converts, these aids enabled catechists to learn religious fundamentals and prayers quickly and to engage their peers with the prevailing oral and visual ways of learning with native-based cultural interpretations. Occasionally, competing outside religious groups adapted the Catholic ladder concept, which underscored its effectiveness. In tandem with technological innovations, the ladders evolved into mass-produced charts with vividly colored pictures and detailed graphic designs. Captioned pictures, companion narratives, and pathways illustrating "two roads" of good and bad conduct became commonplace and were distributed among visual and oral cultures worldwide. But as literacy ascended in subsequent generations, Catholic ladder use waned in favor of standard catechetical texts, some of which employed native languages.

Nonetheless, native people have continued to favor visual and oral learning and to honor their spiritual ancestors, and since the Second Vatican Council, they have participated in the development of catechetical materials using native perspectives. In Canada, these materials have included revised Catholic ladders, and in the United States, Black Elk's canonization cause has prompted efforts to recreate his Two Roads interpretive narrative.

Northwest Indian Evangelization by European Jesuits

GERALD MCKEVITT, S.J.*

" ALL OF MY LIFE," wrote the Jesuit Nicole Point, "I have felt my heart throb at the very sound of the word, 'America.'" The young Frenchman who penned those words while en route to the United States in 1835 voiced a sentiment shared by many nineteenth-century Europeans who longed for missionary careers. Felix Barbelin, who emigrated from France to America in 1831, was so eager to proselytize, his sister recorded, that "he used to practice leaping over chairs, that he might be able to spring clear the ditches in America, whither he was always desirous of going." The future founder of the University of Notre Dame, Father Edward Sorin, entertained the same fantasy, writing in 1842, "I see nothing in the world comparable to the life of a missionary among the savages." Steeped since childhood in exotic accounts of Indian life found in the works of Chateaubriand and other romantic writers, Europeans were further inspired to become missionaries by their religious training. Visits by recruiters and a steady stream of literature about converting Native Americans produced a fascination with the frontier that reaped a bountiful harvest of missionaries for the United States.[1]

---

* This essay was first published as "Northwest Indian Evangelization by European Jesuits, 1841–1909," *Catholic Historical Review* 91, no. 4 (October 2005): 688–713.

1   Cornelius M. Buckley, *Nicholas Point, S.J.: His Life and Northwest Indian Chronicles* (Chicago: Loyola University Press, 1989), 86; Eleanor C. Donnelly, *A Memoir of Father Felix Joseph Barbelin, S.J., that Great and Good Son of St. Ignatius Loyola, who lived and labored for more than Thirty-one Years at Old St. Joseph's Church, Philadelphia* (Philadelphia: St. Joseph's Church, 1886), 23; Sorin, quoted in Marvin R. O'Connell, *Edward Sorin* (Notre Dame, IN: University of Notre Dame Press, 2001), 115. See also Gerald McKevitt, S.J., *Brokers of Culture: Italian Jesuits in the American West, 1848–1919* (Stanford, CA: Stanford University Press, 2007).

The rush of Europeans to frontier America was part of a global migration that saw Christian missionaries scatter to the four corners of the earth in the nineteenth century in unprecedented numbers. "Comparable in size and morale with the expeditionary forces of any great power," in the words of one historian, an army of missionaries achieved remarkable results as Christianity "flung its outposts farther afield and won more converts than in any earlier period of like duration."[2] For the Catholic Church, this burst of energy constituted a striking reversal to what had preceded. At the close of the eighteenth century, Catholic missions had been in a state of near collapse, a consequence of the French Revolution, the temporary suppression of the Jesuit order, and Napoleon's thrashing of the papacy. By the end of the Napoleonic era, the total number of European Catholic priests in all the missions of the world numbered only 270. Yet by the mid-nineteenth century, the Church, led by a succession of strong popes, emerged a revivified and highly centralized institution. As Stephen Neill records in his classic *History of Christian Missions,* "No one at the beginning of the century could possibly have imagined that this apparently moribund Church would produce from within itself those astonishing new manifestations of energy." Not only did missionary work revive; it became international to an unprecedented degree. In the United States, much of that transformation was affected by clergy from France, Belgium, Holland, Ireland, and Italy.[3]

Among male religious orders engaged in ministry to Native Americans, none provided more European volunteers than the Society of Jesus. The most popular destination for Jesuits was the Rocky Mountain Mission in the Pacific Northwest. Founded in 1841 by the Belgian Jesuit Pierre-Jean De Smet, its dominion embraced the modern states of Oregon, Washington, Montana, and Idaho. Personnel were drawn from many nations, but the majority came from Italy, driven from their homeland by the upheavals that accompanied the process of national unification known as the *Risorgimento*

---

2   Carlton J. H. Hayes, *A Generation of Materialism, 1871–1900* (New York: Harper, 1941), 148–150; see also Thomas Bokenkotter, *A Concise History of the Catholic Church*, rev. ed. (Garden City, NY: Image Books, 1979), 368.

3   Stephen Neill, *A History of Christian Missions* (New York: Penguin Books, 1990), 250, 397–400, 437.

("Rebirth"). During that movement, which climaxed in 1870 with the fall of papal Rome, anticlericalism drove members of many religious orders from their homeland. When the kingdom of Piedmont in the north began expelling clergy, many Jesuits from the order's Turin Province took up missionary work in the United States, beginning in 1854 when the *gesuiti piemontesi* assumed administration of the Rocky Mountain Mission.

Although the Rocky Mountain Mission was overseen by the Jesuits' exiled Turin Province, its ethnic membership was strikingly diverse. So appealing was the prospect of converting Indians that men from a wider spectrum of countries volunteered for duty there than in any other Jesuit enterprise in the West. By 1895, the Mission's personnel numbered 160 Jesuit priests, brothers, and scholastics. Nearly fifty percent of these were either Italians or Americans, but another forty percent came from France, Germany, Ireland, and Holland. Fired with missionary zeal, volunteers also flocked to the Northwest from Belgium, Switzerland, Prussia, Malta, Corsica, Scotland, Spain, and Canada. Only four of the fifty priests working in the Rocky Mountain Mission at the turn of the century were born in the United States.[4]

What were the implications of this heterogeneity for Indian evangelization? According to the historian Robert I. Burns, it meant that native peoples were "happily spared the experience of receiving Catholicism at the start from any single ethnic psychology—an Irish, French, Italian, or German Catholicism." Arriving in the United States at a time when the identification between Americanism and Protestantism was almost complete, the alien Jesuits enjoyed an advantage that escaped Protestant missionaries. Indians did not view them as Americans, and hence they were not held accountable for repressive United States policy. "As Protestants never failed to point out," the historian Robert J. Loewenberg writes, the Jesuits had great appeal to the Indian because they had "ambiguous national allegiances." Unburdened with an American

---

4   Statistics found in "Catalogus Primus, Anno 1892–95, Missio Mont. Saxos., Provincial Papers: Histories," and "Catalogus Primus, 1899, Rocky Mountain Mission," Jesuit Oregon Province Archives, Foley Center, Gonzaga University, Spokane, Washington (hereafter JOPA).

background, European clergy were less inclined to "fuse the goals of civilization and Christianity," a mistake which undermined Oregon's early Methodist mission. Although their success in affecting lasting conversions varied from tribe to tribe, foreign birth therefore gave the Jesuits a jump in a variety of ways in winning acceptance from native peoples.[5]

Mediating Cultures

One of the ways in which ethnicity influenced evangelization resulted from the priest's role as arbitrator between cultures. As the historian Anne M. Butler has written, "Whether planned or not, missionaries bridged between communities, serving as mediators in the overlapping social dynamics" of nineteenth-century frontier life.

> While these associations inevitably brought conflict, they also brought exchange, adjustment, and accommodation. People came into contact with languages, customs, and values they had not known. Some they accepted; some they rejected. Either way, the process influenced religious practice as well as secular life. This brokering of cultures constituted a major element in Catholic communities in the West, and the result brought both difficulty and understanding to group relations.[6]

Jesuit missionaries in the Pacific Northwest frequently functioned as mediators during armed conflicts that erupted between

---

5   Robert Ignatius Burns, *The Jesuits and the Indian Wars of the Northwest* (New Haven, CT: Yale University Press, 1966), 54–57; Robert C. Carriker, "Joseph M. Cataldo, S.J.: Courier of Catholicism to the Nez Percés," in *Churchmen and the Western Indians*, ed. by Clyde A. Milner II and Floyd A. O'Neill (Norman, OK: University of Oklahoma Press, 1985), 137; Francis Paul Prucha, *American Indian Policy in Crisis: Christian Reformers and the Indian 1865–1900* (Norman, OK: University of Oklahoma Press, 1976), 158-159; Robert J. Loewenberg, *Equality on the Oregon Frontier: Jason Lee and the Methodist Mission 1834–43* (Seattle: University of Washington Press, 1976), 96–97; Gerald McKevitt, "'The Jump that Saved the Rocky Mountain Mission': Jesuit Recruitment and the Pacific Northwest," *Pacific Historical Review* 55 (1986), 447.

6   Anne M. Butler, "Sacred Contests in the West," *The Frontiers and Catholic Identities*, ed. by Anne M. Butler, Michael E. Engh, S.J., Thomas W. Spalding, C.F.X. (Maryknoll, NY: Orbis, 1999), 53, 107–108.

natives and settlers. From the time of the Whitman Massacre by the Cayuse in 1847 until the end of the so-called Nez Percé War in 1877, the clergy brokered peace between the warring races. Because of their close contact with the tribes and their linguistic fluency, missionaries Nicola Congiato, Joseph Joset, Joseph Menetrey, Antonio Ravalli, and others reconciled opponents during the War of 1858.[7] At the government's request, De Smet was released from his desk job in St. Louis to support the peace effort in the West. "But for the priest's help," Colonel George Wright, commander of the U.S. troops, wrote of Joset after a series of negotiations with several tribes, "the affair would never have been brought to so speedy a conclusion." Twenty years later, Jesuits rode throughout the Northwest calming fearful whites and dissuading wavering Indian bands from joining Chief Joseph and his followers during Nez Percé unrest. Giuseppe Cataldo's mastery of native tongues made him the controlling influence in keeping some tribes at peace and in preventing the spread of hostilities. "If it was not for the restraining influence of the Jesuit fathers," wrote the agent at Colville, John Sims, "there would have been serious trouble in this section long ago."[8]

Participation in the peace process was a precarious exercise because missionaries often sympathized with aggrieved natives. Father Gregorio Gazzoli, who helped persuade the Coeur d'Alenes, Spokanes, and other tribes not to join the belligerent Nez Percés under Chief Joseph, placed blame for the uprising on the government. "From my experience here among the Indians, I am convinced that there never has been necessity for a war with the Indi-

---

7   In 1858, the invasion of gold rushers into Washington Territory precipitated a full-scale war between U.S. forces and the Spokane, Coeur d'Alene, and other tribes. After the cessation of hostilities, the government, assisted by missionaries, inaugurated a campaign to sustain the peace by a series of new treaties that limited native land holdings. The Nez Percé War of 1877 resulted from federal attempts to force some tribal bands to surrender buffalo hunting and settle on a reservation.

8   Wright, quoted in Burns, *The Jesuits and the Indian Wars*, 313. Burns offers the most complete analysis of the Jesuit role in these conflicts; John Sims (Colville) to Brouillet, April 26, 1874, Bureau of Catholic Indian Missions Records, Marquette University, Milwaukee, Wisconsin (hereafter BCIM).

ans if truth and honesty had prevailed in the dealings of the whites with them. A very great responsibility, therefore, rests with those who caused this war," including the local press for its "reckless reporting of murders and Indian atrocities." Gazzoli was loath to blame Chief Joseph for his role in the uprising. "A little kindness I am sure would have deterred him from so desperate an act, and spared so many victims," he wrote. "It is true that for some time he has been preparing to defend his rights with arms, but it is true also that he hesitated to the last moment."[9]

Missionaries also served as middlemen in negotiations between Native Americans and the federal government over tribal boundaries. Confrontation between the races led the United States to the conclusion that unlimited and exclusive Indian occupation of their homelands could not continue, thus prompting decades of treaty-making aimed at preserving the peace and confining once free-roaming tribes to reservations. The Jesuits participated in these negotiations, as missionary Giuseppe Giorda once told President Ulysses S. Grant, with "full knowledge of these matters and with the sincerest desire for the peace of the whites and of the Indians." But they recognized the danger of alienating both sides.[10] "We behaved quite neutral and as a stranger to it, [as] our critical position between Whites and Indians required of us," Antonio Ravalli remarked about attempts to remove the Flatheads from the Bitterroot Valley in the 1870s.[11]

But neutrality was often impossible. "I know very well that over at the Department" of the Interior, Giorda said, "they think that the refusal of the Flatheads to come into the new reservation is attributed to our missionaries' interference." Some priests were understandably reluctant to assume the mantle of advisor. When officials in Washington, D.C., sought Giuseppe Cataldo's intercession in negotiating a treaty with the Nez Percés in 1876, he refused.

---

9   Gregorio Gazzoli (Fort Colville, Washington) to Archbishop Blanchet, clipping, JOPA.

10   Giorda (St. Ignatius Mission) to President Grant, February 21, 1876, 10/10, BCIM.

11   Ravalli (St. Mary's Mission, Montana) to Claggert, October 30, 1871, St. Mary's Collection, JOPA.

"The reason is because I have promised to these Indians several times never to speak to them about making their reservation smaller. . . . And I would lose a great deal of my authority, if I were to busy myself with them about such matters."[12]

Mediation in the peace process, therefore, brought both challenge and opportunity. The priests' presence at treaty negotiations enhanced their position with government officials. In a letter to the Commissioner of Indian Affairs, the agent for the Flathead Reservation in 1873 praised the missionaries "to whom I am indebted for so much success, for it was through them I have succeeded in gaining the confidence of the Indians and with their cooperation I have no doubt of the removal of most if not all the Indians of this tribe before next winter without any trouble."[13] In other instances, mediation enhanced the Jesuits' stature among Indians and rendered them more amenable to clerical influence. The war of 1858 "brought about a change of affairs" among the Spokane Indians, a missionary wrote; "being defeated by the U.S. troops, and greatly compromised, the Indians appealed to the fathers for aid." Some tribes became more open to proselytization. As the historian Howard Harrod has noted, "participation in missionary institutions may provide a needed center of social order and identity for Indians undergoing rapid social change—a conservative, stabilizing function." Since the Blackfeet, for example, "could not return to their old world, although many tried, they were forced to make some adjustments to the institutions and cultural values of white society."[14]

These circumstances gave some priests extraordinary influence. When Pietro Bandini called upon bands of Kootenai on the Flathead Reservation in 1885, he was sought out for his counsel on a variety of issues, including the tribe's negotiation over a right-of-way with the Northern Pacific Railroad. "I listened *pro tribunali coram populo*

---

12 Giorda (St. Ignatius Mission) to Brouillet, February 26, 1876, 10/10, BCIM; Cataldo (Lapwai, Idaho) to S.S. Fenn, January 25, 1876, 9/1, BCIM.

13 D. Shanahan (Flathead Agency, Montana) to Commissioner of Indian Affairs, April 24, 1873, Correspondence, BCIM.

14 L. Van Ree, "The Spokane Indians," *Woodstock Letters* 18 (1889), 354–355; Howard L. Harrod, *Mission Among the Blackfeet* (Norman, OK: University of Oklahoma Press, 1981), xxi, 48.

to everyone," that is, in open court before all the people, he wrote, "adjusting questions of matrimony, clarifying certain doubts and giving them practical instructions on how to take care of themselves during the raging of the typhus." Other individuals "reserved their major problems for a time when they could speak privately with the priest."[15]

In some cases, war and its aftermath hamstrung evangelization. The conflict of 1877 "ruined the Nez Percés physically, morally, and religiously," Cataldo maintained. But "the crowning of all the miseries" was the opening of their reservation to Whites "who literally inundated the country, and entirely drowned the Indians." In such circumstances, missionaries strained to find ears receptive to their message. Treaties mandating the shift of tribal homelands sometimes required the costly relocation of missions. Other compacts left missionary mediators, in Joset's words, "much exposed to the revengeful dispositions" of rebellious native leaders who threatened, "Were the Black Gowns out of the country we would begin again."[16]

"Faith Enters by the Ear"

If outsider status transformed missionaries into brokers of cultures, it also turned them into effective linguists. There was a direct link between a missionary's European origin and his ability to master native languages, a fundamental first step toward effective proselytization. It was also a principle upon which Jesuit tradition placed a high priority. Paul Le Jeune, a seventeenth-century missionary who served among the Montagnais of New France, stated the case for language-learning most succinctly in 1633 when, quoting St. Paul, he declared, "Faith enters by the ear." How did ancestry influence Jesuit linguistic activity in the Northwest? Most of the priests had not only studied classical and European languages before becoming missionaries; they also taught them. Although Native American idioms were strikingly different from those of the

---

15   Bandini letter, 1885, quoted in Robert Bigart and Clarence Woodcock, "St. Ignatius Mission, Montana, Reports from Two Jesuit Missionaries, Part I," *Arizona and the West* 23 (Summer 1981), 165.

16   Cataldo, "Nez Perce Indian Mission," JOPA; Joset, quoted in Burns, *The Jesuits and the Indian Wars*, 315.

Indo-European family, and although their linguistic training was, from a modern viewpoint, limited in its technical aspect, the missionaries' Old World experience did ease their study of New World vernaculars. The international make-up of the Jesuit order in the Northwest also had implications for language learning. Most of the missionaries were from small nations, and since childhood they had been exposed to a diversity of tongues. As Europeans, they were usually not daunted by the prospect of learning a new speech, but recognized it as a necessity of life. That experience freed them from the psychological obstacles that often hinder effective mastery of new languages. It is significant that twenty-three of the twenty-six Jesuit linguists whose papers constitute the Northwest Indian Language Collection of Gonzaga University were foreign-born.[17]

The Jesuits' European origins had other consequences. Many of them came to the United States knowing little or no English. Indeed, Italian so dominated conversation in the Jesuit community at Idaho's Sacred Heart Mission that Father Luigi Parodi thought he was back in Italy when he visited there. Not a few newly arrived missionaries were obliged to simultaneously pick up both English and an indigenous language. In 1874, Filippo Rappagliosi recorded that his chief occupation was "studying two languages at once—English and Kalispel." In some cases this unusual circumstance provided an urgent incentive for mastering the native dialect. Unable to speak with Indians in English, the missionary, if he hoped to communicate, was compelled to master the aboriginal idiom as soon as possible. In some instances, priority was given to acquiring the Indian language. "As I expected to spend all my life amongst savages," the Belgian Brother William Claessens once wrote, "I did not pay much attention to English." Filippo Canestrelli, professor at

---

17 Le Jeune's reference to Romans 10:17 is found in Reuben Gold Thwaites, ed., *The Jesuit Relations and Allied Documents; Travels and Exploration of the Jesuit Missionaries in New France, 1620–1719* (New York: Pageant Book, 1959), V: 191. For a fuller analysis of missionary language-learning, see Gerald McKevitt, "Jesuit Missionary Linguistics in the Pacific Northwest: A Comparative Study," *Western Historical Quarterly* 21 (1990), 291–304; see also Eleanor and Robert C. Carriker, *Guide to Microfilm Edition of the Oregon Province Archives of the Society of Jesus Indian Language Collection: The Pacific Northwest Tribes* (Spokane: Gonzaga University, 1976).

the Roman College, emigrated to America in 1878. From Fort Colville, the new missionary wrote to Cataldo informing him of his safe arrival and stating his assumption that English was the first language he should learn. The reply came back from Cataldo: "No. Kalispel." A decade later, Canestrelli still did not know much English, but he had authored thirteen publications in Kalispel. And of Giorda, a government agent once wrote, "He speaks English poorly," but he "speaks the Blackfoot language fluently."[18]

Most of the priests in the Northwest could express themselves in one or more native dialects. "All our Fathers speak the Flathead" language, Joseph Joset, missionary to the Coeur d'Alenes, reported in 1871, although he did not characterize the level of competency attained by them. The Blackfeet were impressed by Pietro Paulo Prando's knowledge of their language. Kootenai was the specialty of Filippo Canestrelli. Contemporaries judged John Post of Luxembourg "remarkably proficient" in Kalispel, an appraisal borne out by the use modern scholars of linguistics have made of his writings. Mengarini, Canestrelli, Post, and Antonio Morvillo authored useful dictionaries and grammars of Northwest Indian languages. A few of the missionaries were multi-lingual. Giorda's talent for languages was evidenced by his familiarity with the idioms of the Blackfeet, Nez Percés, Flathead, Yakima, Kootenai, and Gros Ventres tribes. Urbano Grassi was allegedly conversant in an equal number. Cataldo, one of the most accomplished linguists, knew ten.[19]

---

18 Parodi, "Reminiscences," JOPA; Filippo Rappagliosi, *Memorie del P. Filippo Rappagliosi D.C.D.G. missionario apostolico nelle Montagne Rocciose*, ed. Victor Garrand (Rome: Tipografia di B. Morini, 1879), 86, JOPA; William Claessens, [n.p.], to unnamed Belgian woman, [n.d.], Claessens Papers, JOPA; Canestrelli story in Mackin, "Wanderings of Fifty Years," Mackin Papers, JOPA; Agent Upson's evaluation of Giorda is quoted in Harrod, *Mission Among the Blackfeet*, 56; see also Carriker, "Joseph M. Cataldo, S.J.: Courier of Catholicism," 9.

19 Joset's remarks in *Letters and Notices* [English Jesuit Province Newsletter] 7 (1871), 322–323, Archivum Romanum Societatis Iesu (hereafter ARSI); Harrod, *Mission Among the Blackfeet*, 58–59; *Helena* (MT) *Daily Herald*, August 12, 1882, news clipping in Giorda Papers, JOPA; data regarding Cataldo is found in Carriker, "Joseph M. Cataldo, S.J.: Courier of Catholicism," 10, 13.

Moving Beyond Words

As in language study, so too in religious instruction, nationality made a difference. Unlike Protestant clergy who drew upon American cultural values and practices, the Jesuit evangelization program relied on European traditions, especially on devotional practices from Italy. The popular piety of southern Europe, with its emphasis on an activist deity, communal worship, and its conception of a world filled with miraculous forces and supernatural beings often complemented Indian religious belief. "Italian popular religion was a complex system of magical practices inherited from a pre-Christian past," one historian has written, "and sustained through centuries of co-existence with Christianity." Imbued with that culture, the Italian missionaries were culturally predisposed to tolerate many Native American expressions of spirituality. As a consequence, two religious systems—Indian and Christian—often overlapped and intermingled in the Northwest, not unlike the blending of pre-Christian and Christian practices that had occurred in Italy many centuries earlier.[20]

When, for example, Roman-born Gregorio Mengarini sought to give the Flatheads "an idea of the ecclesiastical ceremonies that are used in the Catholic church," he borrowed from familiar archetypes. In order to replicate the Forty Hours devotion, in which the Italian faithful honored the Eucharist, he fashioned a throne out of white muslin and two red handkerchiefs, "a rather decent monstrance" carved from "a piece of wood covered with gold leaf," and candles composed of buffalo fat. Thus prepared, "on Easter Sunday I was able to reproduce in miniature the spectacle presented in the Roman College during the Forty Hours devotion."[21] These Italianate

---

20   Jay P. Dolan, *The American Catholic Experience: A History from Colonial Times to the Present* (Garden City, NY: Image Books, 1985), 173–174; James Axtell, *The Invasion Within: The Contest of Cultures in Colonial North America* (New York: Oxford University Press, 1985), 14. For a fuller analysis of the evangelization in the Pacific Northwest, see Gerald McKevitt, "The Art of Conversion: Jesuits and Flatheads in Nineteenth-Century Montana," *U.S. Catholic Historian* 12, no. 4 (Fall 1994), 49–64.

21   James Axtell, "The European Failure to Convert the Indians: An Autopsy," *Papers of the Sixth Algonquian Conference, 1974* (Ottawa: National Museums of Canada, 1975), 280; Mengarini (Vancouver) to Roothaan, September 26, 1844, Mont. Sax. 1001-VI-2, ARSI.

ceremonials elicited a lively response because they appealed to the native psyche with its yearning for the supernatural, the hope for miracles, and the pageant of processions. When teaching catechism, the chief instrument of religious indoctrination, Europe once again supplied the model. "I taught the children catechism by a method commonly followed in Rome," Gregorio Mengarini recorded. After they had memorized "several hundred questions and answers," a public contest was announced.

> On the appointed day, all the competitors, none of whom must be over thirteen years of age, arrange themselves in two lines in the church. The first proposes a question to be answered by his opponent, and so all along the line, each in turn answering or proposing a question. Whoever misses, loses his chance for the prizes. Only one that has seen such a contest can realize its interest. I have seen the Indian boys as pale as their little bronze faces could become, and perspiring profusely, even in the depth of winter; while all around were gathered the parents and relatives of the children waiting anxiously to see who would be the victor.[22]

To facilitate learning, the missionaries inspired competition and they rewarded good performances with prizes just as they had done in the classrooms of Europe. "Every day, for each good answer, tickets of approbation are given," De Smet explained, "one or more, according to the difficulty of the question proposed." Contenders who had won tickets during the week "are rewarded on Sunday with crosses, medals, or ribbons, publicly distributed." Boys who triumphed in Mengarini's Sunday afternoon "catechism bees" received arrows. "The wish to see their children distinguish themselves has attracted almost the whole colony to catechism," De Smet said. "None of the chiefs who have children fail to be there; and there is not less emulation among the parents than among the children themselves."[23]

---

22   Mengarini, "Rocky Mountains," *Woodstock Letters* 18 (1889), 34.

23   Hiram Martin Chittenden and Alfred Talbot Richardson, *Life, Letters and Travels of Father De Smet* (New York: Arno Press, 1969), I: 336–337; see also Gregory Mengarini, *Recollections of the Flathead Mission, Containing Brief Observations both Ancient and Contemporary Concerning this Particular Nation*, ed. and trans. by Gloria Ricci Lothrop (Glendale, CA: Arthur H. Clark, 1977), 31.

Enter Singing

Music quickly emerged as a practical point of convergence between Native Americans and Europeans. The centrality of music in Italian society, which had come to full flower in the eighteenth century, was frequently commented upon by outsiders. "Hardly has one crossed the Alps," a visitor noted, "before music appears quite spontaneously. The violin, the harp, and singing stop you in the streets. The further one advances into Italy, the closer to perfection the music. Even the service in village churches sounds much like a concert."[24] Jesuits were gratified to learn that Indians shared their delight in song. "It is amazing how these natives love music," Mengarini wrote to a friend from the Flathead mission. "Both the young people and the small children have an admirable facility and quickness for learning whatever they are taught." They "love music," affirmed Filippo Rappagliosi, "and when they hear the priests sing, are in ecstasy." Missionaries discovered the importance of chant in indigenous religious practice. As a modern ethnomusicologist observes, "for the Flatheads, the most important single fact about music and its relationship to the total world is its origins in the supernatural sphere." "All true and proper songs, particularly in the past, owe their origin to a variety of contacts experienced by humans with beings which, though a part of this world, are super humans and the source of both individual and tribal powers and skills." Tunes were employed, for example, to attract a guardian spirit who, Mengarini recorded, "would reveal his presence by singing with them." Music, the Jesuit learned, could be used to unstop the ears of the most reluctant congregations. Several Nez Percé families who lived near St. Mary's never entered the church. "But when the music began, they often came to hear it, which provided a good opportunity for them to hear the instruction that is given during a sung mass."[25]

---

24 Maurice Vaussard, *Daily Life in Eighteenth-Century Italy*, trans. by Michael Heron (New York: Macmillan, 1963), 159.

25 Mengarini (Vancouver) to Roothaan, September 26, 1844, Mont. Sax. 1001-V-2, ARSI; Mengarini, *Recollections of the Flathead Mission*, 162, 201; Rappagliosi, *Memorie del P. Filippo Rappagliosi*, 81, 91, JOPA; Alan P. Merriam, *Ethnomusicology of the Flathead Indians* (Chicago: Aldine Publishing, 1967), 3, 127–131.

Having ascertained the centrality of singing among the Flathead, the priests translated Christian liturgical music into Salish. Mengarini wrote a funeral dirge by joining Christian concepts about death to a traditional Flathead lamentation for the departed. For evening prayer, he composed three songs in Salish, two based on scores of his own composition and a third borrowed from a French tune. Popular Italian melodies were transposed into songs in the native tongue. For a Christmas celebration at Montana's St. Peter's Mission in 1875, Rappagliosi translated a traditional holiday hymn, "Tu scendi dalle stelle o Re del cielo," from Italian into the Blackfoot tongue.[26] As early as 1845, Mengarini trained a small band of twelve Indian boys whose instruments included a clarinet, flute, two accordions, a tambourine, piccolo, cymbals, and a base-drum. The ensemble performed an entire Mass score that Mengarini had carried with him from Italy. "We played to notes," he wrote, because "Indians have excellent eyes and ears." "They have learned (who would have believed it?) to sing the 'Gloria,' the 'Credo,' and everything else, and they sing it in plain chant," Rappagliosi rhapsodized in a letter to his parents. Over a century later, these "Bitterroot Valley songs" were still sung among the tribe.[27]

Music was not confined to the liturgy. Unlike Methodist missionaries who said in 1841 that singing "occupied only a secondary place" in the teaching of religion, music occupied a primary place in Jesuit instruction. Pietro Paulo Prando wrote a song in the language of the Crows to impart Christian teachings. "Setting together the words I knew, I made a hymn," he reported in 1883, "and now the hymn is popular in two camps. They have a great desire to learn it by heart and to sing it according to the tune of *Iste Confessor*, a Gregorian chant. Describing his work among the Blackfeet, Prando said, "Their great love of song . . . greatly aids me in teaching the

---

26 Rappagliosi, *Memorie del P. Filippo Rappagliosi*, 122, JOPA; Prando (St. Peter's Mission) to Cataldo, ca. 1881, in *Woodstock Letters* 12 (1883), 311.

27 L. B. Palladino, *Indian and White in the Northwest; or, a History of Catholicity in Montana* (Baltimore: J. Murphy, 1894), 76; Mengarini, "Rocky Mountains," *Woodstock Letters* 18 (1889), 33–34; Rappagliosi, *Memorie del P. Filippo Rappagliosi*, 81, 91, JOPA; Merriam, *Ethnomusicology of the Flathead Indians*, 131.

prayers and truths of religion." The priest even composed a chant to discourage polygamy.[28]

Religious Ritual and Symbol

In their religious rituals, as in their music, the missionaries attempted to bridge the cultural gap between themselves and their converts by finding common ground. As the historian James Axtell has written, Catholic Christianity appealed to Native Americans as "a religion of the liturgy, of colorful and effective ceremony, based on daily habits of prayer and worship." Embracing the human emotions, Catholicism "resembled native religious observances in color, drama, and participation and appealed to the Indians' practical intelligence."[29] Giuseppe Cataldo, for example, let pass no opportunity to incorporate fire and flame into his liturgical services, a practice that complemented the native aesthetic as well as his own "Italian appreciation of many candles in church," as a colleague put it. In his native Sicily, thousands of candles and lanterns transformed the normally dark cathedral into a palace from the *Thousand and One Nights* on the feast of Saint Rosalia. "The whole building was radiant," exclaimed a visitor to Rome's church of the Gesù in 1865. Burning tapers brightened not just every cornice and altar of the interior, but also the temple's ornate facade. Cataldo replicated these spectacles in modest wooden chapels throughout the Indian Northwest. He ordered sacristans to "'lit everything,' meaning *all* the candles"—almost the only slip he made in English, a contemporary observed—whenever large crowds of native worshipers gathered for services.[30]

This blending of traditions served multiple purposes. Elaborate ceremonials sought not only to attract and edify the native faithful, but also to impress upon them that they belonged to a Christian

---

28   Prando (Crow Camp) to Cataldo, September 26, 1883, Prando Papers, JOPA; Prando, *Woodstock Letters* 12 (1883), 326; see also Harrod, *Mission Among the Blackfeet*, 59.

29   Axtell, "The European Failure," 280.

30   Vaussard, *Daily Life in Eighteenth-Century Italy*, 142–143; E.I. Pubrick, "Triduum in Honor of B. John Berchmans at the Roman College," *Letters and Notices* 3 (1865–66), 84–99, ARSI; Michael O'Malley, "Cataldo ms," JOPA.

community that extended far beyond the bounds of their village. This centralizing feature of Italian devotionalism has been examined by the historian Donald Weinstein. Distinguishing between the cult of saints in northern and southern Europe, he maintains that the prototypical holy persons selected for veneration in Germany and the Low Countries were political figures, great prelates and princes. The typical saint of the Mediterranean world, however, was a wonder-worker who was intimately engaged in the miraculous and in the supernatural. Moreover, southern European hagiology, influenced by the papacy, showed a preference for saints who both symbolized and furthered church unity. Among Italians, the cultic veneration of holy persons had a particularly strong centralizing role. This was the type of devotionalism that the Jesuits of Italy brought to native converts of the Pacific Northwest. Through the use of shared symbols—processions, benediction, High Mass, music, patron saints—the missionaries sought to integrate Indian congregations into both a supernatural and a global community. Sermons as well as rituals often aimed at drawing parallels between the natives' experience and that of Christians elsewhere. In 1889, for example, when Cataldo preached to the tribes assembled at Sacred Heart Mission, he focused on the plight of those whose lands were disappearing under the allotment policy. "This morning Fr. Cataldo delivered an eloquent sermon to the Indians," a companion noted, "alluding to Ireland and St. Patrick, [and] how the land of this good people was taken away, and how it nevertheless always kept our Holy Faith."[31]

Right Season, Right Rite

Catholic feast days filled the liturgical year, celebrated with all the pomp and ceremony that a mission's modest circumstances allowed. Indian communities entered into the liturgical cycle of the Catholic Church, beginning with the four weeks of Advent, which culminated with Mass on Christmas Eve. At midnight, the congregation gathered in the vast square before the church where, as in

---

31   Donald Weinstein, *Saints and Society: The Two Worlds of Western Christendom* (Chicago: University of Chicago Press, 1982), 183–185; "De Smet [Sacred Heart Mission] Diary, 1878–1939," entry for March 18, 1889, JOPA.

Italy, an observer wrote in 1895, bonfires lent drama to the event, casting "a truly fairy effect over the deep snow." Among the Nez Percés catechized by Cataldo this ceremony was called "Allakki" (With Fire). As missionary accounts show, it blended Indian and European cultural elements.

> The Indians gather around it in a broken circle, and form a fascinating scene, while the ruddy light of the bonfire plays on their bronze countenances and gay apparel. Some of the chief men, by turns, address the crowd eloquently on the feast [being] commemorated and [on] the various significations of the bonfire. The words are accompanied, as usual, with frequent and graceful gestures. The speeches being ended, all proceed to the church, where prayers, a sermon, and benediction of the Most Holy Sacrament follow.[32]

"The people is (sic) coming with candles," a priest described the Christmas Eve procession at Sacred Heart Mission, and it is a "beautiful sight." In a long line, the worshipers "two by two, left their camp singing, chiefs, soldiers, men and women towards the church." After "the usual speech of the head Indian chief at the door of the church," the congregation sang "Adeste Fideles," marching to the crib of the infant Jesus, where they deposited offering of candles or coins and sang Indian hymns. The high altar "splendidly illuminated with over 200 lights," Mass was celebrated with "the Indians singing from beginning to end." The evening concluded with the firing of guns in the Indian camp (as had been done during high points in the Mass); hence the Indian name for the feast, "Firing of Arms." The Christmas celebration continued for days, ending with the inauguration of the New Year and a ceremonial hand-shaking. After Mass, a Jesuit wrote in 1898, "all the Indians went from the front of the church to the front door of the fathers' dwelling house to shake hands with the fathers, who were there waiting for that purpose, as prearranged with chief Seltice. The Indians went in an interminable long line, beginning with the chiefs, followed by the militia, then all the men followed by the

---

32 "De Smet [Sacred Heart Mission] Diary, 1878–1939," entry for December 25, 1895, JOPA; Cataldo, [Dictation re Nez Percés to O'Malley], JOPA.

women. . . . [Then they] continued their way homeward through the big gate opposite our dwelling house."[33]

Spring brought a new series of feast days, the capstone of which was Easter, a celebration that had originally coincided with the buffalo hunt. The highpoint of the feast was a dramatic reenactment of Christ's death, burial, and resurrection from the tomb. Drawing on a devotion popular in southern Europe since the Middle Ages, the ceremony mixed Indian and Italian traditions. Father Antonio Ravalli carved the wooden corpus used in the pageant with removable arms so that the crucified Christ could be realistically laid out as if dead and borne in procession. The enactment at St. Ignatius Mission in Montana began in the church on Good Friday evening when the people gathered around bonfires in preparation for the grand outdoor procession. Inside the church whose sanctuary had been remodeled into a Mount Calvary, the body of the crucified Christ was removed from the cross and placed on a bier. Preceded by the instruments of crucifixion—nails and crown of thorns—the life-size corpus was conveyed in solemn procession to the village cemetery for burial. Meanwhile, the congregation intoned a Flathead death chant adapted by Canestrelli to the occasion. "Everyone mourned, as is the custom during these days," recorded Pietro Bandini, with wails and other expressions of sorrow.[34]

Other pious practices flowered during the spring. These included devotions to St. Joseph, a practice popularized and promoted by Jesuits in Italy since the seventeenth century. Venerated as the patriarchal protector and defender of Christians, Joseph's statue adorned the chapel of every Indian mission, college, and parish founded by Italians in the West. Joseph's name was affixed to the most improbable objects—from a silver mine in Colorado to a boat in Alaska. The saint's intercession guided even the weather. When a spring shower threatened to dampen the picnic of Indian school boys at St. Ignatius Mission, a grateful Geronimo D'Aste recorded, "It rained some of the morning, but through St.

---

33   "De Smet [Sacred Heart Mission] Diary, 1878–1939," entries for December 24, 1889, December 25, 1897, January 1, 1898, JOPA.

34   Bandini letter, 1885, quoted in Bigart and Woodcock, "St. Ignatius Mission, Part I," *Arizona and the West* 23 (Summer 1981), 170.

Joseph's intercession, it stopped raining until they came back." Conversely, when a downpour rescued the mission's wheat crop from drought, the diarist jubilantly noted, "Rain last night and today. Vivat St. Joseph!"[35]

The practice of dedicating the month of March to Joseph, inaugurated in Rome in 1810, was widely promoted by Italian Jesuits. At the nightly vigil before the feast of St. Joseph on March 19, bonfires were lit and services held in the church before the illumined altar of the saint at Sacred Heart Mission. The congregation heard speeches by their chiefs and a sermon by Cataldo, after which the priest distributed, first to Chief Seltice and then to the congregation, "March blossoms in honor of St. Joseph." These "blossoms," small pieces of paper inscribed with votive offerings to the saint, were deposited before his statue, where they remained until the end of the month. On the saint's day, Indian Catholics enacted the Sicilian ritual known as St. Joseph's Table. According to custom, special foods—notably oranges and lemons—were placed on a table and distributed to honored recipients. A ceremonial honoring the aged missionary Joseph Joset on his nameday, March 19, 1891, illustrated the conflation of Italian and Indian customs. Staged in the school hall of Sacred Heart Mission before a large audience of Coeur d'Alenes, the event began with an address by Chief Seltice, who then ritually "laid an orange on the table in front of the Father."

> Chief Edward then followed in an address and an orange. Then all sang a hymn to St. Joseph, one of Father Giorda's compositions. The men then filed up and next the women each making an offering in turn. Most of the offerings consisted of oranges. One presented chewing gum; several gave eggs; one donated a little whistle; another gave a lead pencil; and a number laid down nickel dimes. When this solemn presentation had ended, Father Joset rose and made a speech in Indian. As soon as he began, Seltice got up and stood by him and every sentence uttered by the Father was repeated in a very loud voice by the Chief. This is a peculiar Indian custom called

---

35 "House Diary, St. Ignatius Mission, 1901–09," entries for May 26, 1903, and May 15, 1906, JOPA.

'Elepskoiyet,' whereby great honor is shown to a speaker. Father Joset then gave his blessing to all. As he was very weak, four Indians picked up his chair and carried him over to his room.[36]

In May, communities honored the Virgin Mary. Although the practice of dedicating the month to her had a long history, its diffusion throughout Italy in the late eighteenth century began with the publication of a small devotional book by the Jesuit theologian Alfonso Muzzarelli. Entitled *Il mese di Maggio* ("The Month of May"), this popular work was published in over 150 editions in the nineteenth century. Its aim was the sanctification of the life of the ordinary Christian through a series of devotions and the practice of specified virtues. During May, participants performed a daily sequence of prayers, hymns, reflections, and virtuous actions selected from a series of *fioretti spirituali* ("spiritual blossoms"). The *fioretti* committed the devotee to good deeds such as visiting someone sick or in prison and offering comfort; performing an act of self-denial; setting aside part of a meal for a poor person; making fifteen minutes of mental prayer; and so forth. Inscribed on small bits of colored paper, the "blossoms" were later deposited as a "bouquet" at a shrine to Mary in whose honor the acts of virtue had been performed. Widely popular in Italy, the devotion was promoted in the United States by Jesuit exiles Salvatore Personè, who translated Muzzarelli's work for distribution in New Mexico, and Lorenzo Palladino, whose *May Blossoms* enjoyed wide use by both Indian and White congregations in the Northwest.[37]

"We have begun, even here, the month of Mary," Rappagliosi wrote from St. Ignatius Mission, Montana, in 1875. "The method we observe is that proposed by Fr. Muzzarelli" and "our functions do not fall short of your Gesù, or the other churches of Rome," Giuseppe Caruana wrote to friends in Italy from Sacred Heart Mission. Devotees among the Coeur d'Alenes gather in the church before "a beautiful painting of the Blessed Virgin" that is "an excel-

---

36   "De Smet [Sacred Heart] Mission Diary, 1878–1939," entry for March 18 and 19, 1889, JOPA; Barnum, "Joset," *Woodstock Letters* 30 (1901), 211.

37   Alfonso Muzzarelli, *Il Mese di Maggio Consacrato a Maria Santissima* (Rome, 1856 ed.).

lent copy of the Madonna in San Carlo in Corso" in Rome. "There is a distribution of acts of virtue to be practiced the next day, the ejaculations and flowerets, just as they are in Fr. Muzzarelli's book." The Roman custom of adorning an image or picture of the Madonna with gifts was transferred to Indian America. Offerings common in Italy ("gold and silver, precious stones and gems") were substituted in the Pacific Northwest with "trinkets of every kind." The Madonna of St. Ignatius Mission, Rappagliosi reported, wears "on her breast a beautiful necklace of shells, and many strings of glass beads of various colors with contrasting big wolf teeth, a bear's claw, and other niceties."[38]

One of the year's greatest celebrations was the feast of Corpus Christi, a June event honoring Christ in the Eucharist. Universal in Europe since the fourteenth century, the great highlight of the feast was public veneration of the host in a public procession that wended its way from the church, through the village, and out into the open countryside. First introduced among the Flatheads at St. Mary's Mission, this devotional spectacle appealed to many tribal communities because it coincided with their annual summer rendezvous to harvest the roots of wild plants. For bands of Spokanes, Coeur d'Alenes, Colvilles, Kalispels and other tribes that lived separately much of the year, these lengthy gatherings provided opportunity for games, trading, visiting relatives, and other communal festivities. When the United States government began to prohibit native ceremonials and powwows, Corpus Christi became even more attractive as a substitute ritual.[39]

The June celebration unfolded in early summer as the pink-petalled bitterroot and the light blue blossoms of the camas dominated the Northwestern landscape. Long before the assembly started, the tribes began flocking to the nearest mission, coming from "the four winds," as one Jesuit put it. At the Colville agency,

---

38   *Letters and Notices* 6 (1869), 226–233, ARSI; Rappagliosi, *Memorie del P. Filippo Rappagliosi*, 115, JOPA.

39   The most complete analysis of the feast is Miri Rubin, *Corpus Christi: The Eucharist in Late Medieval Culture* (New York: Cambridge University Press, 1991); John Fahey, *The Kalispel Indians* (Norman, OK: University of Oklahoma Press, 1986), 32.

a priest reported in 1877, two weeks prior to the feast "caravans of 100, 200, and even 300 arrived at a time and pitched their tents around the church." The grand climax of the day was a solemn procession of the Blessed Sacrament. In preparation for the cavalcade, men of the Kalispel tribe "made a long alley, planting on both sides small pine trees from the church door down [across] the prairie, forming a semi-circle at the end to turn back." In 1877 over 2,300 people participated in the half-mile procession at Colville, "walking two by two about three feet apart from each other singing hymns, reciting the beads." Young men on horseback periodically fired their guns into the air in celebratory volleys as the procession solemnly made its way from one station to the next while the devout venerated the sacrament and preachers and chiefs exhorted the people. The march, which often took an hour to complete, winded through the arbored pathway over a carpet of flowers scattered by children, to several outdoor altars or shrines also abundantly decorated with flowers. For this reason, some tribes dubbed Corpus Christi "the Feast of the Flowers" or "Flower Days."[40]

These popular rituals did not signify that success accompanied every missionary effort. Although they won many converts, the Jesuits were not universally effective by any means; nor was their method of evangelization easily implemented. "I must say, with grief," Pedro Barcelo wrote in 1881, "that the conversion of these Indians is difficult." The priests frequently contrasted the welcome they got from tribes on the western side of the Rocky Mountains with the reception they received farther east. Contact had begun earlier on the western slope, in an era before white settlement and federal supervision had transformed tribal life, thus enabling the priests to exert a stronger and more easily sustained influence. By 1900, Jesuits had Christianized almost all the Native Americans living on the Flathead Reservation—Flatheads, Pend d'Oreilles, and Kootenais. They were unstinting in their praise of the "practical Christianity" of the Coeur d'Alenes, an official of the Bureau of Catholic Indian Missions in Washington, D.C., reported in 1907.

---

40   Sisters of Providence (Colville) to Brouillet, February 1, 1877, 12/3, BCIM; Parodi, "Memoirs," JOPA; Cataldo, "Dictation" [to O'Malley], Cataldo Papers, JOPA; Parodi, "Memoirs," JOPA.

And the federated tribes of the Colville reservation were, in the eyes of the priests, second only to the Coeur d'Alenes.[41]

The ability of the Jesuits to make inroads among tribes on the eastern slope was, however, more problematic. Over-extension by the Rocky Mountain Mission and a lack of personnel partly explained their struggle for acceptance by the Blackfeet, Gros Ventres, Assiniboine, and Crows. These tribes were "very slow and backward in giving ear to the instructions of the Fathers," a missionary complained. While the response of their young people was promising, "whether we shall ever be able to bring the grown people to the faith is not certain." Despite Prando's effectiveness with the Blackfeet, his campaign to introduce Christianity to them remained, one scholar observes, "a complex mixture of resistance, accommodation, and assimilation rather than a simple conversion of Indians to white man's medicine."[42]

A host of factors, some beyond the missionary's control, frustrated evangelization. Shoddy federal administration of many reservations and the social disintegration that accompanied forced relocation often raised formidable barriers. When Pedro Barcelo visited the Blackfeet in 1889, he found them receptive, but distracted by dwindling food supplies. After listening patiently to the priest's appeal, a chief declared "that I should not speak any longer on the matter, that they were starving, that the government should issue rations and provide them with farming implements." This "answer was somewhat rough" but it was "pretty reasonable in the present circumstances," the missionary conceded. "To speak to a starving people about the way to heaven without doing anything to relieve their pressing necessities is simply provoking." The Jesuit Aloysius Van der Velden met similar objections when he approached the Cheyenne. The people "liked priests very much," he wrote, but the government's failure to provide them with rations hindered their

---

41   Barcelo (Helena) to Brouillet, September 14, 1881, 10/9, BCIM; Robert Bigart and Clarence Woodcock, "St. Ignatius Mission, Part II," *Arizona and the West* 23 (Autumn 1981), 268 n58; *Bureau of Catholic Indian Missions Report*, 1907, BCIM.

42   Van Gorp (Spokane) to Martín, July 19, 1897, Mont. Sax. 1003-II-27, ARSI; Harrod, *Mission Among the Blackfeet*, 65.

responsiveness to his message. When a missionary enters their lodges, "their first word is 'Priest, give us something to eat. We are all very hungry. We cannot listen now; we are too hungry.'" "Really, these are good Indians," the missionary said, but "a hungry belly has no ears."[43]

Government policies that frequently redefined the way Indians lived obliged the Jesuits to rethink the way they interacted with them. Geronimo D'Aste, who had begun his ministry among the Flatheads in 1869, believed that missionary work was still spiritually successful three decades later, but "not like it was in earlier times." Confined to reservations and with their lives reshaped by allotment, natives were separated from the mission church by large tracts of land, he noted in 1902. Because the tribe no longer journeyed to the mission for solemn feast days, priests were obliged to go to them, constantly traveling about the reservation. The amount of good one could accomplish in such circumstances, Father Giuseppe Damiani added, "is almost nil."[44]

Americanization

If European dominance of Jesuit operations in the Pacific Northwest made a difference, its decline was also telling. Americanization redefined the order's regional ministry. Since 1880, the Indian Bureau threatened a cessation of government funding to any Native American school that failed to offer English instruction in all subjects. "A mastery of idiomatic English is particularly essential," declared Commissioner Thomas J. Morgan, for teachers charged with "breaking up the use of Indian dialects and the substitution therefore of the English language."[45]

---

43   Barcelo (Miles City, Montana) to Brouillet, November 29, 1889, 10/9, BCIM; [Van der Velden], "The Cheyenne Indians," St. Labre's Mission Collection, JOPA.

44   D'Aste (St. Ignatius, Idaho) to L. Martín, January 30, 1902, Mont. Sax. 1003-VI-17, ARSI; Damiani (Holy Family Mission, Montana) to L. Martín, January 12, 1903, Mont. Sax. 1003-VI-24, ARSI.

45   Thomas J. Morgan, "The Education of American Indians," *Proceedings of the Seventh Annual Meeting of the Lake Mohonk Conference of Friends of the Indian* (Mohonk Lake, NY: Lake Mohonk Conference, 1889), 27.

Such mandates posed a challenge to missionary pedagogues who themselves labored under a linguistic handicap. By the early twentieth century, White congregations, once tolerant of the hiccup of broken language that issued from their pulpits, grew impatient of priests deficient in English. In 1904, Montana's Bishop John P. Carroll angered European clergymen by saying publicly, "only American-born, or Irish priests, would work in this country for the glory of God." In fact, the Jesuits were adding Americans to their ranks at a rapid rate—but not fast enough to satisfy Bishop Carroll and White Catholics.[46] Finding English-speaking priests was becoming more and more indispensable—not only for White parishes but also for Indian congregations. By 1900, about 1,000 of the 1,621 Indians on the Flathead reservation spoke English. So widespread was its usage that Europeans who volunteered for missionary work in the United States were no longer welcome if they could not speak the dominant idiom. "Knowledge of English, real knowledge, not just mediocre, is absolutely necessary in our Indian missions today," Mission Superior George De la Motte wrote in 1909. "A good half of our European fathers, especially Italian, speak very poor English." "In the majority of our missions," he went on, "the young Indians know English—better than the majority of our Italian, German, or European missionaries." Priests not fluent in English were, he said, "almost completely useless."[47]

No single event more profoundly signaled—indeed propelled—the shift in ministries than the Jesuit decision to open colleges. With the founding of Gonzaga College in 1887 and the starting of Seattle College four years later, the Rocky Mountain missionaries committed themselves irrevocably to the White man. Under European leadership, the Mission's motto had long been *Sumus primo pro Indianis* ("We are here primarily for the Indians"). Once drummed into every missionary who stepped off the boat, this principle was

---

46   Carroll is quoted in J.D. D'Aste (St. Ignatius Mission) to G. De la Motte, August 30, 1908, D'Aste Papers, JOPA.

47   De la Motte (St. Francis Regis Mission) to Wernz, May 3, 1909, Calif. 1005-I-10, ARSI; Bigart and Woodcock, "St. Ignatius Mission, Part II," 272n73.

replaced by another that committed the Jesuits to serving White as well as native populations.[48]

With Americanization, the European phase of missionary work was passing. In 1880, 158 Jesuits, half of the personnel of Italy's Turin Province, had been stationed in the American West. That number dwindled steadily in the decade that followed as old timers passed from the scene and as fewer young Europeans replaced them. Declining emigration to America was traceable to the restoration of the Society of Jesus in European countries from which they had once been exiled. The flow of Turinese Jesuits to the United States slowed and then ceased entirely. "We presently find ourselves with such scarcity of men," an official wrote in 1892, "that we don't even have enough to run our houses in Europe." The difficulty of finding men suited for administrative posts and a desire to provide better training for seminarians led in 1907 to the merger of the Jesuits' Rocky Mountain and the California missions. Three years later, only thirty-eight Italians, most of them aged and infirm, remained on the West Coast. That small cohort represented only 9 percent of the province's total membership of 416 men, proof that Italian manpower resources were now centered almost entirely on rebuilding in Europe. The historic tie between Europe and the American West was quickly unraveling.[49]

Separation

With growing Americanization and waning European influence, Jesuits lobbied to end Italian oversight of operations in the United States. When they proposed that the Rocky Mountain Mission sever its dependence upon Italy and merge with an American jurisdiction, many Europeans protested. Cutting the bond with Italy

---

48   Cataldo, quoted in Victor Garrand (Seattle) to Franz Wernz, January 10, 1893, Mont. Sax. 1003-IV-34, ARSI. According to Cataldo, that principle had first been established by the Jesuit Father General. See Cataldo (St. Ignatius Mission) to Carlo Torti, January 3, 1888, Archives of the Turin Province of the Society of Jesus, Villa S. Maurizio, Strada comunale di Superga 70, Turin, Italy.

49   *Catalogus Sociorum e Officiorum Prov. Taurinensis, 1880*, 52–53; F. Giudice (Chieri) to Anderledy, July 29, 1892, Taur. 1011-III-34, ARSI; De la Motte (Santa Clara) to Wernz, March 19, 1909, Calif. 1005-1-7, ARSI.

would be "utterly ruinous and destructive," veteran missionaries argued, because it would "mean the total ruin of the Indian missions." Why? Because, according to Turin provincial, Giacomo Razzini, no American "thinks the missions are worthwhile." Not only were they prejudiced against native peoples, but "even the best of them" could not put up with the "privations and uncomfortable traveling" of missionary life.[50]

That prophecy proved true. As opponents anticipated, the severance of ties with Italy in 1909 was followed by a declining ministry among Native Americans. By 1919, according to a report of the Bureau of Catholic Indian Missions, there were 147 Catholic priests engaged in missionary work nationwide. Of these, only forty-four men (about a third) were born in the United States. Among Jesuits, the percentage of native-born priests was even smaller—only nine out of thirty-eight. "All of the priests of other orders and a large majority of secular priests engaged in work for Indians," the Bureau wrote, "are foreign born." The implication was clear. Without the influx of clergy from abroad, the Catholic commitment to Indian evangelization would continue to shrink.[51]

Among Jesuits, other factors too accounted for the drop-off. European interest in missionary work had already begun to shift before the severance of ties between Italy and the West Coast in 1909. The gradual withdrawal of federal subsidies to Indian schools run by missionaries in the Pacific Northwest had dealt a severe blow to Jesuit institutions and to missionary morale. Moreover, by century's end, the preferred destination of Jesuits in Italy was no longer the Rocky Mountain Mission but a new field of endeavor that had opened in 1886. Of twenty-six men in the Turin Province who petitioned Rome for missionary assignments at the end of the century, half listed Alaska as their first choice. This novel arena appealed to young Jesuits for the same reasons the Rocky Mountain Mission had charmed religious idealists of an earlier time. As vol-

---

50 Diomedi (Spokane) to Beckx, January 17, 1887, Mont. Sax. 1003-IV-1, ARSI; De la Motte (Spokane) to Sasia, July 19, 1895, Calif. 1003-VII-6, ARSI; Razzini (Turin) to Martín, May 20, 1889, Taur. 1011-11-37b, ARSI.

51 *Bureau of Catholic Indian Missions Report, 1909* (Washington, DC), 46–47, BCIM.

unteers put it, Alaska seemed to have greatest need for workers; it was "the hardest mission of the Society," and it seemed a "paradise of poverty and humility."[52] Replete with sweet challenges, Alaska even enticed experienced missionaries for whom the Pacific Northwest had become too tame. Descriptions of life among the Aleuts and Eskimos stirred up rosy memories of early days among the Flatheads and the Coeur d'Alenes. Recruitment literature abounded with appealing accounts, as did a report sent from Alaska in 1907. "Our Indians are so perfectly nomadic in their habits and disposition that we have to be always on the move, if we wish to be with them." Jesuits were drawn to such possibilities. They "wanted to go where the glamour was," a chronicler writes, "and where the danger could be found." For the more adventurous, that place was no longer Washington, Oregon, or Montana, but Alaska.[53] Consequently, just as foreign influence had once shaped the Catholic ministry to aboriginal people in the Pacific Northwest, that same dynamic now began to unfold in Alaska. The shift of interest to a new frontier did not mark the end of Jesuit ministry to Indians in the Pacific Northwest. Members of the order continued to staff schools and missions throughout the region, but on a scale reduced from what had prevailed a half-century earlier.

European evangelization of Indians left a mixed legacy. Although less ethnocentric than many contemporary American missionaries, the Europeans' understanding of the aboriginal world of the Pacific Northwest was filtered through both their limits and their strengths. They opposed the liquidation of communal land ownership and the imposition of severalty. But the Jesuits cooperated with the government by forcing so-called civilization upon the tribes through schooling, thus contributing to the eradication of native culture with programs of religious and educational assimilation. On the other hand, they paradoxically helped preserve other aspects of Indian tradition through linguistic studies that conserved

---

52 "Epistolae Missiones Petentium," Taur. 1012-XIII-1 to 36, ARSI: "Obituary of Crispino Rossi," Rossi file, JOPA.

53 Julius Jette, "Alaska: An Autumn Trip," *Woodstock Letters* 36 (1907), 277; Wilfred P. Schoenberg, *Paths to the Northwest: A Jesuit History of the Oregon Province* (Chicago: Loyola University Press, 1982), 183.

languages that might otherwise have been lost. And schools established by the missionaries, despite their obvious shortcomings, enabled some tribes to survive in the White world. The fact that many Indians remained Catholic is in large part attributable to the enthusiasm with which European clerics dedicated themselves to missionary careers in mid-nineteenth-century America. Even today the historian Andrew F. Rolle writes, still-flourishing churches on many reservations in the Pacific Northwest represent "the tangible results of a far-flung missionary system rivaling the Spanish California mission chain of adobe and brick."[54]

---

54   Andrew P. Rolle, *The Immigrant Upraised* (Norman, OK: University of Oklahoma Press, 1968), 197.

Native Americans on the Path to the Catholic Church: Cultural Crisis and Missionary Adaptation

ROSS ENOCHS*

TO HELP UNDERSTAND the conversion of Native Americans to Catholicism, historians need to take into account the historical and social context of the Native American community at the time when many Native Americans were leaving their ancient Stone Age religion and adopting Christianity. Native American religions were closely linked to their hunting, farming or raiding economies, and by the 1890s their ancient lifestyle would end. The United States government placed most of the Western Native Americans on reservations from 1850 to 1890, and it was during this turbulent period that missionaries established permanent missions among them. In addition to their effort to convert Native Americans, Catholic missionaries had to help them adapt to a new economy, land boundaries, diet, social rules, marital rules, morals, and political system. In contrast, when Jesuit missionaries went to China in the seventeenth century, they did not attempt to make radical changes to Chinese culture, but rather focused on spreading the Catholic faith. In the Native American missions, religion and culture had to change together. Catholic missionaries, however, were not agents of the American government. They were representatives of a modern American Catholic culture that often tried to distinguish itself from many American social trends. With the movement of white population into the American West, Native Americans faced some of the most rapid and dramatic cultural changes in history. These profound economic and social changes were the primary forces that brought an end to traditional Native American religions.

*An earlier version of this essay was published in *U.S. Catholic Historian* 27, no. 1 (Winter 2009), 71–88.

Challenges to Native American Culture and Religion

A central aspect of Native American religion that could not survive the encounter with modern culture was the institution of shamanism. Most Native American tribes had shamans who were the healers and religious leaders of the community. Shamans operated under the theory that breaking religious rules would bring sickness to the individual or would have adverse effects on hunting or farming. Diagnosis and treatment of illness and poor hunting was the shamans' responsibility. The tragic outbreak of smallpox and other diseases among Native Americans had the effect of discrediting the shamans who were powerless to hinder the devastation of the diseases. At times, Catholic missionaries themselves administered medicines to Native Americans and vaccinated them against disease.[1] When priests, nuns, or white doctors provided medical care, modern medicine began to replace the shamans' remedies and through this process a central part of Native American religion began to erode.

Changes in trade and the introduction of Western goods also degraded Native American culture, and the fur trade was a profound example. One of the hallmarks of Native American religion was the interdependent relationship between the animals and the people. Native Americans saw the animals as spirits or supernatural beings. To ensure a good hunt, the Native Americans would invoke and propitiate the animal spirits. Native Americans would participate in elaborate rituals in which they honored the animals that they hunted. In turn the animals would allow themselves to be killed by the people according to Native American beliefs. In Native American religion, the idea that the animals sacrificed themselves for the good of the people was a common theme.[2] The fur trade, however, brought an end to this benevolent relationship between the hunters and the hunted. The French traded their copper pots, steel knives, wool blankets, cotton cloth, and alcohol

---

1   Charles M. Buchanan, "Reverend Eugene Casmir Chirouse, O.M.I." *Indian Sentinel* 1 (January 1918), 10–11.

2   Stith Thompson, *Tales of the North American Indians* (Cambridge, MA: Harvard University Press, 1929), 169–173; Joseph Epes Brown, *The Sacred Pipe* (Norman, OK: University of Oklahoma Press, 1953), 67–100.

for the beaver pelts. In the seventeenth and eighteenth centuries, Native American overhunting decimated beaver populations in the Great Lakes area.[3] Native Americans' desire for these modern goods changed their relationship with the animals. No longer were the fur-bearing animals hunted for food with accompanying rituals that honored their sacrifice. The fur trade changed the animals from self-sacrificing spirits into commodities. Native Americans abandoned the animal spirits for copper, iron, rum, and other material goods. Since, in the past, Native Americans did not have metal pots, cooking was difficult. Furthermore, the metal knives and hatchets were much more effective than the flint or obsidian knives. Of course, they would want better tools. However, the new material things that people acquired changed their culture and religion radically. Just look how the introduction of the cellphone has changed the way people behave. If the Native Americans were really attached to their conception of the balance of nature, the avoidance of overhunting, and their worship of the animal spirits, why did their desire for material goods trump this fundamental religious orientation? Similar questions could be asked of most modern people as well in regard to their desire for possessions and the amount of time they spend on the internet. Nevertheless, the results of the fur trade caused Native Americans to lose their relationship with the animals which was one of the central pillars of their religious faith.

Several Native American tribes like the Navajo had beliefs about witches and ghosts that were also challenged by the new culture that they entered. A large portion of Navajo rituals were designed to seek protection from ghosts and witches or to exorcise their influence. According to Navajo religion, ghosts and witches were malevolent spirits that sought to damage the lives of the people. For example, if a Navajo unexpectedly died in his hogan or house, Navajos believed that the ghost of that person would wreak havoc on those who remained living in that house. They would have to abandon the house to find peace. When a man or woman died, his or her possessions had to be buried or the ghost of the deceased would cause

---

3   Shepard Krech, *The Ecological Indian* (New York: W.W. Norton, 1999), 173–209.

trouble for whoever used the possessions. If the deceased had a horse, the Navajos would sometimes kill the horse so that no one could use it. The beliefs that ghosts and witches caused sickness dominated Navajo religion. Such beliefs simply did not hold up in modern culture where it became difficult to abandon houses or all the possessions of the dead. Modern American culture was far more materialistic than Native American culture, and the idea of abandoning wealth was anathema to modern Americans.

The effect of possessions on Native American culture was profound and should not be underestimated. One of the cardinal virtues of Native American religion was charity. Among many tribes, during a funeral or marriage ceremony, a family member would hold a potlatch or "give-away" ceremony in which he or she would allow the other members of the community to take most of his or her possessions. Through these ceremonies and through their myths, many of which stressed this same theme, Native Americans learned not to be attached to their possessions. The early Jesuit missionaries in New France remarked on their charity. Jean de Brebeuf, S.J., in 1635 commented on the Hurons:

> We see shining among them some rather noble moral virtues. You note, in the first place, a great love and union, which they are careful to cultivate by means of their marriages, of their presents, of their feasts, and of their frequent visits. On returning from their fishing, their hunting, and their trading, they exchange many gifts; if they have thus obtained something unusually good, even if they have bought it, or if it has been given to them, they make a feast to the whole village with it. Their hospitality towards all sorts of strangers is remarkable; they present to them, in their feasts, the best of what they have prepared, and, as I have already said, I do not know if anything similar, in this regard, is to be found anywhere. They never close the door upon a stranger, and once having received him into their houses, they share with him the best they have; they never send him away, and when he goes away of his own accord, he repays them by a simple "thank you."[4]

---

4   Edna Kenton, ed., *The Jesuit Relations and Allied Document, Travels and Explorations of the Jesuit Missionaries in New France, 1610–1791* (New York: Vanguard Press, 1954), 113–114.

Similarly, Jerome Lalemant, S.J., in 1648 wrote:

> It seems as if innocence, banished from the majority of the Empires and Kingdoms of the World, had withdrawn into these great forests where these people [the Montagnais] dwell. Their nature has something, I know not what, of the goodness of the terrestrial paradise before sin entered it. Their practices manifest none of the luxury, the ambition, the avarice, or the pleasures that corrupt our cities.[5]

In most Native American tribes, chiefs did not have more material wealth than other people. Chiefs did not live in grand houses or wear clothing much different from the rest of the people. The Jesuit missionaries of the seventeenth century were impressed that the charity of Native Americans in many respects exceeded that of Catholic countries, and they saw this as evidence that Native Americans found some truths through the natural law.[6] From 1880 to 1930, however, the government discouraged the practice of many Native American rituals including the give-away.[7] As time passed, Native Americans began to lose those practices that reinforced the egalitarian nature of their communities.

Archaic religion, an aspect of Native American religion that would be threatened by forces unrelated to the efforts of the missionaries, was characterized by worship in sacred places. To act out many of their rituals, Native Americans had to travel to specific sites at which they believed sacred events occurred. Their difficulty was that when the U.S. government restricted them to reservations, often they no longer had access to these sites, and therefore were unable to practice these rituals. The Native American attitude toward sacred places contrasted with the Christian view. In the Gospel of John, the Samaritan woman asked Jesus if the place to worship was in Jerusalem or in Samaria, and Jesus' response indi-

---

5   Reuben Gold Thwaites, *The Jesuit Relations and Allied Documents, Travels and Explorations of the Jesuit Missionaries in New France, 1610–1791* (New York: Pageant Book Company, 1959), 32: 283; James Moore, *Indian and Jesuit* (Chicago: Loyola University Press, 1982), 56–57.

6   Moore, *Indian and Jesuit*, 41–58.

7   Christopher Vecsey, "Prologue," in *Handbook of American Indian Religious Freedom,* ed. by Christopher Vecsey (New York: Crossroad, 1991), 16.

cated that worship was not restricted to any place. This allowed Christianity to spread since place was not essential and Christians could worship God anywhere. Archaic tribal religions like Native American religion were bound by sacred spaces. When the land on which these sacred places existed was seized by the U.S. government, and when so many Native Americans were forced off their land, they lost another aspect of their religion.

In the 1880s the collapse of the buffalo population, due to white overhunting, helped end the traditional economy of Western Native Americans. Prior to the 1880s, Western Native Americans produced food, clothing, houses, tools, ropes, and fuel from the buffalo. Many of their traditional rituals, like the Sun Dance, were based on buffalo hunting and when they no longer could make a living from the buffalo hunt, their culture was altered dramatically forever. Similarly, many Southwestern Native Americans traditionally farmed corn and other crops for subsistence. After they were placed on reservations, they eventually gave up their traditional farming lifestyle. The religious rituals of many Southwestern Native Americans—the Sacred Clown ceremonies, the Corn Dances, and the Snake Dances—were based on bringing fertility to the land. Many of these fertility rituals also contained sexual imagery and explicit sexual practices because Native Americans believed that the sexuality of the people was linked with the fertility of the land. The Native American economies of hunting or farming were so closely linked with the religious rituals, that the two were inseparable. The way they planted the corn or the way they hunted the buffalo were in themselves religious rituals. They needed to participate in these activities to perpetuate their religion. Fertility and healing were at the center of Native American religion. Modern medicine replaced shamanism. Modern agriculture replaced the idea that Father Sky fertilized Mother Earth and that human sexual activity caused it to rain.

A central ritual that declined after Native Americans began life on the reservation was the menstrual ritual that mediated the passage of a girl from childhood to adulthood. Native American religion was not simply an individual practice but rather involved the entire community. The whole community had to cooperate to celebrate the menstrual rituals and this became increasingly difficult after the U.S. government placed Native Americans on reservations. Traditionally, when a girl had her first menstrual period, Native Americans believed, the spiritual power that she was experiencing was a danger to the community. The power that she received had to be ordered through the ritual so that she would be a blessing to the community. In many tribes, whenever a woman had her period, she had to separate herself from the tribe or observe additional restrictions during this time. When a young woman had her first period, she had to perform the work that she would be responsible for during her life—gathering firewood, making clothing, grinding corn, and taking care of children. Soon after the government placed Native Americans on reservations, women no longer had the tasks of grinding corn and making clothing from skins. The old taboos that they had observed no longer fit in with reservation life, and they began to abandon the menstrual rituals that were such a significant part of women's spirituality. During these rituals, the girls were symbolically linked with the Mother Earth whose fertility and power, they believed, passed into the young girl.[8] When the Native American economy no longer depended on hunting and farming, the symbolism of the earth as mother became more distant because Native Americans increasingly depended on the government for sustenance or purchased their food. Going to a store and buying food was different from planting, harvesting, grinding corn all to the accompaniment of fertility rituals and religious stories that linked corn to the flesh of the gods.[9] Since the roles of Native American women changed and since modern Americans did not believe that menstruation made women dangerous, the menstrual rituals began to fall out of practice.

The presence of inquisitive anthropologists and other white people that came to the reservations was another factor that forever changed Native American religion. Native American dances were not designed to be shows for entertainment, but were religious rituals in which the entire community participated and from

---

8   Brown, *The Sacred Pipe*, 116–126; Peggy Beck and Anna Walters, *The Sacred: Ways of Knowledge, Sources of Life* (Tsaile, AZ: Navajo Community College Press, 1995), 209–223.

9   Alice Marriott and Carol Rachlin, *American Indian Mythology* (New York: Thomas Crowell, 1968), 100–111.

which the community learned about their faith. The presence of white people at the rituals changed this atmosphere. For example, Hopis formerly performed the Snake Dance that involved collecting numerous live rattlesnakes and dancing with live snakes held in their mouths. The purpose of the dance was fertility, and they asked the snakes to bring their prayers for rain to the gods. In the 1880s, white people started to attend the dances.[10] As the word got out, more white people wanted to sample the exotic and in the next few decades groups of tourists traveled to observe this event. The Hopis were a very tight knit community and they held on to their traditions longer than most Native Americans. The Hopis, however, began to alter their rituals in response to the white audience. For example, the Hopi Clown Dances involved the sacred clowns performing overt sexual behavior that offended some white observers. One of the Hopi sacred clowns recounted an event in which he confronted a white man who was witnessing a Clown Dance. In this ritual he was getting ready to simulate intercourse on a man (referred to in the following text as the "lady") who was dressed up as the Corn Maiden. Hopis believed that the simulated sexual act would stimulate the fertility of the land and bring rain.

> The principal was still watching, but we decided to take our reward in spite of him. We dragged the "lady" around the corner out of his sight and placed her on a sheepskin. . . . I made ready, then glanced around and saw the white man had moved in to get a better view and was leaning forward, looking. The people laughed but I was angry. We called off the demonstration led the old Katchina to our "House," gave her some corn meal, and told her to take our prayers to the Six-Point-Cloud-People [the gods]. She seemed very pleased and said, "All right your reward will be rain." Then I turned to my partners and said, "I'm going to fix that white man." I walked up to him, shook hands, and said in Hopi, "Well white man, you want to see what goes on, don't you? You have spoiled our prayers, and it may not rain. You think this business is vulgar, but it means something sacred to us. This old Katchina is impersonating the Corn Maiden; therefore we must have inter-

---

10   Earle Forrest, *The Snake Dance of the Hopi Indians* (Los Angeles: Westernlore Press, 1961), 141.

course with her so that our corn will increase and our people live in plenty. If this were evil we would not be doing it."[11]

In response to the presence of a critical white person, the Hopis removed an essential aspect of this ritual. Native Americans found it difficult to ignore government officials, tourists, and others who increasingly attended their sacred rituals. Simple contact between white and Native American cultures began to change the way Native Americans practiced their religion.

New Native Religions

The push of the settlers into the American West brought a great deal of turmoil to Native American tribes and also brought new religions, such as the Ghost Dance and Peyote Religion. These two religions were a blend of Native American and Christian influences. Even before the conquest of America, Native American religion was in flux and different tribes borrowed religious stories and practices from each other. When white settlers came, Native Americans formed new religions by combining Christian and Native American concepts. Many Native Americans who converted to Christianity were not converted from their traditional religions but were converts from these new blended religions.

The Ghost Dance Religion was an apocalyptic religion that spread through the United States from 1870 to 1890, and dozens of tribes in the American West adopted this new religion. At this time, Western Native Americans were experiencing a number of hardships and their morale was low. They were cheated out of their land by the government and confined to reservations. The buffalo population declined precipitously, various diseases swept through their tribes, and their traditional religions were in decline. Into this religious vacuum came the Ghost Dance with its apocalyptic prediction that Jesus or some other god was going to destroy all white people, raise the dead Native Americans, return the buffalo, and inaugurate a paradise in which no one became sick or died. To hasten the

---

11   Leo Simmons, *Sun Chief: The Autobiography of a Hopi Indian* (New Haven, CT: Yale University Press, 1942), 190.

coming of the apocalypse, Ghost Dancers performed dances that lasted all night. Even though this apocalyptic theme was not traditional to Native American religion, the Ghost Dance spread quickly through the country. Prior to the introduction of this new religion, each tribe had its own distinct religion, but from 1870 to 1890 many tribes embraced this new religion.

The doctrine of the Ghost Dance emphasized a return to the hunting economy and to the traditional clothing that was made from the animals. At many of the actual dances, Ghost Dancers symbolically shed their Western clothing and adopted buckskin Ghost Shirts. James Mooney, an agent sent by the government to investigate the movement, commented: "In accordance with the general idea of the return to aboriginal habits, the believers, as far as possible, discarded white man's dress and utensils. Those who could procure buckskin—which is now very scarce in Sioux country—resumed buckskin dress. . . . "[12] Many also banned metal ornaments from the dances.[13] After the apocalypse, they believed there would be a return to the times of dressing in skins. For Ghost Dancers, the buckskin Ghost Shirts symbolized their rejection of white culture.

The Ghost Dance also changed Native American funeral practices and theories concerning war. Before the emergence of the Ghost Dance, violent behavior often accompanied funeral ceremonies. The doctrine of the Ghost Dance prohibited such displays:

> [The Ghost Dance] forbids the extravagant mourning customs formerly common among the tribes. "When your friends die, you must not cry," which is interpreted by the prairie tribes as forbidding the killing of horses, the burning of tipis and the destruction of property, the cutting of hair and the gashing of the body with knives, all of which were formerly the sickening rule at every death until forbidden by the new doctrine. As an Arapahoe said to me when his little boy died, "I shall not shoot

---

12   James Mooney, *The Ghost Dance Religion and the Sioux Outbreak of 1890* (Chicago: University of Chicago Press, 1965), 30, originally published as the *Fourteenth Annual Report of the Bureau of Ethnology to the Secretary of the Smithsonian Institution, 1892–93* (Washington, DC: Government Printing Office, 1896).

13   Mooney, *The Ghost Dance Religion*, 30.

my ponies, and my wife will not gash her arms. We used to do this when our friends died, because we thought we would never see them again, and it made us feel bad. But now we know we shall all be united again."[14]

Traditionally, Native Americans encouraged their warriors to be brave and they often competed in testing their bravery in raids of other cultures. Writing in 1892, James Mooney noted that the Ghost Dance doctrine, among most of its adherents, forbade war with white people:

> [The Ghost Dance] preaches peace with the whites and obedience to authority until the day of deliverance shall come. Above all it forbids war—"*You must not fight. . . .*" Now comes a prophet as a messenger from God to forbid not only war, but all that savors of war—the war dance, the scalp dance, and even the bloody torture of the sun dance—and his teaching is accepted and his words obeyed by four-fifths of all the predatory tribes of the mountains and the Great Plains. Only those who have known the deadly hatred that once animated Ute, Cheyenne, and Pawnee, one toward another, and are able to contrast it with their present spirit of mutual brotherly love, can know what the Ghost-dance religion has accomplished. . . .[15]

Lieutenant H.L. Scott writing in 1891 made a similar comment about the Ghost Dance prophet:

> He has given these people a better religion than they ever had before, taught them precepts which, if faithfully carried out, will bring them into better accord with their white neighbors, and has prepared the way for their final Christianization.[16]

Scott noticed that the Ghost Dance was a phase that changed the Native Americans' moral orientation. As a result, many of the missionaries who encountered Native Americans in the late 1800s were evangelizing people who were practicing a new pan-Native American religion that had already modified their traditional religious beliefs.

---

14   Mooney, *The Ghost Dance Religion*, 24.
15   Mooney, *The Ghost Dance Religion*, 25.
16   Mooney, *The Ghost Dance Religion*, 25.

The Ghost Dance religion, however, did not last long. In the winter of 1890 at Wounded Knee Creek in South Dakota, the Seventh Cavalry massacred about 300 Sioux Ghost Dancers, most of whom were unarmed men, women, and children. Prior to the battle, Sioux Ghost Dancers believed that their Ghost Shirts would be invulnerable to the soldiers' bullets. A woman wounded at the massacre was asked if she would allow her Ghost Shirt to be removed so they could treat her wounds and she said, "Yes; take it off. They told me a bullet would not go through. Now I do not want it anymore."[17] Additionally, Sioux Ghost Dancers predicted that the apocalypse would come in the spring of 1891. As with many apocalyptic movements that set down a specific time for the end time, the followers lost confidence when the predicted time passed. After the failure of the Ghost Dance to produce tangible results, many Native Americans were more receptive to Christianity. The religious vacuum caused by the collapse of the Ghost Dance was filled by the Christian missionaries who were already present on the reservations. The Ghost Dance took Native Americans one step further away from their traditional religions, and the failure of the apocalyptic predictions dashed their hope to return to their traditional way of life.

The Peyote Religion was another new religion that sprang up and spread throughout North America in the 1870s in response to the same social conditions that influenced the Ghost Dance. The Peyote Religion was a different sort of response but it became the dominant form of Native American religion. The central practice of this religion involved the ingestion of the peyote cactus. It was eaten raw, dried, or taken as tea. Since peyote contains hallucinogenic alkaloids, the person who ingested it might experience a hallucination, or, from the perspective of the Peyote devotee, a vision from Father Peyote or Jesus. According to the adherents of this faith, the vision led the devotee to God. This was a mystical religion that was a blend of Christianity and Huichol religion adapted to a time when Native Americans forgot their tribal rivalries and saw themselves as brothers and sisters. In regard to ethics, this new faith emphasized that Native Americans should live peacefully with

---

17   Mooney, *The Ghost Dance Religion*, 34.

white people and other tribes. It was also a religion that discouraged the use of alcohol and promoted family unity. Unlike their traditional religions, this faith was not connected to hunting, farming or raiding economies, but was a new mystical religion that replaced most traditional rituals with the Peyote ritual. During the all-night ritual, devotees ingested peyote, sang songs, prayed, and meditated on the visions they received. The ritual took place anywhere and anytime the group decided to get together. Often ceremonies were performed for the purposes of healing or protection from evil. Since peyote grew only in the desert around Northern Mexico, traditionally only the Huichol Native Americans and a few other Mexican Native American tribes used peyote. It was only after the 1870s that this faith spread through North America, and therefore the Peyote Religion was not a traditional religion for the Native Americans of the United States. Many devotees of the Peyote Religion identified Jesus as their God and source of truth. As J.S. Slotkin, the notable scholar of the Peyote Religion, said, "From the viewpoint of almost all Peyotists, the religion is a Native American version of Christianity. White Christian theology, ethics, and eschatology have been adopted with modifications which make them more compatible with traditional Indian culture."[18] The Peyote Religion served as further evidence that Native Americans were, of their own accord, already leaving many of their old religious rituals and beliefs at the time when the Catholic missionaries came to the reservations.

Missionary Approaches and Encounters

Native Americans saw Catholic missionaries, who they called "Blackrobes," as a distinct group of white people. Realizing that they were often betrayed by the U.S. government, Native Americans did not lump the Catholic missionaries into the same group as the representatives of the government. Catholic missionaries were celibate, a vocation that was almost unknown among Native Americans, and this helped to distinguish Catholic missionaries from other white people. Another characteristic that distinguished the

---

18   J.S. Slotkin, "The Peyote Way," in *Teachings from the American Earth: Indian Religion and Philosophy,* ed. by Dennis Tedlock and Barbara Tedlock (New York: Liveright, 1975), 96.

missionaries was their proficiency in Native American languages. In the early 1900s, the Bureau of Catholic Indian Missions encouraged missionaries to learn Native American languages so they could communicate the Catholic faith in a way Native Americans would understand.[19] Just the ability to speak to Native Americans in their own language created a great deal of good will toward the Catholic missionaries. Catholic missionaries also spoke about religion and even if Native Americans did not accept the ideas that they promoted, Native Americans were interested in religious matters and were patient listeners. Throughout their history Native Americans borrowed religious ideas, stories, and rituals from neighboring tribes, and therefore tended to have an open-minded view of other religious traditions.

Catholic missionaries saw their missionary work not just in terms of religious education and the dispensing of the sacraments, but as a charitable effort to give Native American tribes the material assistance that they needed to make the transition to the American lifestyle. Among the Navajos, Franciscan missionaries saw a need for surveying skills to help define the boundaries of Navajo land and to help settle property disputes. Anselm Weber, O.F.M., took it upon himself to learn this skill and thereby aided the Navajos in these legal disputes.[20] Catholic missionaries often distributed food and medicine to the Native Americans as a part of their missionary work. After the Wounded Knee Massacre, Franciscan sisters tended the wounded Native Americans and this added to their good reputation.[21] Catholic missionaries identified the needs of the Native Americans and tried to help them in ways that they would not or could not help themselves.

The moral message of Catholic missionaries encouraged Native Americans to leave behind a number of tribal practices and further

---

19   "St. Michael's Mission and School for the Navajo Indians," *Indian Sentinel* (1908), 20; Editorial, *Indian Sentinel* 1 (January 1917), 20.

20   Robert Wilken, *Anselm Weber, O.F.M.: Missionary to the Navajo* (Milwaukee: Bruce Publishing, 1955), 202–203.

21   Emil Perrig, S.J., diary, December 31, 1890, St. Francis Mission Collection, series 7, box 5, folders 14–15, Marquette University Archives, Milwaukee, Wisconsin.

adapt to American culture. Since many Native Americans were polygynous, the missionaries sought to convince them to have only one wife. Furthermore, Native Americans often allowed arranged marriages and child marriages which Catholic missionaries sought to discourage.[22] Catholic missionaries were also leading Native Americans from a set of tribal ethics to a universal set of ethics. In tribal religions, the ethical systems generally advocated treating members of the tribe with a benevolence and fairness that was not extended to those outside the tribe. For example, Paul Mary Ponziglione, S.J., missionary to the Osage Native Americans, described a situation in which a Kaw Native American stole a horse from an Osage:

> Now you ask: "Do these Indians see any harm in stealing?" Yes they do, that is among themselves. They very seldom steal from each other, though they have many a chance for the wig-wams and lodges are always open. But . . . they see no harm in appropriating the property of their enemies.[23]

Ponziglione was making the point that traditionally, Native Americans were prohibited from stealing from members of their own tribe, but it was, however, acceptable to steal from a neighboring or enemy tribe. To lead Native Americans into the modern world, Catholic missionaries realized that these ancient tribal ideas had to be replaced with universal moral laws.

Catholic missionaries trained Native American catechists to help instruct the Native Americans in Catholic ethics and doctrine. These catechists even traveled to visit other Native American tribes to help spread the Catholic faith.[24] Training for the priesthood was a vocation that Native Americans were generally reluctant to seek

---

22   Nicholas Point, S.J., "Recollections of the Rocky Mountains," *Woodstock Letters* 12 (1883), 263–264; Peter Prando, S.J., to Father Superior, [1883] *Woodstock Letters* 12 (1883), 329.

23   Paul Mary Ponziglione, S.J., to Father Superior, July 7, 1881, *Woodstock Letters* 10 (1881), 292.

24   William Ketcham [Director of the Bureau of Catholic Indian Missions] to Henry Westropp, S.J., December 11, 1907, Bureau of Catholic Indian Missions Collection, series 1, box 55, folder 3, Marquette University Archives, Milwaukee, Wisconsin.

out because celibacy was not a part of their culture. The position of catechist, however, gave a leadership position in the community that was open to married men. Often commenting on the profound effectiveness of Native American catechists,[25] Catholic missionaries realized that Native American catechists had some advantages in communicating with other Native Americans because they shared many cultural experiences and could communicate with other Native Americans through familiar images and symbols.

An aid to missionaries and catechists in spreading the Catholic faith among Native Americans was the similarity of Catholic and Native understandings of the nature of ritual. The difficulty in converting indigenous people to Catholicism did, to some extent, depend on the degree to which their religion was structurally similar to Catholicism. Both Catholics and Native Americans shared the same idea that grace or sacred power could be invoked though ritual and communicated to the individuals involved. Native Americans had confession ceremonies that were similar to the sacrament of confession. Many Native Americans also believed that each person had his or her own helper spirit who aided that person in times of trouble. Early on in the missions, priests realized that these beliefs were not that different from the Catholic belief in guardian angels.[26] Furthermore, the adoption ceremony of the Sioux was similar to the Catholic sacrament of marriage. In both rituals, two unrelated people were bound together by divine power and they exchanged gifts as a symbol of this bond. Through both of these rituals, two people gained mutual obligations that endured through their lives. Similar to the idea expressed in Ephesians 5:25 that husbands must love their wives as Christ loved the Church, the Sioux believed that the relationship created through the adoption ceremony was a reflection of the relationship that existed between the Great Spirit and the people.[27] Traditional Native American religion also emphasized large outdoor rituals and Catholic missionaries were happy to accommodate their desires for these types of ceremonies. Corpus Christi processions and Rogation days rituals were

---

25 *Indian Sentinel* 1 (October 1918), 8.
26 Moore, *Indian and Jesuit,* 109.
27 Brown, *The Sacred Pipe,* 101–115.

common on the reservations.[28] In the Southwest, Native Americans celebrated saints' days with Native American dances that were encouraged or tolerated by Catholic missionaries.[29]

In addition to accepting many Native American dances, Catholic missionaries participated in other traditional Native American customs. For example, some tribes adopted Catholic missionaries into their families through traditional religious rituals.[30] Also from the beginning of the missions, many priests smoked the sacred pipe with the Native Americans.[31] The sacred pipe, Native Americans believed, was given to them by the gods for the purpose of sending their prayers to the gods. Catholic missionaries knew that they were participating in a religious ritual by partaking in the sacred pipe ceremony because prayer was the central aspect of this ritual. There were many examples of Catholic missionaries accepting the pipe as an inoffensive aspect of Native American culture even though missionaries universally condemned the use of other types of paraphernalia that were linked to shamanic rituals. Catholic missionaries knew that by trying to reject all aspects of Native American culture, Native Americans would be less likely to listen to the message they brought.

Missionaries adapted in those situations where they thought the preservation of Native rituals or ideas did not conflict with Catholic doctrine. For example, Benedictines and Jesuits in the Dakotas used the Sioux term *Wakan Tanka,* meaning "Great Spirit," as a transla-

---

28 Paul Mary Ponziglione, S.J., letter to Father Superior, January 1, 1876, *Woodstock Letters* 5 (1876), 144–148; Pierre Chone, S.J., to Father Superior, July 6, 1876, *Woodstock Letters* 5 (1876), 229–233.

29   Jerome Hesse, O.F.M., "The Keres Indian Tribe and Cochitenes," *Indian Sentinel* (1914), 27; Pablo Abeita, "The Pueblo Indian Question," *Franciscan Missions of the Southwest* 6 (1918), 7–8.

30   Albert Reister, S.J., "Sioux Trails all Lead to Big Road," *Indian Sentinel* 11 (Winter 1930–1931), 7; Louis Hennepin, O.F.M., *A Description of Louisiana* (Ann Arbor, MI: University Microfilms, 1966), 106–108.

31   Zephyrin Engelhardt, O.F.M., "The Venerable Antonio Margil de Jesus, O.F.M.," *Indian Sentinel* 1 (January 1919), 11; Hiram Martin Chittenden, *Life, Letters and Travels of Pierre-Jean De Smet* (New York: Francis Harper, 1905), 1: 211–212; Nicholas Point, S.J., "Recollections of the Rocky Mountains," *Woodstock Letters* 12 (1883), 8.

tion for "God" in their prayer books and catechisms as early as 1899.[32] This showed that Catholic missionaries accepted that the Sioux had naturally found some notion of the true God. In contrast, the Franciscan missionaries to the Navajo were not able to adapt in this way because the Navajo religion was clearly polytheistic and the gods were not necessarily benevolent. The Navajos' understanding of the gods and rituals was so different from the Catholic view that the Franciscans rejected and discouraged most Navajo religious beliefs and rituals.[33] Catholic missionaries did, however, encourage or tolerate certain Native American traditions when those traditions did not conflict with Catholic doctrine.[34]

In their efforts to preserve tribal unity, Catholic missionaries adapted to Native American culture. On Sioux Reservations, Jesuits set up Catholic Sioux Congresses that would meet each year on one of the several Sioux reservations that were located in different parts of North and South Dakota. Some Sioux Catholics would travel hundreds of miles just to come to the Congress. On the reservation on which the Congress was held, Sioux Catholics would work together to prepare for the Congress. They would usually erect a scaffolding resembling the Sun Dance grounds at which they would celebrate the Mass. The sacrifice of the Mass replaced the sacrifice of the Sun Dance, but they did retain some of the other traditions associated with the Sun Dance. The Catholic Sioux Congresses were designed to retain the feel and structure of these old meetings but change the religious content. By calling the Catholic Sioux together each year, the Church helped to maintain the tribal unity of the Sioux while also providing a large Catholic ritual that in some ways resembled the traditional Native American rituals.

---

32   Jerome Hunt, O.S.B., *Katholic Wocekiye Wowapi* (Fort Totten, ND: Catholic Indian Mission at Fort Totten, 1899); Eugene Buechel and Jesuit Fathers of St. Francis Mission, *Lakota Wocekiye na Olowan Wowapi: Sioux Indian Prayer and Hymn Book* (St. Louis, MO: Central Bureau of the Catholic Central Verein of America, 1927).

33   Ross Enochs, "The Franciscan Mission to the Navajos: Mission Method and Indigenous Religion, 1898–1940," *Catholic Historical Review* 92, no. 1 (January 2006), 46–73.

34   Ross Enochs, *The Jesuit Mission to the Lakota Sioux: Pastoral Theology and Ministry, 1886–1945* (Kansas City, MO: Sheed and Ward, 1996), 89–150.

The mission schools were also crucial in leading Native Americans to the Catholic Church, and in the 1880s and 90s, the Catholic mission schools were able to secure direct federal funding. Most of these early schools were boarding schools and they had the effect of cutting Native American children off from their traditional culture for much of the year. Since the houses on the reservations were often spread out over the reservations, it was impossible to have day schools. There were no roads on the reservations, and trucks or buses only came in the 1930s. Mission schools fed, clothed, disciplined, and educated the students in religion as well as traditional academic subjects. During this time in their lives, young Native Americans were immersed in Catholic and American culture in the schools. Students who attended mission schools went with the approval of their parents who had to sign a form indicating that they desired their children to attend.[35] Since missionaries could not force children into their schools, they took pains to meet with Native American elders and persuade them of the benefits of the schools. In 1908 Anselm Weber, O.F.M., missionary to the Navajos, wrote of his numerous visits to members of the tribe:

> I also laid special stress upon the fact that we had come to stay; that, after their children had left our school, we would consider them our special friends, would remain in touch with them, and would assist them in making practical use of what they had learned at school—a point in which the Government had been singularly deficient. I also dwelled on the fact that I could not use any force or drastic means to induce them to send their children; if they did not see the advantage of a good education and did not care to send their children voluntarily, why, we did not want them. [A government agent tried to force the Navajo children to attend public school ten years before.] Even such as had been at the point of going upon the warpath ten years previous not to be forced to send their children to school, [the Navajos] promised to send them to us stating that until now they simply had been told they must send their children to school, but I having explained to them why

---

35   "Editorial," *Indian Sentinel* (1905–1906), 33–34. For a complete discussion of this issue, see Francis Paul Prucha, *The Churches and the Indian Schools* (Lincoln: University of Nebraska, 1979).

they should send them, they saw the advantages and would send them with pleasure.[36]

Even though the schools taught material that contradicted tribal traditions, parents still allowed the students to attend. For example, Navajos avoided buildings in which people died because Navajos were afraid of ghosts. On the Navajo reservation, Franciscan missionaries set up a school with an infirmary, and there were some who died in the infirmary. Navajos told their children to avoid such places but the Franciscans directly contradicted this traditional belief and persuaded the children to dismiss what the friars saw as "superstition."[37] Missionaries taught the students industrial skills such as farming, carpentry, sewing, baking, shoe making, cattle farming, electrical work, blacksmith work, and other skills so that they would be able to secure jobs in the new economy that they were entering.[38] Parents knew they would need these skills to succeed in this new world. In the case of the Sioux, parents sent their children to Catholic schools because most of the Sioux elders were Catholic themselves. In contrast, Navajos, whose elders tended not to convert to Catholicism, nevertheless were not opposed to allowing their children to attend Catholic schools and learn the new ways.[39]

As evidence of their support for the mission schools, there were many instances of Native American tribes asking for Catholic missionaries to set up schools among them. In 1890, John B. Masskogijigwek, a Catholic Ojibwa, wrote to the Bureau of Catholic Indian Missions:

> We Catholic Indians of Red Lake are writing you a letter today telling you what is going on here. . . . We are perfectly satisfied with the Sisters' school here. Our children are taught well; this

---

36 Anselm Weber, O.F.M., "St. Michaels' Mission and School for the Navajo Indians," *Indian Sentinel* (1908), 22.

37 Weber, "St. Michaels' Mission and School for the Navajo Indians," 23; Anselm Weber, O.F.M., "Origin, Religion, and Superstitions of the Navajo," *Indian Sentinel* 1 (April 1918), 5.

38 "A Little Indian Life," *Indian Sentinel* (1902–1903), 17; "St. Boniface's Industrial School, Banning, California," *Indian Sentinel* (1905–1906), 21–23; "St. Francis School," *Indian Sentinel* (1907), 22–23.

39 Anselm Weber, O.F.M., "On Navajo Myths and Superstitions," *Franciscan Missions of the Southwest* 4 (1916), 45.

is indeed a great benefit to them. And they are coming more and more into the school; at present there are 55–60 children here in the Sisters' school. We tell you this, if you would help, that the school building be enlarged, a little, especially for the boys, so that afterwards also a "brother" could come and teach the boys in the school.[40]

Similarly, in 1877 in a series of speeches to President Rutherford Hayes, Red Cloud, Head Chief of the Lakota Sioux said:

> I want schools to enable my children to read and write, so they will be as wise as the white man's children. . . . I want you to give me school teachers, so that we will have a good school house and learn my children how to read and write. Catholic priests are good, and I want you to give me one of them also. . . . We would like to have Catholic priests and nuns, so they could teach our people to read and write.[41]

These statements are only two of the Native Americans' numerous petitions in support of the mission schools. Native Americans knew that they had no alternative but to adapt to the new culture, and the schools played a central part in helping their children to become immersed in American Catholic culture.

Despite the pressures to abandon traditional religions, some Native Americans continue to practice rituals resembling past practices. Although it was prohibited on the reservations,[42] the Sun Dance endures to the present, in some form, as do some of the Rain and Corn dances of the Southwestern Native Americans. These dances are expressions of Native Americans' resistance to becoming completely Americanized. Through these dances, they seek to maintain their cultural identity. These dances, however, do not

---

40   Marie Therese Archambault, Mark Thiel, and Christopher Vecsey, eds., *The Crossing of Two Roads: Being Catholic and Native in the United States* (Maryknoll, NY: Orbis, 2003), 107.

41   Transcript of the Meeting between Chiefs Red Cloud, Spotted Tail, and other Chiefs and President Hayes, Executive Mansion, September 26, 1877, Council Proceedings, May 26, 1875–April 19, 1894, 201, 216, 226, RG 75, box 779, National Archives and Records Administration, Kansas City Branch.

42   Sharon O'Brien, "A Legal Analysis of the American Indian Religious Freedom Act," in Vecsey, *Handbook of American Indian Religious Freedom*, 28.

have the same religious significance that they once had because the hunting and farming traditions associated with these rituals have been lost. Originally, the central focus of the Sun Dance was to honor the buffalo for their sacrifice and to induce the buffalo to continue sacrificing themselves for the tribe. In this ritual, Native Americans offered their own flesh and blood as a reciprocal sacrifice to the buffalo. Primarily this was a hunting ritual and when the Native Americans no longer hunted buffalo, the significance of the ritual changed.

Cultural Change: Acceptance and Rejection

To understand the conversion of Western Native Americans, it is necessary to consider their mindset and culture at the time when Catholic missionaries established permanent missions in the American West. Native Americans went through the fastest cultural change possible. They made the transition from the Stone Age to the age of trains and cars. Their traditional culture went through a crisis and collapsed under the weight of modern culture. In a short period of time, their traditional ideas about tribal warfare, hunting, farming, healing, ethics, property, ghosts, and marriage drastically changed. The pressures on Native American culture did not originate with the Catholic missionaries, who were often blamed for the decline of Native American religion. Native American religion declined primarily in response to the modern culture that surrounded it. Catholic missionaries of the late 1800s and early 1900s certainly did try to help Native Americans adapt to the new culture and were emissaries of modern culture, but there were many other forces involved in the decline of Native American religion that had nothing to do with the missionaries. Native American religion was inextricably linked to the hunting and farming economies and when they no longer hunted or farmed, their religions were bound to decline. Additionally, the Ghost Dance and Peyote Religion were signs that Native Americans were not just passively accepting all that the missionaries told them. Through these new religions, the Native Americans themselves reacted to modern culture and also began to discard traditional aspects of their religions. Ultimately, Native American culture and religion could not withstand the changes that the new material possessions, new medicine, and new economy brought to them.

Many people believe that the reason Native American religion declined was that the Native Americans were persecuted and forced to abandon their religion by white settlers backed by the U.S. government; however, this explanation for the decline of Native American religion is inadequate. Certainly, Native Americans did experience severe and horrible persecution in the United States. Persecution in itself, however, does not always cause the decline of religion. Despite persecution, Judaism has survived because it is a modern religion. Unlike archaic religions, Judaism is monotheistic; it does not have fertility rituals or shamans. Judaism is not linked to a particular hunting, farming, or raiding economy. For thousands of years, Judaism has been a moral and philosophical religion that was able to survive in modern culture. In contrast, many of the assumptions and practices of Native American religion were so contrary to those of modern American culture that the Native American religious beliefs fell away as the Native Americans became enmeshed in modern culture.

Though Catholic missionaries rejected some aspects of Native American culture like shamanism, the violent rituals of mourning the dead, and fertility rituals, Catholic missionaries accepted many aspects of their culture like the pipe ceremony, adoption ceremony, sweat lodges, and several traditional dances. Native Americans who converted to Catholicism realized that the missionaries' toleration of these customs demonstrated the missionaries' respect for certain aspects of Native American culture. Through history Native Americans altered their religions due to contact with other tribes. When Catholic missionaries arrived, Native Americans adapted their dances and other ceremonies so they fit in with Catholic celebrations. Since Native Americans and Catholics emphasized rituals and had similar notions about how rituals functioned, Native Americans found many familiar ideas in the Catholic faith. By the 1880s and 1890s, Native Americans were already giving up their tribal ethics and rivalries. By this time, the Catholic missionaries' emphasis on universal ethics was not difficult for Native Americans to accept. In the midst of a cultural crisis, Catholic missionaries arrived on reservations to establish permanent missions. Their efforts to speak the Native American languages and accept some of their traditions allowed many Native Americans to trust the missionaries to help them make the transition to a new culture and religion.

Hindsight and Foresight:
The Catholic Church and
Native North Americans, 1965–1997

CARL F. STARKLOFF, S.J.*

> In the past the churches concentrated on pressing Indians to
> accept what they had to offer. Now they must learn how to let
> the Indians receive the offer in their own way, and they will
> be able to do so only as they learn to receive from the Indians.
> If such mutuality can be established, the hostility to Christian-
> ity evident in many quarters today may yet prove to have been
> a no that means yes.[1]
> —John Webster Grant, *Moon of Wintertime*

THUS HISTORIAN John Webster Grant concludes his study of
Protestant and Catholic missions in Canada—a study that,
mutatis mutandis, applies to the United States as well. Grant is one
of those historians who is sympathetic to Christian mission, even if
highly critical of its methods in the past. In a similar vein, another
sympathetic critic, Henry Warner Bowden, writes,

> For American society, Indian life points the way to greater
> diversity and expanded tolerance. Ethnic persistence is already
> a fact, whether today's demographers recognize the impor-
> tance of it or not. If the nation as a whole restricts the Indians'
> freedom to act and worship along indigenous lines, it will per-
> petuate a shortsighted parochialism and deny what is best for
> itself as an amalgam of many peoples.[2]

---

*This essay originally appeared in *U.S. Catholic Historian* 16, no. 2 (Spring
1998), 107–121.

1   John Webster Grant, *Moon of Wintertime: Missionaries and the Indians of
Canada in Encounter Since 1534* (Toronto: University of Toronto Press, 1984),
266.

2   Henry Warner Bowden, *American Indians and Christian Missions: Studies
in Cultural Conflict* (Chicago: University of Chicago Press, 1981), 1.

I choose to cite these friendly Christian critics, rather than any of the host of hostile ones, simply to illustrate that even those scholars within "the fold" are pressed by their data to call all the churches to a continuing self-examination on mission policies and practices. Both of these authors were writing at the height of a dialogical era that saw many attempts to reconcile the various Christian churches with the spiritual traditions of native peoples. This is the era about which I intend to reflect in the following pages, about its conflicts as well as its dialogues.[3]

If the present article can be categorized, it might best be called a personal narrative of the last thirty years, or perhaps even a "memoir" of pastoral and scholarly experience in the area of mission to North American aboriginal peoples. I ask pardon for a number of references to the first person, but the essay is in fact drawn at least as much from personal experience as from "scientific" scholarship—with both the perils and promises of such an approach. The procedure here is what Clifford Geertz has called an "after the fact" examination. In his book by that name, Geertz revisits some of his own earlier projects in order to analyze them afresh through some degree of hindsight. He cites one of Soren Kierkegaard's numerous quotable aphorisms that "Life is lived forward but it is understood backward."[4]

Geertz here indulges once again his penchant for epistemology as he turns several clever phrases and concocts a scholarly pun to describe what he is about. The word "fact" first describes the obsession of anthropologists with pursuing "the facts." His method is an "ex post interpretation, the main way (perhaps the only way) one

---

3   For a summary history of mission in North America (including Canada up to the nineteenth century), see Carl F. Starkloff, S.J., "The Catholic Church and Native Americans," in *Encyclopedia of American Catholic History,* ed. by Michael Glazier and Thomas J. Shelley (Collegeville, MN: Liturgical Press, 1997). For a much more detailed treatment, see Christopher Vecsey's three-volume history of American Indian Catholics: *On the Padres' Trail* (Notre Dame, IN: University of Notre Dame Press, 1996), *The Paths of Kateri's Kin* (Notre Dame, IN: University of Notre Dame Press, 1997), and *Where the Two Roads Meet* (Notre Dame, IN: University of Notre Dame Press, 1999).

4   Clifford Geertz, *After the Fact: Two Countries, Four Decades, One Anthropologist* (Cambridge, MA: Harvard University Press, 1995), 166.

can come to terms with the sorts of lived-forward, unhistorical backward phenomena anthropologists are condemned to deal with."[5] But Geertz further intends his method to serve as "a post-positivist critique of empirical realism, the move away from simple correspondence theories of truth and knowledge which makes the very term 'fact' a delicate matter."[6]

It is just such an interpretation that I offer here: I embrace Geertz's concern to transcend a naive realist obsession with pure facts. While I am trying to interpret a lived history "objectively," it is after all a history in which I have been deeply involved, and not always as a searcher for facts. Nonetheless, it is offered with the hope that readers will take it for at least one factual reality—that it represents a quest for the kind of truth that is salvific for both the Church and human cultures. The upshot of this point is that I am writing as a Christian believer who believes in sharing his faith with others, and, if they are drawn by grace, even inviting them to join me in my faith community. Needless to say, that community has some extensive reassessment to do as to its approach to this "mission," and that reassessment is central to this personal history of mine. I live in a community of saints/sinners, Luther's *simul justi et peccatores*, but being one of them, I cannot reject the community and its mission.

My date lines are not purely arbitrary, but rather represent three short mini-eras within the period of three decades that I intend to describe and review. I call them, 1) "confrontation and dialogue," 1965–1979; 2) "participant observation," 1979–1989; and 3) "backlash on inculturation," 1989–1997.[7] To be sure, these

---

5   Geertz, *After the Fact*, 167.
6   Geertz, *After the Fact*, 168.
7   To avoid the widespread misinterpretation about the meaning of inculturation, readers are referred to the simple and serviceable work of J. Peter Schineller, S.J., *A Handbook on Inculturation* (New York: Paulist Press, 1990). A more complex synthesis of theology and anthropology is Gerald A. Arbuckle, S.M., *Earthing the Gospel: An Inculturation Handbook for the Pastoral Worker* (Maryknoll, NY: Orbis Books, 1990). For some further implications and complexities of the terminology, see Carl F. Starkloff, S.J., "Inculturation and Cultural Systems," *Theological Studies* 55, no. 1 (March 1994), 66–81, and 55, no. 2 (June 1994), 274–294.

time-lines are not entirely detached selections, since they represent certain turning points in my own life and work. However, they also represent significant dates in the history of Catholic mission among native North Americans.

Confrontation and Dialogue: 1965–1979

1965 is a highly symbolic date simply because it marks the conclusion of the Second Vatican Council, which produced, among many other dramatic documents, a decree on the missions (*Ad Gentes*) which has led to vast reappraisal of missionary activity. I point out here, though, that such documents did not spring miraculously from that short three-year period, although I believe that the Holy Spirit was indeed dramatically active there. In its documents on missions, as well as on interfaith dialogue and on religious tolerance, Vatican II was reaching back to roots in the Acts of the Apostles, in such apostolic fathers as Justin Martyr, and to the culminating point of the patristic period in Gregory the Great. Analogously, I point out that the dialogical attitude that followed this council was not entirely new to missionaries in North America. One thinks here of the superb linguistic and ethnological work of Berard Haile, O.F.M., among the Navahos, Eugene Buechel, S.J., among the Sioux, and J.B. Sifton, S.J., among the Gros Ventres and Arapahos. My own earliest efforts to understand Arapaho culture and my later knowledge of Ojibway traditions were based on Sifton's field notes and the monographs of Sister Mary Inez Hilger, O.S.B.[8] All of these pre-Vatican II personalities represent the kind of relatively unbiased "attention" to which we are called today.

But what was so special about Vatican II? It effectively symbolized, I believe, a "paradigm shift" in consciousness, in that it began to advocate listening to traditional cultures and spiritualities, not simply as objects of study, but as "subjects" of history and as partners in a conversation. This dialogical quality struck me with some

---

8   See Sister Mary Inez Hilger, O.S.B., *Chippewa Child Life and its Cultural Background* (Washington, DC: Smithsonian Institution, Bureau of American Ethnology, 1951), 146, and Sister Mary Inez Hilger, O.S.B., *Arapaho Child Life and its Cultural Background* (Washington, DC: Smithsonian Institution, Bureau of American Ethnology, 1952), 148.

force in the summer of 1965, my ordination summer, when I returned to the Wind River Reservation, the site of my earlier teaching years, to assist with pastoral ministry. While celebrating the Sunday Eucharist at the Northern Arapaho Pow Wow grounds, I made what I would later realize was one of my first gestures toward an "analogical imagination" (in the words of David Tracy). In my homily, I repeated a story I had recently read, about the encounter between an Inca king and one of his priests. The priest had rebuked the king for blasphemously gazing directly into the setting sun. In reply, the king argued that the sun was not the sovereign deity, as the priest claimed, since it too traveled and seemed to be doing the bidding of Another.

I suppose, in retrospect, I saw myself as a modern version of St. Paul speaking in the Areopagus about the "unknown god" of the Athenians. But I was soon shown that my thought was far from original, when John J. O'Hara, S.J., who was later to become one of my most valued teachers, told me later that this was exactly how his people viewed the sun whenever the participants in the "Sun Dance" sang and danced facing it or under it. The honor and worship was being given to the Creator of the sun. This sharing was perhaps not in itself so unusual, but it stirred in me the beginnings of a desire to explore the goodness and beauty in aboriginal traditions.

By the end of the 1960s, such conversations as this could be seen growing at mission sites, especially among the Benedictines of Blue Cloud Abbey in South Dakota, among the Jesuits in South Dakota and the Pacific Northwest, among the Capuchins in Montana, and among the Friars Minor and Blessed Sacrament Sisters in the American Southwest. One of the most striking of such ongoing conversations was that inaugurated by William Stolzman, then a Jesuit on the Rosebud Reservation and later a diocesan priest in Minnesota. By the early 1970s, Stolzman had initiated fortnightly dinner conversations among Sioux medicine men and spiritual leaders, and the Catholic and Protestant clergy of the area. These conversations proceeded largely along the lines of analogy: that is, the participants tried to approach all comparison between Lakota and Christian symbolism with the position that they were "in some ways alike and in some ways different." The sessions continued over some half-dozen years, and led to the publication of Stolzman's *The Pipe and Christ* in 1986.[9] This book has been criticized, with some justification, I believe, for an excessively Catholic bias and conclusions. But it has also been undeservedly and sometimes viciously vilified by some who accept no place at all for the Church among native peoples, or for any synthesis of aboriginal and Christian spirituality. But whatever one's viewpoint, it symbolizes a striking method of dialogue in the spirit of Vatican II.

My own initial feelers into conversations in 1969 and 1970 among the Northern Arapahos led to an article in 1971 on "confrontation and dialogue" between Christianity and native traditions.[10] My approach here differed somewhat from Stolzman's in that it employed categories from the history, sociology, and phenomenology of religions in an effort to find common ground for conversation. In a similar line of thought, I followed this with a small book using further categories and somewhat wider field experience.[11] This book too has been criticized—justly, I believe—for some oversimplifications, perhaps too much "Catholic" bias, and several misinterpretations.[12] I do not, however, repent of my posi-

---

9   William Stolzman, S.J., *The Pipe and Christ: A Christian-Sioux Dialogue* (Chamberlain, SD: St. Joseph's Indian School, 1986).

10   Carl F. Starkloff, S.J., "American Indian Religion and Christianity: Confrontation and Dialogue," *Journal of Ecumenical Studies* 8, no. 2 (1971): 317–340.

11   Carl F. Starkloff, S.J., *The People of the Center: American Indian Religion and Christianity* (New York: Seabury, 1974). The historian of religion, Ake Hultkrantz, in *The Study of American Indian Religions* (New York: Crossroad, 1983), has relegated this book to the ranks of "propagandistic studies." As he warns his readers, ". . . this kind of writing only too often has a restricted empirical value. . . ." I most willingly plead guilty. The book is a very early, and sometimes clumsy, effort to begin a process of dialogue and healing, and it is intended to be pre-eminently pastoral. As anyone who carefully reads the Preface and Introduction will realize, I never at any time express the least desire that the book should serve as a database for academics.

12   For example, my study of possible Arapaho words for God (30-33) has progressed considerably since publication of this book, thanks to more extended conversations with tribal leaders. A record of this can be found in two more articles: "Aboriginal Cultures and the Christ," *Theological Studies* 53, no. 2 (March 1992), 288–312, esp. 298–312, and "In Search of the 'Ultimate Meaning' in Arapaho Tradition and Contemporary Experience," *Ultimate Reality and Meaning: Interdisciplinary Studies in the Philosophy of Understanding* 18, no. 4 (December 1995): 249–263.

tion that a reformed Christianity might still be salvific for native peoples, as long as they are free to reject it or accept it. While the book was premature, written too early in my field experience, it seems to have struck a surprisingly strong chord among a number of native people. It has been used as an educational tool or topic of discussion in some theological schools, in parish discussions, and, in one case that I was informed of, in a prison, to defend the freedom of religion for native practitioners there.

A third colleague of mine, Paul Steinmetz, S.J., had likewise been venturing into dialogue on the Pine Ridge Reservation beginning in the late 1960s; his work eventuated in the publication of a more specified and scholarly study in 1980 on contemporary religious movements among the Oglala Lakota (Sioux) people.[13] This book too has received considerable acclaim and some invective—again illustrating, along with the earlier mentioned works, the neuralgic atmosphere that has continued around the encounter between native traditions and Christianity. If nothing else, all such literature of the period contributes to the picture of deep-seated anger and antagonism as well as fervent longings for spiritual dialogue and growth.

One might best characterize the period between 1965 and 1979 as one of "participant observation," a phrase used by many scholars, as suggested some years ago by Wilfred Cantwell Smith, to describe a creative process of interfaith dialogue.[14] One need not be a "theological pluralist" like Professor Smith in order to embrace participant observation with sincerity and openness. In any case, such participation by missionaries began to grow when, after a period of quite justified suspicion on the part of native people, their spiritual leaders started to accept missionaries into certain of their cere-

---

13   Paul B. Steinmetz, S.J., *Pipe, Bible, and Peyote among the Oglala Lakota: A Study in Religious Identity*, rev. ed. (Syracuse, NY: Syracuse University Press, 1998).

14   See Wilfred Cantwell Smith, "Participation: The Changing Christian Role in Other Cultures," in *Mission Trends No. 2*, ed. by Gerald H. Anderson and Thomas F. Stransky (New York and Grand Rapids, MI: Paulist and Eerdmans, 1975), 218–229. Smith has since developed this line of thought in many works, but space allows only for this citation here.

monies. Theological reflection grew, based very often on the question being put to Christian leaders, "How can I be both a Christian and an Indian?" Some aboriginal leaders, as early as 1970, were inquiring into ways in which they might help their people to integrate the native and received traditions. To be sure, this question seems not to have troubled many of them originally, since they had long before made peace with either an unofficial "syncretism" of ways, or with a more "compartmentalized" approach to dual belongings, such as still exists among the Pueblos. The dominant "world view" in these cases obviously had to be aboriginal, but it expressed itself by means of two sets of symbolic observances. Many writers have described the conditions that made this approach even more imperative than it had to be, especially the situation provoked by the failure of church leaders to listen to native people.

Participant observation in native ceremonies led naturally into the question as to how traditional practices figure in the lives of Christian native people. By this time, most missionaries of my acquaintance had accepted the validity of tribal ritual life for their parishioners. There was, of course, a residual "right wing" viewpoint (which included some native persons) that these rituals symbolized a "pagan" or "idolatrous" mentality, and that they could not be detached from a "bad medicine" use of symbols and power. There was likewise the "left wing" thinking, carried on even to the point of arguing that the tribal rituals themselves were enough for aboriginal Christian people and that the "European" practices were harmful and useless. My personal experience was that most Arapaho Christians desired the blessing of the Church on their native traditions.[15]

An equally delicate issue during this period was the importation of native symbolism into the liturgy of the Church, again featuring a full spectrum of opinions—from conservative Christian to conservative tribal-traditional, both of which feared "adulteration," or, in the language of many Christians, "syncretism." Some churches built or remodeled during this time reflect indigenous

---

15   For a further exploratory missiological essay on these issues, see Carl F. Starkloff, S.J., "Mission Method and the American Indian," *Theological Studies* 38, no. 4 (December 1977), 621–653.

themes; one thinks here of newer structures such as the church at St. Labre Mission in Ashland, Montana, Immaculate Conception Church at West Bay, Ontario, and the main chapel at Anishinabe Spiritual Centre at Anderson Lake, Ontario. The parish church at St. Stephen's Mission in Wyoming has passed through at least three remodeling phases, each one turning increasingly toward indigenous symbolism, all created by Arapaho artists.

The mission policy of St. Stephen's was to carry on a constant conversation with native spiritual leaders and elders as to fitting or unfitting forms of inculturation. The use of drums in church, especially at funerals, received nearly universal Arapaho approval even as early as 1970, and the practice of "cedaring" or "smudging" (incensing native style) was widely accepted as constitutive of the opening penitential rite of the Eucharist. Several translations of one of the basic Eucharistic prayers were made into Lakota, Crow, Cree, Arapaho, and Ojibway, to mention a few. The Arapaho text features considerable usage of "functional substitution" of Arapaho words for conventional European words, although the words of institution have been translated as literally as possible. Some proposals were explored as to the use of the sweat lodge as the context for a rite of reconciliation, but this has not become widespread. One Sioux deacon did employ the lodge for ceremonies, especially of communion.

Finally, during this period, issues of injustice to aboriginal people by both secular and ecclesiastical leaders were becoming ever more shrilly enumerated. It was the period, after all, of The American Indian Movement (AIM) and its 1973 seizure of the site of the massacre and burial of some two hundred mostly unarmed Sioux at Wounded Knee in 1890. This time marked the appearance of a trilogy of trenchant critical books by Sioux lawyer and philosopher Vine Deloria, Jr.—*Custer Died for Your Sins*; *We Talk, You Listen*; and *God is Red*. Hyemeyohsts Storm's *Seven Arrows* portrayed the suffering of a Cheyenne family at the hands of explorers, government, and the churches, while N. Scott Momaday published several powerful novels about native life, with *House Made of Dawn* being an especially tragic one. Margaret Craven's *I Heard the Owl Call My Name*, about the last year or so of a terminally ill Anglican curate sent to work among the Kwakiutls, dealt much more gently with the Church, but cast it as a listener and learner.

Such listening marked the growth of a most effectively wide-spread organization of Catholic native people—the Tekakwitha Conference. This conference had begun in 1939 as a small mutual support group for missionaries, continuing in that mode for nearly thirty years.[16] In 1977, however, many of the missionaries and a few native persons decided that the conference had outlived its usefulness in this form. But rather than disband it, they chose Father Gilbert Hemauer, a Capuchin from Ashland, Montana, and two native persons, Francis (later Deacon) Hairy Chin and Sister Genevieve Cuny, O.S.F., to reform and revitalize the conference. The ensuing gathering in 1978 saw a growth of participants from thirty to nearly two hundred, with perhaps a third of them being native persons. Its agenda featured issues discussed by native people and requests for recommendations from them.

The 1979 gathering marked the end of the first epoch, featuring as it did a highly vocal native minority. The conference leaders had committed what turned out to be a *felix culpa*, by extravagantly praising the missionary endeavors of the past, and thus unintentionally regressing from the hopes expressed the year before. Under the leadership of Beatrice Swanson, an Ojibway from Minneapolis, the native people burst out into an excoriation of the conference agenda. To their credit, the conference organizers and the four or five bishops present listened quietly, suspended the planned program, and initiated a discussion of how the conference could become a truly "Indian" reality. This event marked the beginning of the end of Church policy of dictating an agenda set by non-natives, even though native leadership of the conference was a decade away.

Dialectical Tension: 1979–1989

I call this the period of "dialectical tension," not simply to use current jargon, but because the period can indeed best be described by that phrase. That is, there was a continuous experience of asser-

---

16 I take this opportunity once again, as I have orally on many occasions, to deny emphatically that the Tekakwitha Conference was or is primarily intended to advocate the canonization of Kateri Tekakwitha. This objective has now become a major one for native people, so it is one that I support, but the conference has a much wider purpose.

tions and counter-assertions in church-aboriginal relations, and each position seemed to contain its own negation within itself. To illustrate, I suggest the matter of the Church's newly found openness to aboriginal experience and spirituality. Using my own context as an example, the "thesis" of the dialectic was placed by our attendance at, not merely the more "secular" (in our language) pow wows, but also at Sun Dance ceremonies, and our participation in rituals such as sweat lodges, "vision quests," and even peyote meetings. This was a startling and even hurtful phenomenon to many native persons who had been raised in conservative Christian traditions. A fitting remark to describe this "dialectic" is one often thrown good-naturedly at me by my Arapaho advisors: "When are you guys gonna make up your minds?" The tension was made more neuralgic by some church persons who uncritically praised all things "Indian," to the point of naively embracing every aspect of traditional spirituality and equating it with some Catholic practice. Such "openness," of course, ignores the fact recognized by all critics of religion, that no religion is without its human frailties.

However, as in all dialectical tensions, there was a creative and renovating aspect to these episodes. Beginning in 1980 at the Denver Tekakwitha Conference, the aboriginal voice grew ever more powerful and influential, whether it was conservatively Catholic, aggressively native, or more commonly, a baffling and often humorous amalgam of these. Thus, the closing liturgy of that conference, held on the lawn under a hot August sun, complete with a cardinal and his retinue, was "delayed" by a half hour of long bidding prayers by native people, some of them extemporaneous, but some in the form of memorized Catholic prayers. One very happy elderly woman announced that she would now say a rosary in thanksgiving, but apparently thought better of it, to the accompaniment of a sigh of relief from other participants!

This increased intensity and extension of the aboriginal voice continued in 1981 at Albuquerque, as some thousand participants, at least half of them native, responded to a survey about their needs and desires for the future. It was during this conference that the magnificent event of the Santo Domingo Pueblo name day featured the twin phenomena of a Catholic pontifical Mass and the traditional harvest and initiation ceremonies. It was especially signifi-

cant, at least to this observer, that each tradition had its "center"—
the Catholic altar in the plaza and the secret Kiva, but that even as
the Eucharist was being completed, Pueblo "clowns" danced across
the plaza to introduce the native element.

It was during the first part of the eighties that other developments began, which would lead to a great deal of creativity as well
as painful tension. The native religious and clergy began their own
support group during this time, with its solidarity as well as its divisions. Another small group, at first under Father Hemauer and then
soon under Sister Genevieve Cuny, began to develop a native catechetical group that continues to the present and has created some
valuable documents. A widened board of directors for the conference, drawn from lay native people, bishops, clergy, and religious
began to advise and at times to openly criticize the director. Task
forces, most notably on liturgy, ministry, catechetics, youth, and
social justice, began to hold seminars, at first mostly under the
direction of non-natives. By the time of the 1982 gathering in
Spokane, native clamor for leadership roles was growing, and this
reached a peak in 1983.

Each annual gathering, as well as the growing number of
regional meetings, now featured both dialogue and confrontation.
The "positive" quality of each dialogue generated its "negative,"
and the ideology behind each was not always easily discernible.
One could hear every possible complaint here, whether it be about
the suppression of native traditions or the loss of the Latin Mass!
One striking symbol of this tension was the opening liturgy in 1982,
led by one of the native parishes in the area: while the language of
the spoken part of the Mass was English, the music was the *Missa
de Angelis*. On the other hand, the participants were also treated to
a prayer session led by women from the Indian Shaker Church that
had grown out of the ecstatic nineteenth-century experience of the
Squaxin John Slocum.

By 1981, my own move to Canada began to distance me from
more intimate involvement in American church activity among
native people. However, I have continued to participate regularly
in the formation of Ojibway people for ministry at Anishinabe Spiritual Centre and occasionally among other reserve communities.

These programs have shown a parallel to developments in the United States, such as those at the Sioux Spiritual Center in South Dakota, Kitchi Manitou Centre in northern Alberta, and centers in Washington State and Montana. From these emerged, and still emerge, trained native leaders and especially deacons, although to my knowledge only one priest has so far emerged. While clerical celibacy is not the only reason for the shortage, it certainly figures largely in the problem.[17]

Also begun under Father Hemauer in 1982 was an orientation seminar of two weeks' duration, for introducing non-native church workers to local contexts. This program still functions, by now under almost total native direction. Such growing influence was symbolic of the process that was leading to a change in the leadership of the Tekakwitha Conference in 1989.

Inculturation: Its Period of Backlash, 1989–1997

I do not intend the title of this section as a completely negative comment on the 1990s; aboriginal leadership has been developing and that is a sign of hope for both church and society. But the inculturation movement, like any "revolution," has generated its reactions, and these have virtually defied classification. The arrival of native leadership in the Tekakwitha Conference, as in other areas both ecclesial and secular, has been a development long desired. But it has generated its own categories of tensions. Almost immediately, in the area of inculturation, there were divisions among native leaders and the clergy over liturgical practices, and not only between these two groups but among native groups as well. My last contact with the conference in any capacity was as a speaker at the Michigan regional meeting near Detroit in 1991. Comments following my address referred to divisions and tensions, but it was difficult to determine very specifically what these were, or who was responsible.

On the positive side, however, some hopeful movements have been taking place "north of the border" in Canada. At first, begin-

---

17   On efforts to address this issue, see David Nazar, S.J., Carl Starkloff, S.J., and Michael Stogre, S.J., "Papers Proposing a Married Native Clergy in the Sault Ste. Marie Diocese," *Mission* (formerly *Kerygma*) 4, no. 1 (1997): 9–28.

ning in 1980 and continuing throughout the decade, there was the Canadian Catholic Amerindian Conference. One local companion to this, in which I have participated several times, has been the Native Peoples' Pastoral Seminar in Thunder Bay, Ontario, started in 1981 and continuing to the present. In this relatively small group of some fifty persons, there has been a more or less like-minded approach to inculturation and native leadership.

The 1990s have also constituted a decade of political confrontations throughout North America. The events at Oka, Kahnasatake, and Kahnawake in southern Quebec, contesting expropriation of native lands by government or private interests, made themselves felt in New York state, which shares the Akwasasne Reserve with Ontario and Quebec. Again, the alignment of opposition was not entirely between Indian and white, since some Mohawks registered fear and suspicion over certain of those claiming to be Mohawk warriors.

Other contests in Canada mirror situations in the United States: the protests of the Cree in northern Quebec over provincial claims to invaluable water reserves have been one grave dimension of the Quebec sovereignty issue. The Teme-Agama Anishinabek (Ojibway) have been struggling against the province of Ontario and the logging industry over stands of virgin timber in Northern Ontario, while their linguistic cousins, the Lubicon Cree of Alberta have filed lawsuits against the Canadian government over a similar issue. Finally, the credibility of the churches has been dealt a severe blow by the emergence of numerous charges of physical and sexual abuse in Canadian residential schools, which are now seen to have emerged from an unfortunate concordat between the federal government and the churches.

One could detail other confrontations in nearly all ten of the Canadian provinces and the two territories, but it may be of more concern to Americans to mention the conflict between natives of the Southwest and the Vatican over the building of an astronomical observatory on Mount Graham in Arizona. This issue was severely complicated by the presence of numerous interest groups, and by the fact that local tribal leaders differed as to whether the observatory was truly intruding on holy ground. As is often the case, it was difficult to hear a consistent "native voice" in this situation.

The 1990s have seen another backlash to inculturation practices. During the 1980s, there was a massive incursion of tourists and "New Agers" into ceremonies on American reservations, which led to a great deal of "appropriation" of indigenous symbols by non-Indians. Many of these began to sell their services as "shamans," "healers," and holy persons or environmental experts. However, the churches' efforts at inculturation have not been spared similar assault, with attacks on clergy and others for employing native symbolism in the liturgy or for participating in tribal ceremonies. The usual objection is that such conduct simply aggravates the rapine already inflicted through the seizure of land and the destruction of languages. Paralleling these charges has been the campaign of "traditionalists" or former Christian natives to draw their compatriots back to "the Good Red Road" as being the only valid one for native people.[18]

All the same, backlash is not the whole story of this decade. It has been my experience, and that of many other church workers, to find a desire to continue the dialogue and to welcome friendly outsiders. Even since 1990, I have been welcomed into ceremonies conducted by Ojibways, Arapahos, Crows, and Shoshones. In the early fall of that year, I was invited, along with two Ojibway deacons, to share in a sweat lodge at Sagamok Point in northern Ontario. This was part of a four-day Sacred Fire ceremony held to support aboriginal representatives at negotiations in Ottawa. Moreover, there continues to be experimentation with native elements in the liturgy, conducted mostly by native persons.

What, then, does this "after the fact" analysis lead me to conclude? Certainly, in hindsight, it tells me that all of us made some mistakes, even our efforts to remedy the errors of the past. So, I fear, will it always be: this is the sadder-but-wiser condition described in the beautiful and melancholy words of Hegel, "The owl of Minerva flies at sunset." That is, wisdom comes only with the sadness of experience, or, sadder still, when it is too late to do anything about it. However, such melancholy wisdom seems more

---

18   See Carl F. Starkloff, S.J., "Religious Renewal in Native North America: The Contemporary Challenge to the Churches," *Missiology* 12 (January 1985): 81–101.

life-giving to me than the arrogance of those who smugly condemn the Church for mistakes, with the usually implied conviction that "I wouldn't have made those stupid mistakes if I had been there."

With hindsight comes also foresight wisdom for another epoch, as Hegel might have put it. Efforts are afoot today, among Catholics and Protestants, in theological schools, outreach programs, parishes, and missions, to prepare native leaders to guide their own churches. Just how prophetic such efforts may prove to be will depend on all the factors I have described above, but also on the openness of hierarchy and church leadership to engage in the "praxis" of inculturation.

In his now famous treatment of the "functional specialty" of history, Bernard Lonergan describes the work of historians as that of identifying in their research those events which were "going forward" at points in the past, and which thus continue to affect events in the present and the future.[19] What might the historian see now as "going forward" from the events I have described? If history is lived forward but understood backward, according to the Geertzian use of Kierkegaard's dictum, what might be critical areas in which the Church can search for deeper historical and theological wisdom?

My first issue is ecclesiological. I have found a deep challenge to such wisdom in the work of anthropologist Victor Turner, in his now famous studies of "liminality." That is, beginning with investigation of the "rites of passage" in tribal societies, Turner eventually went on to employ his data to develop a dynamic theory of stability and change in all societies, including the Church.[20] To my point here is the potential in marginalized cultures and societies for dynamic growth and creativity, separated as they are from the

---

19   Bernard J.F. Lonergan, S.J., *Method in Theology* (New York: Herder and Herder, 1972), chapters 8 and 9, esp. 178.

20   The best known of Turner's works is his *The Ritual Process: Structure and Anti-Structure* (New York: Aldine de Gruyter, 1995, original, 1969). I have developed some of Turner's insights into an incipient theory for stability and change in the Church. See Carl F. Starkloff, S.J., "Church as Structure and Communitas: Victor Turner and Ecclesiology," *Theological Studies* 58, no. 4 (December 1997): 643–668.

more rigid traditional structures. But such liminal conditions, as Turner often insisted, cannot endure without the context of stable structures. With open-minded readiness for conversion within both liminal "communitas" and traditional "structure" (two crucial terms of Turner's), it may be hoped that the Church too will listen more openly to the Holy Spirit.

Part and parcel of these liminal societies is the issue of "syncretism," a word that has struck terror into the hearts of Christians (especially evangelicals) since the seventeenth century. However, there has been an ongoing reappraisal of this phenomenon, leading to the recognition of the fact that the earliest forms of Christianity were already touched by syncretic processes, and that, indeed, all religions are by now to some degree syncretistic. The point, I believe, is not *whether* syncretism, but *how?*

What forms might a valid discernment of syncretic processes take, as we search for a valid praxis of inculturation that respects critically the symbols of all cultures?[21] The methodology needed here, and which I intend to engage in over the coming years, might be called an analysis of "the data of consciousness" as that phrase is described by Bernard Lonergan.[22] The importance of this kind of method is that it is not content simply to gather empirical "facts" that satisfy scholars (to hearken back to Geertz), but seeks to understand the "intentionality" of the other. My own work over the last seventeen years of doing "popular education" and conversation with Ojibways and other native persons has enabled me to see this as the as yet unforged key to an analysis of "syncretism" and therefore the praxis of inculturation.

To complete a trilogy of issues "going forward," one must certainly include crucial problems in the social life of contemporary aboriginal peoples. I have already mentioned many political issues, but perhaps equally as urgent, indeed even more so, are the local

---

21   Towards this end, see Carl F. Starkloff, S.J., "The Problem of Syncretism in the Search for Inculturation," *Mission* 1, no. 1 (1994): 75–94.

22   See Lonergan, *Method in Theology*, esp. 201–203; Bernard Lonergan, *Insight: A Study of Human Understanding* (New York: Philosophical Library, 1956), 72–74, and elsewhere.

problems instigated by the conquerors but which can finally be dealt with only by the native people themselves. I refer to such deadly scourges as alcoholism and chemical abuse, family dysfunction, and such physiological ailments as diabetes and general nutritional deficiencies. In Canada now, especially, local native leaders have been confronting these issues with both increasing technical knowledge and spiritual leadership. Diabetes and nutrition workshops feature not simply scientific education but spiritual healing rites as well, both aboriginal and Christian. Many native leaders now conduct alcohol healing workshops featuring the Twelve-Step Program of Alcoholics Anonymous, the Teachings of the Medicine Wheel, and, more recently, elements of The Spiritual Exercises of St. Ignatius Loyola.

The Church, then, like any other society/community, must understand its history backward and live it forward. It can do so by acting more and more in a facilitating role for aboriginal leaders who are working for creative change. The most powerful dimension to inculturation is that this creative mutual exchange between gospel and culture is finally the domain of local leaders, aided as long as seems necessary and advisable by those who originally introduced them to the faith. As we watch the owl fly into the darkness, we must continue to seek and pray for wisdom, and especially to intensify our powers of memory and imagination, that they may both retain the wisdom of an earlier epoch and project possibilities for the future.

In Native Tongues: Catholic Charismatic Renewal and Montana's Eastern Tribes

MARK CLATTERBUCK*

Introduction: Powerful Memories

During the summer of 2008, I was in Montana interviewing Native Christians on the Rocky Boy's Reservation for an oral history project exploring questions of dual religious identities among the Chippewa and Cree tribes. I spoke with a wide variety of Native Christians on the reservation, including Catholics, Pentecostals, Lutherans, Baptists, and independent Evangelicals. During the course of our conversations, stark differences emerged among the various denominational groups when they explained how free—or restricted—they felt to practice traditional tribal religions alongside their Christian worship.

There was one element in their divergent narratives, however, that seemed to enjoy nearly universal approval, freely transgressing denominational lines, having affected Catholics, Pentecostals, and Traditionalists alike with equal force and emotional weight. In story after story, these Native Christians spoke effusively about a period of spiritual renewal among Montana's tribes that shaped their religious lives unlike any other, a span of roughly ten years that many still regard as a spiritual summit against which they measure all subsequent religious experiences in their lives.

They were speaking of the Catholic Charismatic Renewal that swept across eastern Montana's Native communities from 1975 into the early 1980s. The movement was marked by widespread prayer for physical and inner healing, tongues, the experience of "resting in the Spirit" (also "slain in the Spirit"), prophecies, and a power-

*This essay was originally published in *U.S. Catholic Historian* 28, no. 2 (Spring 2010), 153–180.

fully felt sense of spiritual community. The collective religious experience of those years freely crossed sectarian barriers, often bringing Catholics and Pentecostals together in shared worship on reservations where interdenominational rivalries had deep historical roots. The intensity of those events and their enduring imprint on the religious landscape of these reservations today soon led me back to Montana to give more serious attention to the stories of spiritual awakening and healing that animated the memories and spiritual lives of so many Native Christians who belong today to a wide variety of Christian communities.

Given both the intensity and scope of this phenomenon among Montana's Native people, I believe this is a story that deserves a wider audience than it has received to date. It is also a story best told through the voices of those most affected by the pulse of its life flow and the rhythm of its waves. At the same time, it is a story whose telling is accompanied by a growing sense of urgency; several key players of these events—including the Seneca elder and Franciscan sister José Hobday, the Precious Blood priest Father Paul Schaaf, and the Lakota Sioux elder Joe Red Thunder–have died as a period of more than forty years now separate us from the first rumblings of these extraordinary events. In the summer of 2009, I returned to hear and record the stories of many who were near the center of the movement, Native and non-Native alike. The record of their memories forms the basis of what follows here.[1]

There are always many more voices that ought to be included in a project like this. Nevertheless, I have tried to assemble a fairly representative gathering of those participants largely responsible for the vitality of the movement on three of Montana's reservations where the Catholic Charismatic Renewal (CCR) was experienced most poignantly across the state through the 1970s and 80s: the Fort Belknap Reservation (Gros Ventre and Assiniboine), the Rocky Boy's Reservation (Chippewa and Cree), and the Crow Reservation (Apsáalooke). I include the voices of women and men, Natives and

---

1   The majority of stories recorded here are drawn from one-on-one interviews I conducted on the Belknap, Rocky Boy, and Crow Reservations in July and August of 2009. These interviews have been supplemented by phone conversations, letters, and email correspondence.

non-Natives, lay leaders and clergy, all of whom played key roles in the movement's impact across these tribal communities.

Lighting the Fire: From Devil's Lake to Wolf Point

It began near Devil's Lake, North Dakota. In the early summer of 1975, a regional Catholic Indian Congress was held at St. Michael's Mission on the Spirit Lake Tribe Reservation, not far from Fort Totten. During one of the services, the Lakota Sioux elder Joe Red Thunder was unexpectedly asked to pray for a woman suffering from cancer who was standing beside him. Joe's father had been a Catholic catechist, and Joe himself was steeped in the Catholic faith. He later recounted that all he knew to pray was the "Hail Mary" and the "Our Father." So he put his hand on the woman's forehead and began, nervously, to pray the Lord's Prayer. As he prayed, he felt his legs buckle beneath him and his hands flew upward as a surge of divine power coursed through his body. In the years that followed, many witnesses confirm that the woman experienced a miraculous healing from her cancer that day, and that Joe received a gift of healing that deeply affected him and thousands of Montana Natives for the rest of their lives.[2]

During the business meeting that concluded the Fort Totten Catholic Indian Congress, attendees agreed to hold the following year's congress on the Fort Peck Reservation in northeast Montana, home to Joe Red Thunder. At that time, the primary purpose of the regional congresses was to provide an opportunity for Native Catholics to receive catechetical instruction and sacraments they may have neglected throughout the year—baptism, confirmation, confession, Eucharist, and even marriage. Following his experience at the congress of 1975, Red Thunder's interest was piqued by a news story of a Dominican priest whose prayers purportedly diverted a storm away from a huge charismatic gathering at an outdoor Catholic healing service at the University of Notre Dame football stadium, an event that reportedly attracted 25,000 partici-

---

2   The story of Joe Red Thunder as recorded here comes from an interview with Father Peter Guthneck, priest of St. Mary's Catholic Church, Rocky Boy's Reservation, Montana, August 7, 2009.

pants.[3] That priest was Francis MacNutt, whose bestselling book *Healing* (1974) had recently thrust him onto center stage of an emergent Catholic Charismatic Renewal.[4] Back at Fort Peck, Joe talked to Father Peter Guthneck and Franciscan sister José Hobday (Seneca) about inviting MacNutt to their Catholic Indian Congress the following summer. The recently ordained Guthneck was serving Our Lady of Lourdes at the time, a mixed Native and non-Native parish in the Fort Peck town of Poplar; Hobday was at St. Thomas Church in Brockton, ten miles east of Poplar. Guthneck recalls how Joe wanted to hear this priest "who called upon the powers" during that service at Notre Dame.

MacNutt accepted the invitation to lead the Catholic Indian Congress of 1976. But prior to the congress, MacNutt asked to lead a small retreat for eastern Montana priests given their unfamiliarity with the charismatic movement and, specifically, with healing prayer. According to Father Guthneck, who attended that retreat with roughly ten other priests in early January of 1976, the event was well received, focusing on the necessity of forgiveness as a prerequisite for both physical and inner healing.

At the end of the retreat, MacNutt invited Guthneck and Hobday to join him for a series of charismatic services he was

---

3   For a brief discussion of how the Notre Dame conference (1974)—and, more specifically, the healing Mass led there by MacNutt—contributed to the larger context of the CCR, see R. Andrew Chestnut, *Competitive Spirits: Latin America's New Religious Economy* (New York: Oxford University Press, 2003), 67. See also Barbara Shlemon Ryan, "Restoring the Gifts of Healing: Reflections on Thirty-Five Years of Healing Ministry," *Pentecost Today* (October/November/December 2003): 3–4. Shlemon says the number of attendees at the 1974 Notre Dame conference was "at least 30,000."

4   See Francis MacNutt, O.P., *Healing* (Notre Dame, IN: Ave Maria Press, 1974), and, MacNutt, *The Power to Heal* (Notre Dame, IN: Ave Maria Press, 1977). In one of his most recent books, *The Healing Reawakening* (Grand Rapids, MI: Chosen Books, 2005; second printing, 2008), MacNutt traces what he considers a centuries-long decline in healing prayer among Christians, followed by its recent recovery. The book was originally released in 2005 under the title *The Nearly Perfect Crime*; in a recent phone conversation with MacNutt, he explained that it was retitled after being repeatedly catalogued as a detective/mystery title.

scheduled to lead the following month at a stadium in Barquisimeto, Venezuela. By then, MacNutt was not only a leader of
the CCR in the U.S., but a central player in the spread of the movement to a number of Latin American countries including Mexico,
Colombia, Peru, and Chile.[5] Guthneck, along with Hobday, agreed
to go, and it was on that trip that he ministered beside a number of
influential figures in the burgeoning Catholic charismatic movement. These included Barbara Shlemon, a Catholic laywoman,
author, and international retreat leader; Father Paul Schaaf,
C.PP.S., a co-founder (with Shlemon) of the newly established Association of Christian Therapists (1975); and Jean Hill, a Dominican
sister who frequently traveled as part of MacNutt's healing ministry
team. Guthneck recalls how, among many other experiences, the
trip provided his first direct encounter with the practice known as
deliverance from evil spirits, a particular emphasis in the ministry
of Paul Schaaf.

Following a successful series of services in Barquisimeto, Mac-
Nutt gathered together his ministry team for the Catholic Indian
Congress on the Fort Peck Reservation. Among the team, once
again, were Schaaf, Shlemon, Hill, and brothers Dennis and
Matthew Linn who were both Jesuits at the time with experience in
Native ministry.[6] MacNutt also invited Living Sound, a music group
out of Oral Roberts University, to lead music throughout the con-
ference. The group had recently performed at a concert in Krakow,
Poland, where they were invited into the home of then-Cardinal
Karol Wojtyla. In 1980, two years after his installation as Pope
John Paul II, Wojtyla arranged for Living Sound to perform at the
Vatican before a crowd reported at 64,000.[7] MacNutt's inclusion of

---

5   Chestnut, *Competitive Spirits*, 67.

6   Dennis eventually left the Society of Jesus to marry Sheila Fabricant
Linn in 1989. Since then, the three together have extended their healing ministry, which is rooted in Ignatian spirituality, through international workshops
and retreats. They have also co-authored more than twenty books together on
spirituality and healing.

7   See, "Pentecostal Musician Terry Dalton Remembered for Talent,
Faith," *Charisma Magazine* online, June 9, 2009, https://www.charismamag.
com/site-archives/570-news/featured-news/5688-pentecostal-musician-larry-
dalton-remembered-for-talent-faith-.

Protestant ministers among his pastoral team was not unusual for the Dominican organizer, whose ministry teams, both in the U.S. and abroad, were intentionally ecumenical.

The congress took place June 17–20, 1976, at St. Ann's Chapel on the Fort Peck Reservation, about five miles west of the town of Poplar toward Wolf Point. MacNutt describes a couple hundred participants gathering in a circle and introducing themselves as the meetings opened, a process he recalls taking about an hour and a half. A raucous ceremonial welcoming dance, with dancers in tribal regalia moving to a drumbeat, formally opened the congress. MacNutt humorously recounts that the young boys who were there that day "danced like prairie chickens."[8] The nature of these opening ceremonies demonstrates a dramatic shift that had taken place in the Church's attitude toward traditional Native customs over the previous half century. When the Catholic Sioux Congress met in that same town of Poplar, Montana, in 1920, Native lay Catholics and non-Native Church leaders alike had roundly condemned what they called "the old, wild Indian dances which, of late, have been permitted by the Government and which have done untold harm mentally, physically, and morally, to the young and to the older Indians."[9] Fifty-six years later, the Catholic mission was hosting just such a dance to open the congress.

Publicity posters for the event announced: "Montana-North Dakota Catholic Indian Congress: Praying for Healing of Nations, Inner-Healing, and Body Healing." The advertised theme for the meetings sounded a similar refrain: "The Holy Spirit Healing His People." The services were marked by the laying on of hands, prayers for healing, and teachings on forgiveness as a means to receive God's healing touch. While deliverance from demonic forces often played a significant role in MacNutt's ministry, he says of these meetings that they "went light on deliverance" from evil spirits—adding, "although some deliverance did take place." The focus, instead, remained on reconciliation and forgiveness.[10]

---

8   Francis MacNutt, phone conversation with the author, July 16, 2009.

9   See Bernard Strassmaier, O.S.B., "Catholic Indians in Congress: Sioux Congress of Poplar, Montana," *The Indian Sentinel* (October 1920): 168.

10   Francis MacNutt, phone conversation with author, July 14, 2009.

Estimates of attendance at these meetings ranges from 200 to 400, with participants providing their own lawn chairs for four days of open-air meetings. Those who attended recall a large arbor covered with leafy branches providing shade for the speaker's platform. During the day, there was a lot of singing, teaching by the congress leaders, and testimonies about what was happening across the country as Christians gathered together to pray for healing. The evenings were devoted primarily to prayer. The leaders would typically begin by moving among rows of Native participants who had come up to the arbor for prayer, laying on their hands and praying for individual needs. Then the leaders would invite the congregation to begin praying for one another, instructing the crowds that this was a key component in the ministry of Jesus—empowering his disciples to perform the healing work of the Gospel themselves, rather than looking only to Jesus to do the work.

One attendee of the congress remembers the "fever pitch of expectation" that marked these meetings, as people laid hands on one another and prayed for healing of all kinds.[11] Nowhere was the excitement more palpable than among the Native elders who attended those meetings, according to Michael Ley, who was also among the participants. He tells how John J. Mount, a Gros Ventre Catholic elder from Hays, Montana, saw in these events a return to the old days when the medicine men were powerful and effective healers. He recalls Mount saying during these services, "But those guys are all gone—somehow we lost it. Now, it's coming back."[12]

The preaching and teaching that took place was heavily grounded in the Gospel narratives recounting the healing acts of Jesus. There was also a strong sacramental emphasis, particularly linking the sacraments of Reconciliation and Eucharist to the healing work of Christ. After four days of meetings, Bishop Eldon Bernard Schuster (Great Falls-Billings) presided over the Mass that brought the congress to a close. The energy of those services, however, was only just beginning to gain momentum. On the Fort Peck Reservation in the months following the congress, the nascent CCR took the form of small charismatic meetings in the rectory where

---

11 Michael Ley, phone conversation with the author, March 10, 2010.
12 Michael Ley, phone conversation with the author, March 10, 2010.

Native and non-Native Catholics together regularly gathered for prayer. Their interest in healing and the gifts of the Spirit led to frequent Sunday afternoon drives up to Regina, Canada, to participate in large charismatic prayer meetings taking place there at the time. Guthneck recalls witnessing people jumping up and down in exuberant worship, as well as many speaking in tongues and giving interpretations.[13] Indeed, the movement animating the Catholic community at Poplar in the summer of 1976 did not stay confined to Fort Peck's borders. It rapidly spread to other reservations in the state, beginning with a very enthusiastic reception 200 miles west of St. Ann's Chapel, among the Assiniboine and Gros Ventre tribes on the Fort Belknap Reservation.

The Movement Takes Shape: Fort Belknap and Rocky Boy

Two attendees of that 1976 Catholic Indian Congress were an unlikely pair of near strangers who drove from Hays, Montana, on the Fort Belknap Reservation. Father Joseph Retzel was the Jesuit priest in charge of St. Paul's Mission and Indian School in Hays; Michael Ley was a recently returned Vietnam veteran from Fort Wayne, Indiana, to whom Retzel had casually extended an invitation to join him for the congress. Together, the two would later prove instrumental in bringing the CCR to the Native Catholics of Fort Belknap Reservation.

An unusual set of circumstances had brought these men together. In 1975, a couple years after returning from the war, Ley was running a small construction business with his brother in their hometown of Fort Wayne. When a woman in town organized a garage sale to raise money for a little mission school in Montana that had recently burned to the ground, Ley donated $100 to the cause without thinking much about it. Not long afterward, he received a note from Father Joseph Retzel, thanking him for his contribution to rebuild St. Paul's Mission School. He included an open invitation to visit the school if he was ever in the area. One

---

13   Peter Guthneck, interview with the author, St. Mary's Mission, Rocky Boy, August 7, 2009.

year later, Ley took Father Retzel up on his offer. While hitchhiking his way across Montana on vacation in the spring of 1976, he caught a ride to Fort Belknap to visit the priest and see for himself the newly constructed high school nestled in the scenic foothills of the Little Rocky Mountains.

When Ley arrived, Father Retzel was preparing to head north to Fort Peck for the 1976 congress. Ley joined him for that event, and to this day recalls the excitement and enthusiasm that permeated those meetings. Father Retzel, who served as a minister of the Sacrament of Reconciliation during the conference, was likewise deeply impressed by what took place there. So as the congress drew to a close, Retzel invited Father MacNutt to hold similar services the following year at St. Paul's Mission, an invitation that MacNutt accepted on the spot. That decision would prove decisive in ensuring the spread of the movement across the Native reservation communities of the region.

Although Ley went back to Fort Wayne soon after the 1976 Poplar Congress, he returned to St. Paul's later that summer where he spent the next two years teaching, coaching, and driving a bus for the mission school. He immediately joined Father Retzel as a lead organizer of the upcoming Hays Catholic Indian Congress for which preparations were already underway. A young Native artist named Lester Doney designed the brochure for the event that featured a missionary and a Native Christian kneeling side by side in prayer. When the congress convened in the late spring of 1977, nearly 1,000 people gathered for the four-day event. Although most in attendance were Native people from Montana reservations, there were many— Natives and non-Natives alike—who came from neighboring states (especially North Dakota) and Canada. Tepees, tents, and campers covered the grounds of the mission, and, once again, a large arbor was set up to shade the speakers and musicians throughout the event. There were so many people to feed that organizers set up a horse trough over a fire pit, filled it with water, and boiled an entire cow cut up in large chunks so they could offer family-sized portions to the crowd as services took place nearly around the clock.

Francis MacNutt was accompanied, once more, by many of the same national CCR leaders who had joined him for the Fort Peck

Catholic Indian Congress the previous summer. These included Paul Schaaf, Barbara Shlemon, the Linn brothers, and members of the Living Sound music group from Oral Roberts University. Father Joseph Retzel, who hosted the event, recalls how the emphasis of the teaching that year was again on healing, but this time the focus was primarily on the healing of interpersonal relationships. "Yes, we'll experience healing here," Retzel remembers MacNutt telling the crowds, "but the great healing will be between people." Retzel himself tells stories of white attendees whose negative stereotypes of Native people were permanently altered as a result of the meetings, adding: "When we came together there in the gym, the Spirit between the people, was—you could almost feel it. And there were a lot of Native and white people there; and that's the gift—to me— that was manifest at that gathering. And I believe that the prayer and the healing was between people." While Retzel claims that physical healings did occur, he says it was reconciliation across racial divides that was most memorable.[14]

Michael Ley, who served as co-organizer of these meetings, likewise recalls the emphasis on the healing of relationships, especially noting the healing that took place between tribes historically at odds with one another. He also says that animosity between so-called "half-breeds" and "full-bloods," which was running high at the time, was another key focus of these meetings.[15] Ed Doney, a Gros Ventre and Chippewa from Hays who also participated in these meetings, adds that one of the most important developments of that conference was the reconciliation that began to take place between Native people and the Catholic Church. He explains that his own parents and grandparents had encountered physical abuse at the hands of Catholic boarding school staff, including beatings with a rubber hose when being disobedient or when speaking their tribal language. Therefore, having a white Catholic priest preaching reconciliation and forgiveness to Native Catholics was, according to Doney, really important to Native people at the time. He also recounts large crowds of people gathered together and singing in

---

14   Joseph Retzel, interview with the author, St. Paul's Mission, Hays, Montana, August 7, 2009.

15   Michael Ley, phone conversation with the author, March 10, 2010.

spiritual tongues all at once, a sound he describes as "angelic." He says people would sing in tongues and others would then offer interpretations in English for the benefit of the listeners.[16]

Patty Addy, a Gros Ventre ("with a little bit of Assiniboine") who grew up in Hays before relocating outside the Fort Belknap Agency, humorously recalls Francis MacNutt "dancing in the Spirit" as his head kept hitting the low-hanging arbor above him. Prayer tents were set up on the mission grounds where people could go for healing prayer. Among those who received prayer during those meetings was Patty's daughter, Mary, who was about seven years old at the time. Patty describes Mary being "slain in the Spirit" and receiving a healing for what Patty describes as "bad eyes." According to Patty, these prayer meetings, and the healings and prophecies that accompanied them, sometimes continued all night long.[17] Patty and Ed both attest that there were well over 1,000 people gathered each night at the congress.

Given the size and enthusiasm of the crowds attending these meetings, St. Paul's Mission followed up by hosting another charismatic conference in June of 1978. Heavy rains, however, drove those meetings inside the mission gymnasium and, in turn, produced much smaller crowds than had gathered at the 1977 congress. It did little to quench the excitement of the movement, however. For, by that time, the chief locus of the charismatic movement rippling across Fort Belknap had shifted away from the large, four-day congresses and into the living rooms of the reservation's Native Christians, Catholic and Protestant alike. A key impetus behind this movement was Sister Bartholomew, a Franciscan teacher freshly arrived at St. Paul's from Milwaukee. Under her energetic leadership, the charismatic impulse spread among the students of the mission school and into the homes of Native Christians where weekly prayer and healing meetings started occurring first around Hays, and then all across Belknap.

---

16   Ed Doney, interview with the author, Harlem Assembly of God, Montana, August 9, 2009.

17   Patty Addy, interview with the author, Harlem Assembly of God, Montana, August 9, 2009.

Her force of personality was recognized even by those opposed to her strong charismatic convictions or who bristled at her brazen ministry style, among them the four Franciscan sisters who had been serving together at St. Paul's Mission for four decades before Bartholomew's arrival in 1976. Wherever I traveled collecting stories about this movement—from Belknap to Rocky Boy to Crow—I frequently found myself listening to tales of her powerful prayers, her gifts of healing and tongues, and her belief in God's power over demonic forces. Father Retzel himself credits her for saving his life with a supernatural intervention during an incident at the mission during those days. When a heavily intoxicated man confronted Retzel on the mission grounds one night after dark, Sister Bartholomew was inside praying in tongues for his protection. The man raised a bottle above Retzel's head to strike, but something prevented the attacker from carrying out his threat. Instead of striking, the man simply walked away, never touching the priest. "I'm absolutely certain, to this day," says Retzel, "that she, with God's help, froze his arm so he couldn't do that. I'm convinced of that—that she saved my life."[18]

It was here in these house meetings that the Catholic charismatic movement on the reservations became truly ecumenical. While the large June congresses were, despite the ecumenical ministry teams, distinctly Catholic events grounded squarely in the sacraments, sectarian barriers fell away in the house meetings where Catholic charismatics and Protestant Pentecostals comfortably worshipped side by side in one another's homes. Announcements would be posted each week in the grocery store, gas station, or post office informing passerby when and where the next house meeting would be taking place, and anyone—regardless of denominational affiliation—was welcomed to attend. Everybody brought a Bible, "and there was always a guitar," recalls Michael Ley.[19] The typical service would open with the singing of songs, some from the Catholic missalette and others from a popular pool of interdenominational worship choruses which one participant describes as "half-gospel, half-country western."[20] Attendees would next read sponta-

---

18 Joseph Retzel, interview with the author, August 7, 2009.
19 Michael Ley, phone interview with the author, March 10, 2010.
20 Michael Ley, phone interview with the author, March 10, 2010.

neously selected Scripture passages accompanied by informal reflections based on personal experiences from the week. Then would come a time of prayer for healing. Participants would typically gather in a circle and take turns praying for one another, often laying hands on the supplicant while praying in tongues for various kinds of healing.

The ecumenical nature of the movement was expressed in other ways, as well. Patty Addy, mentioned above, was baptized into the Catholic Church as an infant at St. Paul's Mission. She also attended and graduated from St. Paul's Mission School, just as her parents had done before her, and was later married at the mission. Even so, her initial involvement in the charismatic movement came not through the Catholic Church, but rather through an Assemblies of God congregation in Hudson, Wyoming. In the early 1970s, her husband Don was working as an agricultural extension agent on the Wind River Reservation (Arapaho and Shoshone). While there, they received repeated invitations from the pastor of that Pentecostal church to attend revival services—invitations they repeatedly declined, reminding them "we're very good Catholics." In 1974, the Addys moved to Belknap after Don accepted an extension agent position with the tribe; Patty explains that they had been "born again" by that time. Soon after the move, Sherman Cochran, a Gros Ventre Pentecostal evangelist, came through town and asked Patty and Don to help with some evangelistic tent meetings, which they did. Then, in 1976, the pastor from the Assemblies of God church in Hudson, Wyoming, moved to a church in Shelby, Montana, a few hours' drive from Belknap. On July 4, 1976, the Addys were attending a service at the Shelby church when Patty went forward for prayer "to be filled with the Holy Spirit." "It was the Fourth of July, and that was like fireworks," she says. "I was miraculously filled with the Holy Spirit and started speaking in tongues." She and Don were still Catholic, but they started calling themselves "the Assembly of Catholic," regularly attending both Catholic Mass and Pentecostal worship services.

During these years, the Addys were among those who hosted charismatic prayer meetings in their home, in addition to attending meetings in many other homes as well. They were regularly joined by Ed Doney and his wife Julia, who in 2009 completed a term as president of the Fort Belknap Tribal Council. Ed tells of meetings that took place in reservation houses, or sometimes in the basements of Catholic churches, that numbered up to a hundred people on some nights. He says people mostly came for the healing prayer that included laying on of hands and anointing with oil. Ed and Patty both tell stories about driving carloads of Native friends from Belknap to neighboring reservations—even neighboring states—to attend special meetings held in homes, churches, or in large outdoor gatherings. They made one such trip to take part in informal charismatic meetings led by a Catholic priest at Cherry Creek on the Rosebud Reservation in South Dakota. Ed describes "falling over backward in the Spirit" during one of those meetings while leading worship choruses; he says he kept right on playing while lying on the floor. Ed and Patty also recall a man at one of those services who was demon possessed. Patty says of the demon "it was like it was rolling around in him," adding that the man "was delivered" that night through their prayers. They remember that "lots of people were slain in the Spirit" during those Rosebud meetings.

Meanwhile, back at Belknap, Don's reputation as a powerful spiritual leader was growing legendary. He was known for praying, on the spot, with anyone who asked him (and, sometimes, even with those who did not ask), whether in "K-Mart, Wal-Mart, the grocery store, wherever," says Patty. His commitment to the movement was an important factor in the growth of the CCR on the reservation. Although he was white, the tribe adopted Don in 1998, giving him the name *Wa-Whoa-Ge Yeas*, which means "Likes to Help." Following his death in 2008, the tribe dedicated a park on the reservation to his memory, which stands today as a continuing tribute to his reputation as an influential spiritual leader in the community and a highly effective advocate of the charismatic movement. His influence directly led many Native Christians (both Catholic and Protestant) into the charismatic movement, some of whom later became prominent Pentecostal leaders on Montana's reservations.

According to Patty and Ed, the priest at St. Thomas Catholic Church in Harlem during the late 1970s grew increasingly uncomfortable with the CCR, even "sneaking around the building" during their prayer services to see what was going on. Eventually, they were no longer allowed to hold charismatic meetings in the church building. Patty and Ed say that once the charismatic movement "came in, and then went out" of the Catholic Church in the 1980s, most Catholics they knew in the movement "who were really on fire and touched by the Spirit" stopped attending Mass and became involved in Pentecostal churches. Of the others, they say that some went back to traditional Indian religion, or else started mixing Catholicism and traditional ways. Of the Native Catholics who remained in the Harlem parish, Ed says that the people "started burning sweet grass in the church and bringing in feathers," a mixture he and Patty found regrettable, adding: "the Bible says to come out and be separate."

In 1977, a convergence of charismatic Catholic leadership in the region—lay, religious, and ordained—carried the movement west to Rocky Boy, the smallest of Montana's reservations, located in the north central part of the state about sixty miles from the Canadian border. After St. Thomas Church in Harlem prevented the leadership of the CCR from holding weekly charismatic meetings for the growing number of participants living around the Belknap Agency, Sister Bartholomew and Michael Ley came up from St. Paul's Mission in Hays to drive carloads of Catholic charismatics over to the Rocky Boy's Reservation for Saturday night meetings. Father Peter Guthneck—who was so instrumental in organizing the pivotal Fort Peck Congress in 1976, and who had been serving a mixed Native and non-Native congregation on the Fort Peck Reservation—had just been assigned to St. Mary's Mission on the Rocky Boy's Chippewa-Cree Reservation in August 1977. He opened up the doors of the old St. Mary's Church for these meetings, where Native Catholics from Belknap joined those from Rocky Boy for large, weekly prayer meetings. Joe Red Thunder, whose experience of healing prayer at the Fort Totten Congress of 1975 became the catalyst for the Native charismatic renewal in Montana, also attended these meetings from time to time.

As elsewhere in the CCR, the meetings at Rocky Boy opened with the singing of songs from the missalette mixed with a familiar store of charismatic choruses, followed by members reading and discussing Scripture passages among themselves. But the primary focus of these meetings remained the time of corporate prayer for healing, marked by a variety of physical manifestations. Father Guthneck recounts that the laying on of hands, speaking in tongues, and being slain in the Spirit were regular occurrences at the meetings, although he tried to deemphasize some of these events when he felt they were becoming a distraction to people's spiritual journeys.

The movement at Rocky Boy received a further boost when Michael Ley moved there from Belknap in 1978 where he spent the next three years helping Guthneck build a new chapel and rectory for St. Mary's Mission. During those years, prayer meetings continued at the church and in people's homes with growing enthusiasm and steady attendance. Those who attended the meetings recall many instances of physical and inner healings. Both Guthneck and Ley recall praying one night for a man by the name of Wilbur Parisian who was suffering from a brain aneurism. Guthneck describes how the affected artery was bulging "like a balloon, ready to pop." Doctors said that death was imminent. Witnesses at that meeting, however, claim that Parisian experienced a healing through prayer that defied medical explanation. In the years immediately following that experience, he was among the core group of construction workers who completed the new St. Mary's Church in 1980. According to a conversation with Ley in 2010, Parisian was continuing to enjoy good health.[21]

Connie Morsette was among the many who were profoundly affected by the CCR at Rocky Boy during those years. Connie, a Cree, grew up in the village of Box Elder along the northern edge of the Rocky Boy's Reservation where she was baptized in the Catholic Church as a child. She attended the healing services led by Francis MacNutt at Hays in 1977, which served as her introduction

---

21   The account of Parisian comes from Michael Ley, phone conversation with the author, March 10, 2010, and Peter Guthneck, interview with the author, August 7, 2009. Note: In 1980, Michael Ley left Montana for a time to attend seminary in Milwaukee, receiving ordination in the Roman Catholic Church in 1984. He returned to Montana where he served as a priest for five years. He later married, and, although no longer a priest, he and his wife remain actively involved in Native ministry at St. Mary's Mission on Rocky Boy's Reservation. Michael's brother, Phillip, ordained the same day as Michael in 1984, became a Franciscan priest serving in San Antonio, Texas.

to the Catholic charismatic movement. "I thought these people were kind of crazy the way they were acting," she says today with a smile.[22] Nevertheless, she explains how she was irresistibly drawn to the movement and began attending home prayer meetings near People's Creek on the Fort Belknap Reservation every chance she got. Her husband Ken (Cree and Gros Ventre) also got involved, and it was during these house meetings that Connie was "filled with Spirit." Ken and Connie were among those at Rocky Boy who encouraged the spread of the movement from Belknap to Rocky Boy, joining their efforts with those of Sister Bartholomew, Michael Ley, and Patty and Don Addy to organize charismatic house meetings among the Chippewa and Cree. They also emphasize the role played by Mary Jane LaMere of Rocky Boy, whose son had gone missing in January of 1978. When detectives were unable to locate the young man, Mary Jane attended one of the charismatic meetings at Belknap to seek supernatural assistance. She was not disappointed, receiving a "word of knowledge" from a prayer leader who told her where her son's body could be found. When detectives, following the lead, discovered the body soon afterward, Mary Jane was among those who first urged leaders of the Belknap house meetings to begin holding services at Rocky Boy as well.

Like many others, the Morsettes speak of these years as a time of profound spiritual awakening as a tightly knit community of Native charismatic Catholics met weekly in intimate prayer meetings across the reservations. They also describe Catholic healing services they attended at St. Ignatius on the Flathead Reservation in the western part of the state. Connie's sister-in-law, Alma Swan, tells how Joe Red Thunder prayed over her and her husband, Ron, following one of those meetings. "Ron was healed of drinking," she testifies emphatically. "He was healed of alcoholism that night."

Over time, however, the ecumenical seams of the movement— both at Belknap and Rocky Boy—began showing signs of stress. Several of the Native leaders in the house-meeting movement had,

---

22   Connie Morsette, interview with the author, Box Elder, Montana, August 12, 2009. Also participating in the interview were her husband Ken Morsette, her sister-in-law Alma Swan, and her son Aaron Morsette.

up until the early 1980s, found ways to live comfortably in both the Catholic Church and Pentecostal ministries. But, little by little, they were feeling less at home in their Catholic parishes. Patty and Don Addy, Ed and Julia Doney, and Connie and Ken Morsette were among those who left the Catholic Church by the mid-1980s. The Addys enrolled in ministry programs at Trinity Bible College, an Assemblies of God school in Ellendale, North Dakota. When they returned to Belknap, they became involved in the Harlem Assembly of God congregation rather than St. Thomas Catholic Church where they had once been faithful members and lay leaders. The Doneys joined them, and both families have remained active leaders in the life and ministry of the Harlem Assembly of God congregation. The Morsettes also became active in Assemblies of God churches, both on and off the Rocky Boy Reservation. Alma, too, has left the Catholic Church. She says she is not angry at the Church, but states simply: "I'm glad I left."

Looking back on the movement, Guthneck explains that he was, perhaps, more cautious about the movement than some of the other priests or sisters whose enthusiasm for the miraculous did not always sit well with him. This was particularly the case in reference to those who emphasized the role of the devil and casting out demons, a practice Guthneck continues to view with wariness. Even so, he is clear to state that elements of the movement do continue to influence his ministry at Rocky Boy, including spontaneous prayer, anointing with oil, and the laying on of hands in healing prayer. During a Sunday morning Mass I attended at St. Mary's Mission in July of 2009, congregants were invited to the front of the sanctuary for healing prayer immediately following Communion. Nearly everyone in the church formed a line at the altar, where Guthneck anointed them with oil, one by one, laid his hands on them, and prayed for healing in their lives. As each received prayer, others who were gathered at the altar joined in laying their hands on the supplicant, a practice Guthneck directly attributes to his involvement in the CCR.

Despite those who have left, there remain many Native charismatics at Belknap and Rocky Boy who stayed in the Catholic Church, and for whom the CCR never ended. On the same day I met with the priests of St. Paul's Mission about these events, I later attended a children's Pow Wow that the tribe was holding in the mission gymnasium, an event driven indoors by rain. There I met Lynda Beaudry, a Native (Blackfeet) Catholic woman who, though just past sixty years of age, had moments earlier been dancing lightly alongside the young people at the center of the gym. She pointed around the crowd attending the Pow Wow, noting several others who were once deeply involved in the CCR. While conceding that the movement is no longer as pervasive as it once was, she says that, for some individuals influenced by the events of those years, it is still going strong. She described a dramatic spiritual experience she had in 1992 there at St. Paul's Mission. While leading the singing for a worship service at the mission parish, she suddenly began speaking in tongues. Everyone stopped to listen, and then someone else gave a message of interpretation. Later in the service, while continuing to speak in tongues, she experienced what she describes as "resting in the Spirit" where she felt the presence of God wash over her in an unforgettable way. She says that what happened that night changed the course of her life. As a result of that experience, she determined to become a counselor for teens dealing with drug and alcohol addictions, a profession she still holds today among Native youth on the Blackfeet Reservation in western Montana.

She continues to be involved with Catholic charismatic conferences held annually in Helena, Montana. As a testimony to the ecumenical history of the movement on the reservations, Lynda's involvement in the Catholic Church is paralleled by regular attendance at Protestant full-gospel services to this day where she often serves as worship leader.[23]

"A Natural Charismatic Psyche": The CCR on the Crow Reservation[24]

The Fort Peck Catholic Indian Congress of 1976 stands like a hub at the center of the Catholic charismatic movement in Montana, with spokes extending from those four days of services at St. Ann's

---

23   Lynda Beaudry, interview with the author, Hays, Montana, August 7, 2009.
24   Father Charles Robinson, O.F.M. Cap., on the religious personality of the Crow tribe; phone conversation with the author, July 31, 2009.

Chapel to nearly every Native community in the state. Among those most deeply affected by the movement's impact was the Crow Catholic community 200 miles southwest of Poplar. One of the first Native Catholics to embrace the movement there was Gloria Goes Ahead Cummins, a Crow woman of nearly eighty years of age. I first met Gloria in her home ten miles outside of Lodge Grass on that part of the Crow Reservation known as *Bínneete*—the No Water District.[25]

As a child, Gloria was baptized on the reservation at St. Charles Mission in Pryor. She attended the St. Charles Mission School through the eighth grade before heading off, in 1947, to Flandreau Federal Indian School in South Dakota. She has long attended Our Lady of Loretto Catholic Church in Lodge Grass and takes quiet pride in calling herself the first person "to receive the Holy Spirit" inside the church's new building which was completed in the late 1960s.[26] She describes that evening with deliberate clarity. Deacon Joe Kristufek and three "Spirit filled" Franciscan sisters were leading what she calls a Holy Spirit Seminar at the church at the time. Gloria was attending the seminar, along with one of her daughters and her sister-in-law, Regina Goes Ahead. An invitation was given to go to the front of the church for prayer, and Gloria "felt like someone was pushing her to go up to the front for prayer." She says, "They started praying for us, and we were holding hands, and pretty soon I felt something hit me right here [in the head], and I didn't know what it was—I was really fighting it—it just kind of filled me up . . . and I started shaking, and my hands went up, and I started to cry."

When Gloria and Regina returned to their seats, somebody said to them, "Hey, you two ladies got zapped, didn't you?" They all

---

25   The following material relating to Gloria Goes Ahead Cummins comes from a personal interview conducted at her log home on the Crow Reservation outside of Lodge Grass, Montana, August 11, 2009. Gloria died in 2011. A lengthier first-person account of her spiritual journey can be found in Mark Clatterbuck, *Crow Jesus: Personal Stories of Native Religious Belonging* (Norman: University of Oklahoma Press, 2017), 71–86. The book *Crow Jesus* was co-dedicated to Gloria's memory.

26   The date Gloria gives for this experience at the church is 1977. She qualifies her story by noting there was another woman from the parish who received the Holy Spirit before she did, but the woman was worshipping in a Pentecostal church when the experience took place.

started to laugh, and she repeatedly told me that she had not felt that happy since before her husband's death three years earlier. She explains that "in the Catholic faith, we know the Holy Spirit. But they never taught us how to accept it" like she learned during these charismatic meetings. Of her experience that evening, she says, "It was something so strong, something you feel. It's a good feeling, and you don't want to leave it. I was really high for a week or so after I was baptized in the Holy Spirit; it was really something when that happened to me." She was so happy that her kids started teasing her, saying, "What happened to mom? You better go check. I think she's gone nuts!"

Although her sister-in-law received the gift of tongues that night, Gloria did not speak in tongues until three months later, a spiritual gift she regularly exercises still today. "When I'm alone," she says, "I just pray in tongues. When I can't think up anything else to say, I start praying in tongues and it's really a powerful thing. They say it's just prayer to God, and the Devil don't even understand it when you pray in tongues, so he doesn't know what to do. So it's important that you pray in tongues." Praying in tongues is a legacy Gloria has devotedly passed on to her family. Of her seven children, twenty-three grandchildren, and thirty great grandchildren, she is proud to say that every one has been "filled with the Spirit" and speaks in tongues.

According to Gloria, the Catholic charismatic movement first came to Crow around the year 1976 when Father Noel Hendrick of Our Lady of Loretto Church started holding what she calls "area Masses." These were held on Saturdays, and he would invite "people who were Spirit-filled . . . non-Indians, mostly" from Billings, Montana, and Sheridan, Wyoming, to have Mass and prayer meetings there at the church. "All those people were Spirit-filled, and have testimonies, and shared all their testimonies, and then they started praying, and it was really powerful," she says. She remembers people standing up during these Masses and giving messages in tongues for the entire congregation, followed by others standing up and interpreting them in English.

At about this same time, Gloria also experienced a healing that marked a spiritual turning point in her life. She was enduring chronic stomach pain, but medical tests offered only inconclusive results. One day, when the pain was unbearable, she called her daughters and requested that they take her to the hospital for emergency surgery to get relief. While waiting for them to arrive at her bedside, Gloria opened her Bible to the story that records the miracle of Jesus turning water to wine at a wedding feast in Cana of Galilee, a feat he performed in answer to his mother's pleas. She read and reread the account, unable to make much sense of the story. After reading the passage a third time and praying for help to understand it, she closed her eyes and "the Blessed Virgin Mary talked to me, and she said, 'I want you to trust my son as I have trusted him.'" Gloria admits being startled by the voice, but just then her daughters arrived. She could hardly walk due to the pain in her abdomen, but her daughters helped her into a car and headed to the hospital.

On the way there, Gloria asked to stop at the house where the Franciscan sisters lived, hoping that someone would pray for her. The only one in the house was a sister named Diane who laid her hand on Gloria's stomach and prayed for healing. "And the pain, it just kind of left. And I laid there really still, and I didn't feel it," she explains. "It just left like that." She says they turned around and drove back home, never completing the trip to the hospital. She matter-of-factly concludes: "Anyway, that's what happened." She found out later that the sister had never prayed over anyone like that before.

Like so many others with whom I spoke, Gloria was eager to describe the prayer meetings that began taking place in people's homes and at the Catholic church once the CCR was underway on the Crow Reservation. In Lodge Grass, the meetings occurred every Saturday evening. Many of these meetings took place in Gloria's own home. The informal services usually included singing, praying, laying on of hands, tongues, and falling down under the power of the Spirit. "We'd pray for people and they'd get slain [in the Spirit]," she said, explaining that this was very common during the house meetings. Many of those who attended local house meetings also sought out meetings being held elsewhere on the reservation, and even meetings taking place among non-Natives living off the reservation or in neighboring states. "We'd travel all over, even in winter. Nothing stopped us at the time," she says smiling. These road trips often took groups from Our Lady of Loretto parish to the cities of Billings and Sheridan, where Protestant Pentecostal preachers were holding special healing services.

Despite such instances of ecumenical cooperation among Native charismatic Catholics and white Pentecostals, Gloria describes Pentecostals on the reservation openly deriding the CCR taking place at Crow—a tension apparently rooted in conflicting ideas about how traditional a Native Christian is allowed to remain after conversion to Christianity. She remembers many Pentecostal Indians telling her that "it was a different spirit we [Catholic charismatics] were seeing, because those Pentecostals, they quit everything. They even don't go to dances, or to basketball games. They just kind of quit everything. . . . They think that Indian ways are kind of like an evil thing to do. The beliefs in our cultures—they think that's of the devil." Gloria says that, when attending Pentecostal services today, she still hears preachers condemning the Sun Dance, peyote, and other traditional practices as "evil" and "not of God." To this she simply says: "There's only one Spirit, and that's from Jesus. And that's what we have, too."[27]

In contrast, she explains that in the Catholic Charismatic Renewal there was never really a sense that indigenous Catholics had to leave Indian ways behind, a posture consistent with her own understanding of Native-Christian identity. "My [paternal] grandpa was a real strong Catholic. He was one of the first students that went to that St. Xavier Mission when it opened. So they're real strong Catholics. But they still use their culture, and they have medicine. He's got medicine bundles and believes in the Indian ways, too." Joe Kristufek, the deacon who was instrumental in leading Gloria into the charismatic movement, appears to be living proof of this attitude. No longer at Lodge Grass, Kristufek currently serves Blessed Sacrament Church in Lame Deer, Montana, on the Northern

---

27   For a study of conflicting attitudes regarding traditional Native practices among Catholic and Pentecostal Native congregations in Montana, see Mark Clatterbuck, "Sweet Grass Mass and Pow Wows for Jesus: Catholic and Pentecostal Missions on Rocky Boy's Reservation," *U.S. Catholic Historian* 27, no. 1 (Winter 2009): 89–112.

Cheyenne Reservation, which is located immediately adjacent, to the east, of the Crow Reservation. Although he is not Native himself, he and his wife—a Crow relative of Gloria—actively integrate indigenous languages, songs, and beliefs into their teaching of the Catholic faith. Kristufek works closely with a Catholic Cheyenne medicine man, and, according to the priest now at Lodge Grass, he invites "the Cheyenne spiritual people to do things. He acknowledges their authority; he doesn't take over for them."[28]

In addition to friction between Native Catholic charismatics and Native Pentecostals, other fault lines soon became apparent as the movement grew, including tensions within the Catholic community at Lodge Grass. Gloria explains that some Native Catholics in the parish, especially some of the older congregants, dismissed the CCR as un-Catholic. "You're turning to be Pentecostals now," she remembers them saying to her. Additionally, there was widespread discontent over the CCR movement among non-Native Catholics who attended her parish in the mid- to late-1970s. Gloria remembers the reaction of several white members who walked into a healing service being held at the church, mistaking it for Mass. She describes with a chuckle how they watched people being prayed for and slain in the Spirit, to which they exclaimed, "This is disgusting!" before walking out of the church. According to Gloria, several of those parishioners lodged complaints with the diocese over the movement, and she believes this accounts for the departure of the charismatic Franciscan sisters from the mission that took place soon afterward.

Today, says Gloria, the Catholic charismatic movement at Crow is not active like it used to be. She says some have left the Catholic Church to attend Pentecostal churches, which, she notes favorably, "are starting to change." She adds that "some of the Pentecostals, even the preachers, are beginning to go to [tribal] basketball games" and are not so opposed to the Indian ways like they used to be. Others who were once involved in the movement still attend Catholic Mass while also participating in Pentecostal services and camp meetings. A series of large, outdoor camp meetings were, in

---

28   Jim Antoine, interview with the author, August 10, 2009.

fact, being held by the Crow Agency the week I met with Gloria, and she—along with her sister and a granddaughter—had attended these a few days earlier. Even so, she had mixed feelings about going to the meetings. She stayed in the car, listening to the preaching but not participating in the services. As a Catholic, she says, "sometimes you don't feel welcome; they don't accept us, they don't welcome us." She hopes the charismatic movement comes back into the Native Catholic Church. Until then, her strong charismatic convictions will have to find nourishment outside the Catholic mission, whether by listening to the Protestant camp meeting preachers through her car window, or viewing the Pentecostal televangelists from her living room like she was the day we met.

Father Jim Antoine has served as priest of Our Lady of Loretto Church in Lodge Grass since the late 1970s.[29] On the warm summer day I arrived to speak with him about the Catholic charismatic movement on the Crow Reservation, a Pentecostal congregation was using the church for a large funeral. It was a fitting symbol of the shared history between the Native Catholics and Pentecostals in Lodge Grass during Antoine's three decades at the mission. He first arrived to this small Crow village in 1978, having already encountered the CCR in the late 1960s and early 1970s. The many years he has spent on the reservation and his deep commitment to the people there are reflected in his formal adoption into the tribe in the 1980s under the sponsorship of Clem and Regina Goes Ahead. His first exposure to the CCR occurred when he was a Franciscan novice attending prayer meetings in a friary basement in Huntington, Indiana. It was some time later, while visiting a Franciscan retreat house in Madison, Wisconsin, that he first spoke in tongues—an experience, he says, he did not ask for, but one that found him nonetheless.

He was invited to serve at Lodge Grass by a transitional leadership team overseeing the parish at the time. Father Noel Hendrick had recently left the church after energetically advocating the CCR among the congregation, including his oversight of the "area

---

29   The following material pertaining to Father Jim Antoine primarily comes from an interview with the author held at Our Lady of Loretto Mission in Lodge Grass, Crow Reservation, Montana, August 10, 2009.

Masses" which attracted Native and non-Native Catholic charismatics from across the region, including northern Wyoming. When Father Hendrick left, leadership of the parish passed to Deacon Joe Kristufek and two Franciscan sisters. All three had favorably experienced the charismatic movement and had organized several "Life in the Spirit" seminars, which had attracted Native Catholics from several reservations. Additionally, some Catholics from the Crow Reservation had attended the charismatic Catholic Indian Congresses held in the state the previous two years, including the Fort Peck Congress of 1976 with Francis MacNutt. As a result, many were eager to see a continued emphasis on healing prayer and the power of the Holy Spirit in the Crow Catholic missions.

Therefore, when Father Antoine arrived to Lodge Grass in 1978, the CCR was already underway on the reservation, a movement driven largely by an informal but very active network of charismatic house meetings. "I sort of walked into the charismatic movement," he explains, "because they were already having prayer services in homes on the reservation and most of the time it was a group of people who went to the home and prayed with the people there for God's blessing, God's healing, God's direction in life." The meetings took place nearly every week in the homes of various Native members of the Loretto parish. The meeting location for the week would be published in the church bulletin, although members of other churches would sometimes attend as well.

The order of service was one already well established on Montana's eastern reservations by the late 1970s. There would be food, singing of praise songs, opening prayer, more singing, sharing of Scriptures, personal testimonies, and then a period of prayer marked by the laying on of hands and anointing with oil. Prayers focused on one person at a time. The one requesting prayer typically moved to the center of the room as others gathered around, placed their hands on her, and anointed her with oil. Anyone could offer spontaneous prayers, which often took the form of speaking in tongues. "The presence of God was very strong," recalls Antoine, adding, "It was emotionally and sensibly felt." He says that those attending the meetings often "received an experience of the Holy Spirit, they received tongues, or they received, sometimes, the gift of prophecy—but tongues was more prevalent than prophecy and some of these other things." It was also a common occurrence for those receiving prayer to fall down under the influence of the Holy Spirit, which he calls "resting in the Spirit." Antoine emphasizes that "Scriptures were very important in these services," with laypeople usually selecting several Scripture readings for the evening and offering informal teachings on those passages.

A dramatic event in the movement took place on the Crow Reservation during the summer of 1979. From July 27–29, the Crow Agency Fairgrounds played host to an ecumenical "Healing Power of the Holy Spirit Conference" which enjoyed an estimated attendance of 2,500 people.[30] While clearly following in the wake of the charismatic Catholic Indian Congresses held the previous three years on the Fort Peck and Fort Belknap Reservations, this large outdoor event actively sought to attract Native Christians across denominational lines. Toward this end, the event was formally sponsored *not* by the Catholic mission churches on the reservation, but by the Crow Tribe itself—who also provided use of the fairgrounds, and two buffaloes for meals. The *Billings Gazette* covered the story that weekend, focusing on the communal acts of healing prayer that marked the conference worship services. "Fifteen teams of prayer experts moved efficiently through the crowd, occasionally stopping at a lawn chair that held a sick or injured person. The sick person closed his eyes. The others—sometimes two, sometimes fifteen—put one hand on the sick person and pointed the other skyward," reports one article, continuing: "In chants and tongues, with only an occasional 'praise the lord [sic]' understandable, the groups prayed for the sick person to have strength to heal himself."[31]

On a stormy Friday night during the three-day event, a coincidence of spirit and nature created a circumstance that has entered into the lore of Montana's tribes, an occurrence that is still frequently recounted by Catholics and Pentecostals alike who attended those meetings. As winds blew and lightning flashed in several directions from an approaching storm, tribal police came to

---

30   Lorna Thackeray and Dory Owens, "Rain Mixes with Tears as 'Spirit' Heals," *Billings* [MT] *Gazette*, July 29, 1979, sec. A.

31   Thackeray and Owens, "Rain Mixes with Tears as 'Spirit' Heals."

send away the crowds. But instead of leaving, Bishop Thomas J. Murphy of Great Falls led the people in prayer. "We ask the Lord to disperse the winds and send them in other directions," cites the *Billings Gazette* in an article covering the event. "Let the Spirit come like a gentle breeze to touch us and heal us."[32] According to many witnesses present for the event, the bishop's prayer was answered as the storm split in two, striking Hardin to the north, and Lodge Grass to the south, but dropping no rain on the fairgrounds that night as the conference continued, uninterrupted. This was not the first time a supernaturally diverted storm energized the Catholic Charismatic Renewal among Montana's Native Catholics. It was, after all, news of a very similar event at the University of Notre Dame five years earlier that had caught the attention of Joe Red Thunder and had, in turn, set the stage for MacNutt's involvement in the pivotal Fort Peck Catholic Indian Congress at St. Ann's Mission in 1976.

As it turns out, Joe Red Thunder was among the conference leaders attending the service that night. He was joined by several Catholic Indian mission priests from reservations across the state, as well as national CCR leaders Father Paul Schaaf and Barbara Shlemon. In keeping with the ecumenical intention of its organizers, the conference also included Protestant Pentecostals among the ministry leadership, including Crow musician and evangelist Jay Cummins whose father had left the Catholic Church and raised Jay and his twin brother in a Pentecostal ministry. The ecumenical momentum of that memorable conference carried into the wider spiritual life of the community long after that stormy July night at the Crow Fairgrounds. For following that event, Father Antoine and members of his parish began regularly attending non-Catholic healing services and prayer meetings, many organized by the pastors or lay members of the Assemblies of God or Four Square Pentecostal churches on the Crow Reservation.

The Catholic-Pentecostal relationship grew even tighter when Antoine began a cooperative relationship with a Pentecostal minister named Jerry Lynde whom he met at a Full Gospel Businessmen's

---

32   Thackeray and Owens, "Rain Mixes with Tears as 'Spirit' Heals."

meeting in Sheridan, Wyoming. Father Antoine took a number of Native Catholics from Our Lady of Loretto down to Sheridan to attend services at Pastor Lynde's Pentecostal church. In turn, he invited Lynde to lead a number of Pentecostal tent meetings back in Lodge Grass in the early 1980s. Additionally, several Catholic Crow laypeople took it upon themselves to organize occasional meetings on the reservation where Lynde would offer teachings on some aspect of charismatic living, or "walking in the Spirit," including teachings about overcoming demonic forces. According to Antoine, physical healings, inner healings, and some deliverance from the demonic were all a part of what took place during these meetings. These lay-led, ecumenical services also served to fuel the house meeting movement already underway among Native Catholics on the Crow Reservation. They also reinforced the growing role that Native lay people were taking in the ministry of the Catholic Indian missions throughout the reservation at that time. "A lot of that ministry went on without the help of the Church," Antoine explains. "It was a way people ministered to one another in the community. And certain people were known for their faith in the Holy Spirit, and they were the ones often people went to when they needed help."

While ecumenical cooperation was a welcomed trait of the Native Catholic charismatic movement at the time, not all of its consequences were warmly embraced. "What surprised me with some is that they became a little less Catholic," says Antoine, explaining how some members of his congregation faded out of the congregation through involvement in the movement. According to him, some started to say, "'The Church is not that necessary. We have the Holy Spirit and we have a prayer life the way we want it, and we'll go to whatever church we want.' Smorgasbord faith, I call it. I go and pick out what I want to eat, but I'm not committed to anything, to any group. And I know I have some Catholics like that. They're still connected with the Church, but they're not participating in it."

The collective momentum of the Catholic Charismatic Renewal at Crow had largely subsided by the mid-1980s. Even so, Native members of Our Lady of Loretto these days still ask Father Antoine to lead healing services from time to time, and many still come to him privately for healing prayer. On these occasions, he frequently prays in tongues. His prayer language surprises some of his parishioners for, despite the fact that Antoine does not speak Crow, he says "my tongues have an aspect of the Crow language in it. People can understand what I'm saying, but I don't. When I'm praying, I know some words that are coming out, but I don't think about them ahead of time. I just surrender myself to the Spirit of God, and whatever comes out, comes out. I'm just asking God to carry out whatever he wants for this person."[33]

Twenty miles north of Lodge Grass sits St. Dennis Church by the Crow Agency, another parish deeply influenced by the CCR. The priest at St. Dennis, Father Charles Robinson, O.F.M. Cap., feels that an inclination toward the supernatural accounts, in part, for the popularity of charismatic and Pentecostal Christianity among the Crow tribe. "Crows have almost a natural affinity for speaking in tongues, for searching of visions, for God revealing to them in very private ways," he says. Like Antoine, Robinson believes there are clear parallels between the religious experience of Pentecostalism and traditional Crow religion. He cites the openness that traditional Crow people have for visions, altered states of religious consciousness, and spiritual dreams, suggesting that these practices "seem to dovetail" with the charismatic experience.[34] Robinson himself is decidedly receptive to the miraculous, stating unequivocally: "I certainly believe that we live in an age of miracles."

Father Robinson arrived at St. Dennis in 1987 when the CCR was already in decline on Montana's reservations. Like at Belknap and Rocky Boy, some of the Native Catholics from the parish who were once involved in the charismatic renewal are now in Pentecostal congregations. Even so, important elements of the charis-

---

33   Incidentally, Crow members of Our Lady of Loretto congregation independently confirmed this claim during interviews with them. Gloria Goes Ahead Cummins says she has witnessed this happening to other non-Native speakers as well, including an elderly white man she encountered at a Catholic charismatic area Mass on the reservation in the mid-1970s who started praying in Crow despite having never learned the language. Gloria Goes Ahead Cummins, interview with the author, August 11, 2009.

34   Charles Robinson, O.F.M. Cap., interview with the author, St. Dennis Church, Crow Agency, Montana, August 10, 2009.

matic movement remain an integral part of the religious life in this vibrant Crow Catholic congregation of 150 weekly worshippers. "We have the laying on of hands and healing services right within our church—like at Mass, we always have a communal anointing which is very Pentecostal," explains Robinson. "The congregation stands around the person to be anointed, and many of the people are speaking in tongues, many of the people have their hands raised, kind of a traditional Pentecostal prayer." He performs the anointing with oil during Mass whenever a church member makes the request. Others in the congregation will gather around the person seeking prayer, laying on their hands and speaking in tongues. Although Robinson himself does not speak in tongues, it is a very common practice among his Native congregants. "It's just part and parcel of their prayer form," he says.

Father Robinson performs the laying on of hands in prayer for his congregation several times a year, especially during the seasons of Advent and Lent. During these services, he says it is not uncommon for people to be "slain in the Spirit" as he lays his hands on them. On the Friday before we met to talk, Robinson was praying for a young man seeking recovery from substance abuse when he started to sway; the boy's aunt hurried behind the boy to catch him when he fell. Robinson insists he does nothing special to make this happen. He describes the first time he was slain in the Spirit in the 1970s during a prayer service when a priest laid hands on him, despite being quite unfamiliar with—and even skeptical of—the practice. It was then during a prayer service in Medjugorje that he first laid hands on people in prayer, and one or two of those he prayed for went over in the Spirit. Of the following time, he says: "Almost every person I laid hands on fell. And that's when I felt that if this wasn't *the* gift I had, it was *a* gift."

Closing Reflections

Each of the stories told by these leaders and participants of the CCR among three reservation communities in Montana reflect deeply personal experiences in the lives of the tellers, experiences that continue to shape and animate the spiritual journeys of these speakers through powerful memories now stretching across decades. And yet, despite the personal nature of the experiences recounted here, the Catholic Charismatic Renewal was, first and foremost, a communal happening, both in terms of its initial manifestations and the nature of its enduring impact on those communities affected by its manifest presence.

Taken together, these stories, therefore, resurrect a significant chapter in the collective religious narrative of the communities under consideration, a common narrative whose impact depended on a coincidence of several social factors working in synchronicity to produce the effects still being felt today. Although different recollections of—and distinct reactions to—these events establish each of their tales as unique, participants repeatedly returned to three underlying elements of the CCR that help to explain the surprising scope and intensity of the movement among them: supernaturalism, community, and ecumenism.

The shared emphasis on physical manifestations of the Divine in both the CCR and traditional Native religions may be the most important factor in accounting for the astounding popularity of the charismatic renewal among the reservations at the height of the movement. Both the CCR and the indigenous tribal traditions considered here embrace and promote the experience of direct, immediate, and sensibly perceived contact with God—whether in the form of losing consciousness and falling over in the Spirit, having dreams or visions, hearing audible voices, or uttering messages in "tongues" unknown to the speaker. Speaking as a Native charismatic, Patty Addy asserts that "Native American people are very spiritual people—very open." And it is that spiritual disposition, according to her, that best explains the movement's widespread and powerful appeal once it reached Montana's tribes. Father Jim Antoine offers a similar explanation when he says, "I believe that what attracts Native people to Pentecostalism is the experience of sensing the power of God," adding: "Native people here [on the Crow Reservation] are very sensitive to that, to the spiritual world, and this is an experience of being touched by the spiritual world." As Michael Ley heard one Native elder from Belknap explain during the years of the CCR, the movement filled a vacuum created when the traditional healing rites of medicine men on the reservation entered decline after decades of federal and missionary assimilationist policies.

Father Peter Guthneck, whose involvement in Native ministry spans nearly forty years, suggests that the apparent openness of Native people to the supernatural may be rooted in the social realities of reservation life. "On the reservation," he explains, "people maybe are a little bit more dependent on God, on the Spirit, on the power of asking God for . . . something to eat, healing, blessing. They don't have the economic means all the time to satisfy their needs." He adds, "People are a little bit more aware of the spiritual, and they allow God in on their daily life." He notes that healing options such as professional counseling or medication, while typical avenues of solace for non-Natives, are often regarded among the tribes as inadequate. For many on the reservations, "God's the only thing that's going to make any sense."

A second factor in the movement's appeal was the sense of community it engendered not only within tribes, but across tribal affiliations. Over and over, participants described the feeling of being "a big family" as they worshipped in each other's homes and logged hundreds of hours on the road together to attend charismatic prayer meetings and healing services. Vine Deloria, Jr., has pointedly accused the Catholic Church, among other Christian denominations, of creating what he calls a "religious vacuum" in Native communities through their systematic dismantling of traditional social and religious structures without offering, in their place, effective alternatives for creating social cohesion.[35] In some ways, the CCR—with its reliance on Native leadership, its rootedness in Native homes, its emphasis on experiential encounters with the Divine, and its non-hierarchical structure—provided, for many Native families, an effective, alternative context for intra- and even inter-tribal connectedness. In this way, the movement's success mirrors the popularity enjoyed by Catholic societies in the early 1900s among the Lakota of Rosebud, South Dakota. According to Lakota deacon Ben Black Bear, Jr., Catholic societies were so warmly embraced by Native Catholics because they functioned analogously to the tribe's traditional social structure known as *okolakiciye* fol-

---

35 Vine Deloria, Jr., "Missionaries and the Religious Vacuum," in Deloria, *Custer Died for Your Sins* (New York: Macmillan, 1969; revised ed., Norman: University of Oklahoma Press, 1988), 101–124.

lowing decades of federal efforts to eradicate them.[36] As Father
Retzel says of the CCR at Belknap, "It was a happening, and they
experienced community, and that's what blessed them."

A third characteristic of the CCR which helps to account for the
movement's popularity was its inherently ecumenical nature. As
alluded to above, the movement's emphasis on direct, experiential
encounter with God required neither strict ecclesial loyalties nor
hierarchical mediation. Although priests and religious sisters were,
indisputably, essential in promoting the CCR among Montana's
tribes, one of the most striking aspects of the movement was the
extent to which it was driven by Native lay Catholics. A number of
important consequences followed from this dynamic. For one, Native
Catholics collectively assumed a leadership role in the spiritual life of
the Montana mission churches that was, perhaps, unprecedented in
the story of Catholic Indian missions in the state. As many observers
of Catholic Indian missions have noted, the inability—or unwilling-
ness—of the Catholic Church to attract, train, and retain an indigenous clergy must surely be counted among its greater historic fail-
ings.[37] Although hardly compensating for this failure, the Catholic
charismatic movement of the 1970s and early 80s offered indigenous
lay Catholics the chance to assume meaningful leadership roles in the
liturgical and sacramental life of the Church unknown to earlier generations of indigenous Catholics. This was certainly the case in the
ubiquitous prayer meetings that took place across the reservations
during these years. As the priest could not possibly attend all the
meetings taking place, it fell to the laity to take the lead. Even when
the priest was in attendance, Native laypeople were equal partners
with him in the leading of prayers, in the laying on of hands, in the
reading and explication of Scriptures, and in exhorting fellow Christians in the faith. As Father Jim Antoine notes, "A lot of that ministry

---

36   See Marie Therese Archambault, O.S.F., ed., "Ben Black Bear, Jr.: A
Lakota Deacon and a 'Radical Catholic' Tells His Own Story," *U.S. Catholic Historian* 16, no. 2 (Spring 1998): 90–93.

37   Vine Deloria identifies this failure to train Native leaders toward
assuming leadership of Native parishes—thus keeping them in a perpetual state
of mission status—as the single greatest sin of the Christian churches against
Native people in this country. See Deloria, "Missionaries and the Religious
Vacuum," in Deloria, *Custer Died for Your Sins*, 112.

went on without the help of the Church. It was a way people ministered to each another in the community. And certain people were known for their faith in the Holy Spirit, and they were the ones often people went to when they needed help."[38]

The movement's institutional fluidity had other consequences. From the beginning, there was considerable crossover between the Catholic missions and Pentecostal churches, two groups on the reservations who previously shared little interaction. At times, Catholic priests known for their healing prayer attracted to their services nearly as many non-Catholics as Catholics. Meanwhile, some Native Catholics were attending Mass and Pentecostal camp meetings with equal frequency, sometimes organizing open-air prayer meetings themselves that featured non-Catholic Pentecostal preachers.

Much of this ecumenical cross-fertilization was welcomed by the priests advocating the CCR. Some of it was not. For not only did many Native charismatic Catholics end up leaving the Catholic Church in preference for their Pentecostal neighbors, but many who remained Catholic became, in the words of one priest, "less Catholic." Focused, as it was, on experiencing God beyond the traditional context of Mass, priest, and sacraments, the movement had a tendency among some to deemphasize ecclesial loyalties in a way that, at times, frustrated Church leaders. We might recall Father Antoine's muted annoyance with this trend when he stated, "They will say, 'The Church is not that necessary. We have the Holy Spirit and we have a prayer life the way we want it and we'll go to whatever church we want.' . . . I know I have some Catholics like that. They're still connected with the Church, but they're not participating in it."

By the early- to mid-1980s, many Native Catholics who had been involved in the CCR had moved into Pentecostal churches. Others had drifted away from Christian churches altogether, preferring primary identification with indigenous religious traditions. Of the many who remained in the Catholic Church, some carried into their private devotions various charismatic beliefs such as healing prayer and tongues; sometimes they even requested small and spo-

---

38   Jim Antoine, interview with author, August 10, 2009.

radic healing services to be led by a willing priest. For many Native Catholics, however, the movement simply faded away as the collective energy necessary to perpetuate the CCR proved impossible to sustain indefinitely, or as priests and sisters who had been strong advocates of the CCR moved out of the state, replaced by those either less enthusiastic or unfamiliar with the movement.

Today, several decades on the other side of the movement's apex, there are some Native Catholics (or, more often, former Catholics) who feel like the Catholic Church abandoned them during the most important stage of their spiritual journeys. One Native former Catholic, who was baptized by Father Retzel at St. Paul's Mission at the height of the charismatic renewal, barely conceals his frustration with the loss of support many Native Catholics felt in the early 1980s when some parishes moved away from the CCR. In the context of what he views as the Church's religious coercion among previous generations of his family, he says, "With Native people, Catholicism was essentially shoved down their throat. . . . They were taught, instructed in Catholicism; there was no choice. At the same time, there was a deep need for spirituality, and they found it [in the CCR]—but it was quashed."[39] His parents, and many other family members, are now involved in Pentecostal churches.

The Catholic Charismatic Renewal is now discussed mostly in the past tense on Montana's reservations. Even so, it is not forgotten as the passionately told stories above should remind us. Father Retzel of St. Paul's Mission says there are those in the mission parish who from time to time ask "about bringing something like the charismatic movement back."[40] Father Bob Erickson, also of St. Paul's Mission, acknowledges that the Catholic community in Hays could use the kind of excitement that animated the parish during those years. "We need something," he says. "Maybe it is for the charismatic movement to come back. But we need something to rekindle the faith."[41]

---

39   Aaron Morsette, interview with the author, August 12, 2009.
40   Joseph Retzel, interview with the author, August 7, 2009.
41   Bob Erickson, interview with the author, August 7, 2009.

Natives and Nationalism:
The Americanization of Kateri Tekakwitha

ALLAN GREER*

IN THE HISTORY of the United States, the figure of the Indigenous person as "Indian" has played an important part in discourses of national self-definition. Since colonial times, according to Jill Lepore, Americans constructed a "triangulated" identity, in relation to the native Other, but also in relation to "another Other," the European.[1] Ancient colonial tropes of the evil savage and the Noble savage were available to nationalists seeking to distinguish the United States, either from the wild, untamed New World or from the decadent Old World. At times, the Indian was demonized and rejected so that the republic could be cast as the embodiment of civilization triumphing over cruel barbarity. At other moments, the Indian was idealized and incorporated into the American identity as the emblem of virtues that distinguished the United States from European civilization. The last two decades of the nineteenth century was one of those intervals when positive images tended to prevail.

The fact that Indigenous nations no longer posed a serious military threat at the time encouraged the emergence of this comparatively favorable view. In the immediate aftermath of the Civil War, the resistance of the Sioux and other western tribes had favored the

*A version of this paper was presented at the spring meeting of the American Catholic Historical Association, Santa Fe, New Mexico, April 29, 2000. The author wishes to thank Todd Webb for research assistance and Ann Little for her comments on an earlier draft. This essay was originally published in *Catholic Historical Review* 90, no. 2 (April 2004): 260–272.

1   See Jill Lepore, *The Name of War: King Philip's War and the Origins of American Identity* (New York: Knopf, 1998). See also, Robert F. Berkhofer, *The White Man's Indian: Images of the American Indian from Columbus to the Present* (New York: Vintage Books, 1979).

resurgence of blood-thirsty images of "savage red-skins," but by the 1880s the West had been "won."[2] It was in that decade that reforming voices (mainly Eastern voices) began to clamor more insistently and effectively than in the past for an end to violence and broken treaty promises and for assistance to bring the poor Indian into the American mainstream.[3] Real Indigenous people, it was thought, needed to shed their distinctive culture as quickly as possible—it was doomed in any case—in order to enter into the national body politic for their own good. Military conquest was to give way to cultural annihilation, as the Dawes Act, Indian schools, and other similar initiatives undermined the bases of a separate way of life. Imaginary Indians, on the other hand, uncontaminated natives inhabiting some timeless region of the past, were to be cherished for the symbolic work they performed contributing their natural and primordially American qualities to the nation's identity.

Fin-de-siècle primitivism, Philip Deloria reminds us, represented the obverse side of modernism, rather than its negation.[4] The primitive—associated with colonized peoples, but also with the working class and with women generally—gave definition through contrast to the progressive and the modern, while providing a focus for fantasies generated by the tensions and anxieties inherent in modern life. Primitivism was a theme found throughout Western culture at the time, but Americans had a special fascination with Indians. Industry, urbanization, the rapid growth of powerful corporations, labor militancy, and class conflict were disturbing developments in Europe as well as America, but in the United States they were accompanied by massive immigration. Here the economically degraded and politically radical "foreign laborer" became emblematic of a constellation of "alien" forces that were transforming the

---

2   Roger L. Nichols, *Indians in the United States and Canada: A Comparative History* (Lincoln: University of Nebraska Press, 1998), 213–220.

3   See Francis Paul Prucha, *American Indian Policy in Crisis: Christian Reformers and the Indian, 1865–1900* (Norman: University of Oklahoma Press, 1976), 134–147, 161–165; Brian W. Dippie, *The Vanishing American: White Attitudes and U.S. Indian Policy* (Lawrence: University of Kansas Press, 1982), 156–176.

4   Philip J. Deloria, *Playing Indian* (New Haven: Yale University Press, 1998).

United States and threatening its traditional self-image.[5] In the xenophobic atmosphere of the times, images of the Indigenous had a special appeal, not only because of their general association with Nature, the Past, and the Land, but also because they represented specifically the negation of immigration. Hence the popularity of Wild West shows, summer camps with native motifs, and exculpating stories of love and harmony such as the Pocahontas legend.

In these unquiet late nineteenth-century times, the American Catholic Church had its own reasons for invoking Indian symbols. Catholicism had always occupied an insecure situation in a country where civic traditions were steeped in Protestant Christianity and where "papist" religion had long been demonized.[6] But with impoverished Catholic workers pouring into the country from Ireland, French Canada, and southern Europe, old patterns of religious prejudice united with thoroughly modern class conflict to produce an upsurge of nativist anti-Catholicism. This was indeed the period when the Church emerged as—to quote James Hennesey—"preeminently the church of laborer and city-dweller, of ghetto and slum."[7] In the xenophobic imagination, all that was Catholic tended to be identified with all that was "foreign," degraded, "radical" and menacing. Thus, as bishops gathered for the great Plenary Council of Baltimore in 1884, they felt an urgent need to affirm the Church's American identity.

Kateri Tekakwitha's Story and the Need for an American Saint

Among proposals for rooting Catholicism more firmly in United States soil came the suggestion that genuinely American saints were

---

5   Robert H. Wiebe, *The Search for Order: 1877–1920* (New York: Hill and Wang, 1967); John Higham, *Strangers in the Land: Patterns of American Nativism, 1860–1925* (New York: Atheneum, 1963).

6   Ray Allen Billington, *The Protestant Crusade, 1800–1860: A Study of the Origins of American Nativism* (New York: Macmillan, 1938); Higham, *Strangers in the Land.*

7   James Hennesey, S.J., *American Catholics: A History of the Roman Catholic Community in the United States* (New York: Oxford University Press, 1981), 175.

needed. An article in the *Catholic World* asked: "Where does America stand in this vast spiritual empire of the communion of saints? We have our share, it is true, in the common treasures of the church, which are inexhaustible. . . . But where are our national saints and shrines? This is one of the coming questions of the hour."[8] Various names came forward—the Jesuit martyrs René Goupil and Isaac Jogues, among others—but a Mohawk convert to Catholicism, Catherine (later known as Kateri) Tekakwitha, emerged as the favorite candidate for canonization. Tekakwitha seemed the perfect symbolic antidote to the negative associations then burdening the Church in the United States. An Indigenous innocent from the distant colonial past, she could serve as a screen on which to project primitivist fantasies and as a symbol connecting Catholicism to Nature and the Land and to a primordial American essence that was the antithesis of industry, immigration, urban grime, and class conflict.

The Tekakwitha story was a standard hagiographic narrative, remarkable not so much for its form as for its subject, a colonized "savage" cast in the role of the saintly figure.[9] It had first been committed to paper by two French Jesuits who had known her well and who became convinced after her death in 1680 that she was a saint.[10] Born in an Iroquois village in the Mohawk valley in 1656, Tekakwitha was a sickly and reclusive orphan who converted to Catholicism as a teenager, taking the baptismal name "Catherine." After suffering persecution at the hands of her "pagan" fellow-villagers, she fled to the Jesuit mission of Sault St-Louis (Kahnawake), near Montreal, and there she joined a group of young Iroquois women who had renounced sex and marriage in favor of a life of religious perfection. Tekakwitha's "penances" (fasting, self-flagellation, sleep deprivation, etc.) were particularly severe, her dreams and visions exceptionally illuminating. She died at the age of twenty-four and,

---

8 R.H. Clarke, "Beatification asked for American Servants of God," *Catholic World* 40 (March 1885): 808. See also, *The Pilot* (Boston), March 7, 1885.

9 Allan Greer, "Colonial Saints: Gender, Race, and Hagiography in New France," *William and Mary Quarterly*, 3rd Ser, 57 (April 2000): 323–348.

10 Allan Greer, *Mohawk Saint: Catherine Tekakwitha and the Jesuits* (New York: Oxford University Press, 2005).

beginning almost immediately after her death, she became the object of a cult among Native and French-Canadian Catholics.

The Tekakwitha story was published in French in 1717, and then subsequently translated into other European languages. Appealing to exotic tastes, but conforming to the familiar conventions of the hagiographic genre, this Indian *vita sanctorum* found a substantial audience in Catholic Europe and Latin America from the eighteenth century down to the present. However, until the 1880s the United States seems to have been comparatively untouched. To readers in other parts of the world, Tekakwitha had been represented as an Iroquois, as a Native, and as a child of the New World, but the only attempts to nationalize her image had been Canadian and French.[11] Then, suddenly, about the time of the Baltimore council, it was discovered that this holy Indian had been born in the state of New York and was therefore, in effect, a deceased citizen of the United States. Historically-minded Jesuits and local clergy of the Albany region were the original promoters of this post-mortem naturalization, but before long, Tekakwitha had been thoroughly Americanized and was being put forward by the U.S. bishops as a candidate for beatification.[12]

---

11   The French-Canadian Church showed an interest in Tekakwitha in the nineteenth century as a potential Canadian saint, but primitivist Indian imagery was less prevalent in nineteenth-century Quebec than in the United States and so the Canadian Church gave priority to the Jesuit martyrs as symbols of patriotic Catholicism. Guy Laflèche, *Les saints martyrs canadiens*, 5 vols., Vol. 1, *Histoire du mythe* (Laval: les Editions du Singulier, 1988), 229–336.

The rather unlikely enlistment of Tekakwitha as a national icon for France was the work of the royalist Romantic François-René de Chateaubriand. In *Les Natchez*, he presents her crossing the sky in a celestial chariot, the embodiment of "la France sauvage." See Gilbert Chinard, ed., *Les Natchez* (Baltimore: Johns Hopkins Press, 1932), 167–173.

12   The bishops forwarded to Rome a brief for beatification with their collective episcopal backing in 1884, but the Sacred Congregation of Rites waited decades before instituting formal proceedings. When action did come, the case of the Jesuit martyrs took precedence over that of the Mohawk Virgin. Political influence has always determined which cases are introduced onto the agenda of the Sacred Congregation of Rites, and it seems that Tekakwitha was shouldered out of the way at this time partly because the French-Canadian hierarchy pushed more strongly in favor of the martyrs, joining their influence to

Doubly Americanized: The Walworths' Promotion of Kateri

A central figure in the Tekakwitha campaign was Father Clarence Walworth, a native of Saratoga Springs, New York, and a parish priest in Albany.[13] Walworth sprang from a prominent New York family, Presbyterian in religion and of old-stock Yankee background, but he had converted as a young man after reading the tracts of Newman, Pusey, and other Anglo-Catholic writers. His Romantic temperament made him susceptible to the Oxford Movement's aesthetic evocation of the picturesque splendors of pre-Reformation Christianity.[14] After studying and taking ordination in

---

that of the American bishops where Goupil and Jogues were concerned, but also adding four other slain Jesuits to the list. Eventually, the Vatican announced the beatification of Goupil and Jogues, as well as Jean de Brébeuf, Gabriel Lalemant, Antoine Daniel, and Charles Garnier, in 1925. Five years later they were canonized as saints. The case of Tekakwitha moved much more slowly, the formal process beginning only in 1932, after the Jesuits had been taken care of. Finally, the Iroquois woman was beatified in 1980 by Pope John Paul II and canonized in 2012 by Pope Benedict XVI. See the statement by the "General Relator," F. Antonelli, in Robert Holland, ed., *The Positio of the Historical Section of the Sacred Congregation of Rites on the Cause for Canonization and Beatification and on the Virtues of the Servant of God, Katherine Tekakwitha, the Lily of the Mohawks, Being Original Documents First Published and Presented for the Edification of the Faithful* (New York: Fordham University Press, 1940), 6; more generally, Kenneth L. Woodward, *Making Saints: How the Catholic Church Determines Who Becomes a Saint, Who Doesn't and Why* (New York: Simon and Schuster, 1990) and Kathleen Sprows Cummings, *A Saint of Our Own: How the Quest for a Holy Hero Helped Catholics Become American* (Chapel Hill: University of North Carolina Press, 2019).

13 On Walworth, see *Appleton's Cyclopedia of American Biography*, 6 vols. (New York: D. Appleton, 1889), 6: 345; Joseph McSorley, *Father Hecker and his Friends: Studies and Reminiscences* (St. Louis: B. Herder, 1952), 106–118; Ellen H. Walworth, *Life Sketches of Father Walworth with Notes and Letters* (Albany: J.B. Lyon, 1907); John J. Dillon, *The Historic Story of St. Mary's, Albany, N.Y.: First-Second-Third Church* (New York: P.J. Kenedy & Sons, 1933), 196–212; David J. O'Brien, *Isaac Hecker: An American Catholic* (New York: Paulist Press, 1992).

14 Clarence Walworth, *The Oxford Movement in America* [1895] (New York: United States Catholic Historical Society, 1974); George Shriver, "Romantic Religion," in Charles H. Lippy and Peter W. Williams, ed., *Encyclopedia of American Religious Experience: Studies of Traditions and Movements*, 3 vols. (New York: Charles Scribner, 1988), 2: 1103–1115.

Belgium, Walworth returned to America as a Catholic revival preacher with the Paulist Fathers, before leaving the order and settling down in the Albany parish of St. Mary's.

By his own account, Indians were Clarence Walworth's "hobby,"[15] and so when he heard about Tekakwitha he threw himself into the task of promoting her cause and researching her story. Accompanied by his niece Ellen Walworth (under Clarence's influence, her parents had converted and raised their children in the Catholic faith), he set out to map the Mohawk village sites west of Albany. Then, in September 1884, the pair traveled to Montreal and Kahnawake to visit Tekakwitha's grave and consult with the bishop and his assistant about the historical documentation, as well as the procedures for preparing a case for canonization or beatification.[16] Even after passing this material on to the council of bishops, Walworth continued to pursue his "hobby," following Tekakwitha's pathway through the old Iroquois lands from the Mohawk River to the St. Lawrence. Finding the girl's grave site sadly neglected, he personally financed a thousand-dollar granite monument at Kahnawake in a much-appreciated gesture of international cooperation.[17]

Nation-states and rigid borders had no place in the ancient traditions of either the Iroquois peoples or the Catholic Church and, in that light, Clarence Walworth's cooperation with the French-Canadian clergy and his contribution to commemorating the resting-place of Tekakwitha seem perfectly appropriate. And yet, there was something fundamentally national about the modern cult of the "Lily of the Mohawk." The U.S. bishops were interested in promoting her beatification only to the degree that she could be enlisted as an *American* Catholic symbol. It is clear that the French-Canadian Church understood this as a project of appropriation and accordingly its cooperation was less than whole-hearted. From the late nineteenth century down to the present, there have been two

---

15   Walworth, *Life Sketches of Father Walworth*, 244.

16   C.A. Walworth to Mgr. E.-C. Fabre, October 16, 1884; C.A. Walworth to Rev. T. Harel, November 3, 1884, Archives du diocèse de St-Jean-de-Québec.

17   Nicholas Burtin, *Vie de Catherine Tekakwitha, vierge iroquoise, décedée en odeur de sainteté à l'ancien village du Sault Saint-Louis le 17 avril 1680* (Quebec: L. Brousseau, 1894), 66–72.

Tekakwitha shrines drawing pilgrims respectively to Kahnawake, Quebec, and Fonda, New York. Moreover, there were two official canonization campaigns with separate Canadian and American vice-postulators. At the unofficial level, veneration of the Mohawk virgin has taken many forms, including one shaped by a Native American movement of continental, even hemispheric, scope.[18] Yet the force that supplied the initial impetus to set in motion the modern cult of Tekakwitha was nationalism acting on and through the Catholic Church of the United States.

While Clarence Walworth dedicated himself to the Americanization of Tekakwitha through his contribution to the U.S. Church's beatification campaign, his niece was busy Americanizing Tekakwitha in a different way. Ellen Walworth came from a remarkable upstate New York family: her grandfather had served as the last chancellor of New York state and her mother was a founder of the Daughters of the American Revolution. "Nelly," as she was known in the family, had been educated by nuns at Kenwood school in Albany and, while still an adolescent, she had accompanied her uncle Clarence on a voyage around the world. Her first book, published at the ripe age of eighteen, was *An Old World as Seen through Young Eyes*, and it recounted their adventures in Europe and Asia.[19] It was eight years later, when Nelly was teaching school in Saratoga Springs, that her uncle suggested she write a book on Tekakwitha. She readily accepted the challenge and threw herself into the task with "a fixed determination to explore so tempting a field of romance and archaeology."[20]

"Romance and archeology" were Nelly Walworth's first thoughts, not religion and piety; it was apparent from the outset

---

18   Carl F. Starkloff, S.J., "Native Americans and the Catholic Church," in *The Encyclopedia of American Catholic History*, ed. Michael Glazier and Thomas J. Shelley (Collegeville, MN: Liturgical Press, 1997), 1019–1021; Christopher Vecsey, *The Paths of Kateri's Kin* (Notre Dame, IN: University of Notre Dame Press, 1997).

19   Ellen Walworth, *An Old World as Seen through Young Eyes; or, Travels around the World* (New York: D. and J. Sadlier, 1877).

20   Ellen Hardin Walworth, *The Life and Times of Kateri Tekakwitha: The Lily of the Mohawks, 1656–1680* (Buffalo: P. Paul, 1891), v.

that her whole approach to the life of the saintly Mohawk would be different from that of all her predecessors. When others told the story of Tekakwitha, they had acted as pious translators and paraphrasers, borrowing their narrative from earlier works of sacred biography and adding embellishments and discussions of the story's religious implications. Nelly Walworth attacked her subject as a historian, gathering together seventeenth-century sources and ransacking the archaeological and ethnographic literature for background information.

Traveling to Montreal, Quebec, and Paris, she carefully copied the manuscripts of Chauchetière and Cholenec, Tekakwitha's original hagiographers. By themselves, semi-sacred texts could not bring the Mohawk woman to life in the way Nelly Walworth had in mind, and so she turned to works on the colonial history of New France and New Netherlands, as well as writings emanating from the fledgling science of anthropology. She visited and corresponded with amateur scholars and missionaries, anyone with expertise bearing on her subject. By chance, she ran into "Mr. [Horatio] Hale of Philadelphia, author of the Iroquois 'Book of Rites,'" on a steamboat on the St. Lawrence and spent the voyage picking his brain about Mohawk culture.[21] Not content to rely exclusively on the outsider's knowledge of white experts, she also sought out and cultivated native informants, among them a man named Pierce at the Onondaga Reservation and Grand Chief Joseph Williams of Kahnawake.[22] Though she never mastered the Mohawk language, she did her best to learn about it, and her book is liberally sprinkled with Iroquois words and phrases. Her linguistic, historical, and ethnographic research really was extensive, but it was research in the service of imagination.

Neither conventional hagiography nor dry scholarship, Walworth's biography is above all a work of literary invention. The largest part of the book is devoted to Tekakwitha's early years, before the move to Kahnawake. This was the phase of her life when the Mohawk saint could still be considered an honorary cit-

---

21 Walworth, *Life Sketches of Father Walworth*, 254.

22 Walworth, *Life Sketches of Father Walworth*, 252, 255; Walworth, *The Life and Times of Kateri Tekakwitha*, vii.

izen of the United States of America and when she still walked the paths of Nelly's beloved home region. Before the visions and heroic penances started, she also seemed a more human subject and that clearly suited the author's taste. But Tekakwitha's first twenty years are thinly documented. Since the Jesuit chroniclers had to rely on secondhand memories, shaped no doubt by the later belief that the girl had always been God's chosen vessel, they left the biographer with a sketchy account, short on solid facts about the young Tekakwitha. This was not entirely a bad thing from the point of view of a writer whose enthusiasms ran in the direction of "romance and archaeology." Walworth, therefore, left the saintly phase of Tekakwitha's career to Chauchetière and Cholenec, relying extensively on quotations from their hagiographic texts in the later chapters of her book. This left her the task of fleshing out the story of the subject's New York girlhood, and she approached this challenge by confronting the meager evidence directly bearing on that phase of the life with what she could find out about Mohawk culture and the history of French and Dutch colonization. On that well-researched basis, she then imagined a life for Tekakwitha, complete with homey episodes of domestic routine and dangerous wartime adventures.

In *The Life and Times of Kateri Tekakwitha*, the wars, treaties, epidemics, and evangelization campaigns of the seventeenth century form the backdrop for invented personal vignettes. For example, the resumption of war between the Five Nations and the French in 1658 enters the narrative with the matron Anastasia rushing to tell the news to Tekakwitha's mother and finding the Algonquin woman romping on the longhouse floor with the toddler. "Catching the child from the clean-swept earthen floor, the mother holds it laughing and struggling in her lap, while she sings the Algonquin 'Song of the Little Owl.'" Eight years later, a French army approaches the Mohawk country in the dead of winter. Young Tekakwitha, who had been out in a blizzard gathering firewood in an attempt to win the affection of her grumpy aunt, alerts the village to the danger.[23] Other episodes are less dramatic, but equally the product of historically informed invention.

---

23   Walworth, *The Life and Times of Kateri Tekakwitha*, 27, 69–71.

In Nelly Walworth's hands, the story of Tekakwitha is thoroughly feminized.[24] Her biography concentrates on sentiment and emotions, especially feelings concerning personal relations with family and friends. Tekakwitha's "pangs of regret" on quitting the country of her birth, her joy on meeting with a warm welcome at Kahnawake, her wounded feelings on being falsely accused of adultery: all are recounted in poignant detail. In this telling, God plays a comparatively unobtrusive part in Tekakwitha's emotional life.

Certainly her treatment of Tekakwitha tends to center on the adolescent girl's struggle to discover and assert her identity. When her aunts try to pressure her into marriage, this docile child "showed at this time a sudden development of will, with inherent force to mold its own fate, and a strength of character that had not before asserted itself." On the trail to Kahnawake, after the pangs of separation had passed, she experiences the thrill of "sudden freedom, then, from all the bonds that bound her to her lodge and tribe." Finally, she takes a vow of perpetual virginity, and this too becomes an assertion of autonomy: "However others might look upon her act, this solemn engagement with God gave her a feeling of freedom rather than of thraldom. At last she had an acknowledged right to live her own life in her own way."[25] Since the seventeenth century, the story of the Mohawk Virgin had always been constructed around clashes between an emergent self and (mostly hostile) others, but it took a "New Woman" of the late nineteenth century to reshape the narrative into a psychological drama in which the thoroughly modern quest for personal autonomy provided a central dynamic.[26]

---

24   In case it does not go without saying, I use the term "feminize," not in any absolute sense, but historically. In *The Feminization of American Culture* (New York: Knopf, 1977), Ann Douglas charts the development of a sentimental style through which disenfranchised women exerted a powerful influence over the culture of Victorian America. Walworth's biography exemplifies several aspects of the tendency Douglas describes: sentimentality in literature, a preference for feeling over theology in religion, the substitution of nostalgia for history. See also Carroll Smith-Rosenberg, "The Female World of Love and Ritual: Relations Between Women in Nineteenth-Century America," in *Disorderly Conduct: Visions of Gender in Victorian America* (New York: Knopf, 1985), 53–76.

25   Walworth, *The Life and Times of Kateri Tekakwitha*, 131, 185, 253.

26   See Charles Taylor, *The Malaise of Modernity* (Concord, ON: House of Anansi, 1991).

Nelly Walworth's book is modern too in its nostalgic attitude towards the colonial past. Not only the Mohawk village of Tekakwitha's birth, but also Dutch Fort Orange and French Montreal, into both of which she is imagined wandering, are described as picturesque and quaint. Walworth repeatedly evokes the landscape of upstate New York, emphasizing the contrast between a bustling present and a dreamlike past. "In the Mohawk Valley, the great artery of our nation's life, the tide of human travel now ebbs and flows with ever-swelling force; here the New York Central Railway levels out the course of four broad tracks; here the great canal bears heavy burdens east and west. . . ."[27] And here in the midst of the forest, she continues, stood Iroquois "castles" and Dutch trading posts in Tekakwitha's day. Sometimes the author inserts herself into the scene and, reminiscing about research field trips, indulges in a double layer of nostalgia: "The past had become like the present that day; and what was then present, all blended with sunshine that blotted out the tragic and left the heroic parts of the picture, has since become past."[28] Although the "heroic parts" of the colonial past included wars and battles, there is a striking absence of fundamental conflict between natives and colonizers in Walworth's version of colonial history. She manages to lionize the French Jesuits without demonizing the Iroquois or slighting the English and the Dutch, the latter described as sturdy "early settlers of our State."[29] Europeans and natives all take their place in this picturesque tableau without any hint that one group is flourishing at the expense of the other.

And yet, Tekakwitha's people have vanished from the Mohawk Valley, where the sound of throbbing locomotives now resounds. "The Mohawks have gone from us, indeed, leaving us only a memory, all inwrought in a thick array of Indian names. Let us try at least to understand and to preserve these names, in honor of the brave race that once peopled our hills and valleys, our forests and streams."[30] In Nelly Walworth's mind—and her views were basically in harmony with contemporary currents in anthropology and

---

27 Walworth, *The Life and Times of Kateri Tekakwitha*, 3.
28 Walworth, *The Life and Times of Kateri Tekakwitha*, 38.
29 Walworth, *The Life and Times of Kateri Tekakwitha*, 19.
30 Walworth, *The Life and Times of Kateri Tekakwitha*, 102.

modernism generally—natives were more than a distinct racial or cultural category; they were inhabitants of a different *time*. Her primitivist longing for that authentic "brave race" should actually be read as an affirmation, rather than a rejection, of modernity. "To reaffirm modern identity," writes Philip Deloria,

> Americans needed to experience that which was *not* modern. Just as one visited nature in order to be able to live in the city and enjoyed leisure in order to work more effectively, one acted out a heuristic encounter with the primitive. Indian Others, constructed firmly outside American society and temporality, represented this break not only historically, but also racially, socially, and developmentally.[31]

As researcher and writer, Walworth's most strenuous efforts are directed to recapturing the lost Indigenous world. Touches of ethnographic verisimilitude abound: descriptions of Mohawk houses, costumes, songs, and crafts, mostly based on the writings of Jesuit missionaries and modern ethnographers. At the same time, she has difficulty resisting the temptation to merge her subject's specifically Mohawk identity into a larger, more generic Indian identity, one in which women are "squaws," men are "braves," hunting is the main economic pursuit, and people are most at home in the forest. The association of Indians and nature, so basic to all writings about Tekakwitha, is particularly visible in Nelly Walworth's biography:

> Her whole life had been the life of an untamed Indian. She had accepted Christianity in the only way in which under the circumstances it could possibly have been offered to her,—that is to say, Christianity pure and simple, with few of the trappings of European civilization. . . . She was still a child of the woods, and out of her element elsewhere.[32]

Thus, the genuinely serious attempt to recreate the seventeenth-century Iroquois world of Tekakwitha keeps running aground on the sand bars of this timeless essence of savage humanity.

---

31 Deloria, *Playing Indian*, 105.
32 Walworth, *The Life and Times of Kateri Tekakwitha*, 239.

In keeping with this nostalgic longing for something pure and lost to time, Walworth is at pains to maintain her heroine's "Indian" identity undefiled and, to that end, she goes so far as to give her a new name. Until this book appeared, writers had always referred to the Mohawk virgin as "Catherine Tegakouita." The girl's aboriginal name was rendered as "Tegakouita" or "Tekakwitha" by European writers seeking to approximate the Mohawk sound of a Mohawk name (Iroquois languages have a consonant somewhere between the sound of a "k" and a hard "g" in English; the French tend to avoid the letter w: hence the variant spellings). At age eighteen, she was baptized in the name of Catarina di Siena and so she acquired that saint's name, though she still retained her Iroquois name. In their writings, the Jesuits sometimes referred to native converts by their baptismal name followed by their original name, which might have given the impression that "Catherine Tegakouita" was a personal name-sur-name pair, which it was not. Rather it was a coupling of two personal names reflecting one woman's multiple affiliations and layered identities. Such a complicated badge of colonial hybridity would hardly do for a portrait of unadulterated Indianness, however, and so Walworth rechristened her subject "Kateri Tekakwitha." Where did the name "Kateri" come from? The author explains in a footnote that this is "the Iroquois form of the Christian name Katherine,"[33] leaving us to surmise that she acquired this information either from Mohawk people at Kahnawake or from one of the priests who knew their language. Two hundred years after her death, Tekakwitha's people were referring to her by the European name they heard at church, rather than her original native name (at least in public and cross-cultural situations; possibly they called her Tekakwitha in their own homes). But in their own tongue they could not duplicate the sounds of the French name, just as the Jesuits could only approximate the sound of "Tekakwitha." Thus, Nelly Walworth, anxious to eliminate the blatantly European "Catherine" from her title, was using a Mohawk mispronunciation of an Italian saint's name, linked to a French approximation of a Mohawk name, to clothe her heroine in an identity designed to look immaculately indigenous. The gambit was a complete success and, ever since, Tekakwitha/Catherine has been known around the world as "Kateri Tekakwitha."

---

33   Walworth, *The Life and Times of Kateri Tekakwitha*, 1.

Nelly Walworth's biography of Tekakwitha was more than a simple repackaging: it represented an important break with the traditions of hagiography. The book is filled with pious sentiments, but its treatment of Kateri's religious life, and particularly the extravagant asceticism that had made her famous, is rather perfunctory. She accords no special significance to her virginity (Victorian prudishness? Yes, but also a desacralizing of sexual abstinence); and the miracles that followed her death are hardly mentioned at all. Indeed, what distinguishes *The Life and Times of Kateri Tekakwitha* most emphatically from any hagiography is the way Walworth treats the subject's death as an end rather than a beginning. Tekakwitha's deathbed provides, not a launching pad for glorification, but the setting for a touching conclusion to a short and eventful life. This is, in the end, a secular text about a religious person, rather than a religious text about divine intervention in the affairs of humanity.

The product of a modern and essentially secular sensibility, Ellen Walworth's book is a worthy complement to her uncle's campaign to provide the Catholic Church of the United States with a symbol in the form of an Indian maiden from another century that could anchor this "foreign" religion in American soil. The legend of Tekakwitha was doubly Americanized.

Kindred Spirits and Sacred Bonds: Irish Catholics and Native Americans

CONOR J. DONNAN*

O N A DARK NIGHT in 1859, the Irish-born Father Patrick O'Reilly boarded a canoe to visit the Hupa, a Native American tribe near Hoopa, California.[1] Father O'Reilly had been sent to the American West from All Hallows College, a seminary in Dublin, Ireland, that trained priests for both ministry to Irish worldwide and to combat Protestant and Anglo-Saxon influences. O'Reilly came to minister to Irish soldiers, but he was more interested in the "great chief of the neighboring tribes" who lived across the bay. His letters to All Hallows were filled with curiosity when describing his visit to the Hupa campground. While he had never met a Native American, he had been told that they were the "enemy." On his journey, an innkeeper vehemently warned, "If . . . you see an Indian, shoot him, or he will shoot you." Nevertheless, O'Reilly spent time with the Hupa and found the chief to be "a man of judgment, forecast, and natural ability."[2] Unnamed in O'Reilly's letters, other sources identify the chief as Captain John (ca. 1837–1912).[3] He and the priest had deep philosophical and theological conversations about the nature of the world and the afterlife. The Hupa leader explained that "in the other world, the good Indian will have fine hunting; the bad Indian will have no game at all." Captain John's belief in an

---

*This essay originally appeared as "Kindred Spirits and Sacred Bonds: Irish Catholics, Native Americans, and the Battle Against Anglo-Protestant Imperialism, 1840–1930," in *U.S. Catholic Historian* 38, no. 3 (Summer 2020): 1–23.

1 Father Patrick O'Reilly to Father Bennett, December 28, 1863, found in *Annals of All Hallows College for The Year 1863* (Dublin: John F. Fowler, 1863), 92–98.

2 O'Reilly to Bennett, December 28, 1863, in *Annals of All Hallows College for The Year 1863*.

3 Byron Nelson and Laura Bayer, *Our Home Forever: A Hupa Tribal History* (Hoopa, CA: Hupa Tribe, 1978), 68.

afterlife and in the divine (an "above old man") convinced O'Reilly that there were similarities between Native religion and Catholicism. After spending considerable time together, O'Reilly finally bade the Indians farewell for the evening, but an Irish soldier invited the "Indians to come over the next day to see the garrison" at Fort Gaston and witness the celebration of Mass.[4]

The Irish soldiers enthusiastically welcomed the Hupa at Mass, but their military superiors, who were not Irish, did not. Although, according to O'Reilly, the "Indians are well aware that the whites are the cause of all this evil to them," they trusted the Irishmen to keep them safe during a tour of the garrison.[5] The settlers had committed unspeakable crimes against Indigenous peoples, selling children into slavery, confiscating their guns, and murdering family members.[6] The garrison's leader (most likely Edmund Underwood or David Snyder) welcomed the priest because he believed it would enforce "obedience on the [Irish] men," yet he was "exceedingly apprehensive lest the savage Indians, who were very numerous, might make an attack upon him." Captain Snyder had previously attempted to intimidate the chief by firing "several cannons in his presence" when he brought the chief to San Francisco for a tour of its fortifications.[7]

This story offers insight about the relationships between Native and settler communities in the borderlands of the American West. Fort Gaston's purpose was to ensure that the Hupa did not supply resources or weapons to more hostile tribes.[8] Captains Underwood and Snyder feared that the Native Americans would violently resist the American empire, but they also feared the Irish soldiers' disobedience. In their quest for imperial expansion, the Anglo-Saxons

---

4   O'Reilly to Bennett, December 28, 1863, in *Annals of All Hallows College for The Year 1863*.

5   O'Reilly to Bennett, December 28, 1863, in *Annals of All Hallows College for The Year 1863*.

6   Nelson and Bayer, *Our Home Forever*, 64–80.

7   Father Patrick O'Reilly to Father Bennett, December 28, 1863, found in *Annals of All Hallows College for The Year 1863*; Nelson and Bayer, *Our Home Forever*, 64–80.

8   David Levering Lewis, et al., *Neither Wolf Nor Dog: American Indians, Environment, and Agrarian Change* (New York: Oxford University Press, 1994), 80–90.

sought to control the colonized Indigenous nations through military force and the Irish soldiers through religious obedience and discipline. Despite this, the Native Americans and Irishmen built a relationship of mutual trust, and perhaps even admiration.

Their relationship formed against the backdrop of imperial expansion, industrialization, and capitalistic growth in the American West. Manu Karuka demonstrates that corporations and the government worked side by side to develop a war-finance nexus. Irish Catholics became part of the emerging nexus that fought Native Americans and advanced the causes of imperialism, capitalism, and Anglo-Saxonism.[9] American forces killed tens of thousands of Indigenous people in the American West, including at the Massacres of Washita (1868) and Wounded Knee (1890).[10] In 1866 General Thomas Francis Meagher, the former Irish revolutionary turned acting governor of Montana, called for the creation of a 500-man militia to "wipe out the rascally red skins" in his state.[11] The Irish were part of the imperial army described by the Hupa as "a menace so large that no man could imagine it and no barricade could stop it."[12] The Native Americans' suppression paved the way for Irish Catholic migration to places such as Montana and Nevada, with many seeking a fortune in the gold or mining industries. Some became millionaires and sponsored additional Irish arrivals. Nonetheless, as David Emmons concludes, the Irish were primarily "instruments of conquest, not conquerors."[13] American imperial-

---

9   Manu Karuka, *Empire's Tracks: Indigenous Nations, Chinese Workers, and the Transcontinental Railroad* (Oakland: University of California Press, 2019), 42–46.

10   Peter Cozzens, *The Earth Is Weeping: The Epic Story of the Indian Wars for the American West* (New York: Alfred A. Knopf, 2017), 54; Thomas Powers, *The Killing of Crazy Horse* (New York: Alfred A. Knopf, 2011), 210–214.

11   William Lovell to General Meagher, January 31, 1866, in Thomas Francis Meagher Collection, 1846–1946, Montana Historical Society, Helena, Montana.

12   Nelson and Bayer, *Our Home Forever,* 77.

13   Michael P. Malone, *The Battle for Butte: Mining and Politics on the Northern Frontier, 1864–1906* (Seattle: University of Washington Press, 2012), 80–83; David M. Emmons, *The Butte Irish: Class and Ethnicity in an American Mining Town, 1875–1925* (Chicago: University of Illinois Press, 1989), 19–21; David M. Emmons, *Beyond the American Pale: The Irish in the West, 1845–1910* (Norman, OK: University of Oklahoma Press, 2010), 154.

ism's primary driving force was Anglo-Protestantism's capitalist and individualistic ideology.

While the Irish's bloodstained role in the American West cannot be excused, unique commonalities connected the Irish experience with Indigenous North Americans. Irish Catholics became intertwined socially, politically, and economically with the natives in ways that Anglo-Americans could not. The Irish related to being victims of the Anglo-Protestant imperialism forged in Britain and embedded in American society.[14] Historians like Daniel Richter have rightfully argued that the U.S.'s plantation model of colonization originated with the conquest of Ireland.[15] In fact, many of America's Anglo colonizers were from the same families that settled Ireland. Moreover, Anglo-Protestantism viewed both Catholicism and Indigenous religions as primitive and attempted to eradicate their spiritual worlds. But the rituals, traditions, and mystical outlets central to Catholicism made the Irish more relatable to Native Americans than Protestants. The relationship between Irish Catholics and Native Americans in the American West indicates that because they shared a history of oppression, both groups used anti-colonial language, political solidarity, and religious collaboration to counter Anglo-Protestant hegemony, offering an alternative to conquest and imperialism.

Anti-Colonial and Anti-Anglo Discourse

Due to their experiences of persecution, the Irish and Native Americans understood, sympathized with, and participated in resistance movements. The Irish revolted numerous times against the British. In 1848, the Young Irelander rebellion saw Irish revolutionaries exiled from their land, while the leaders of the 1916 Easter Rising were brutally executed.[16]

---

14 Roxanne Dunbar-Ortiz, *An Indigenous Peoples' History of the United States* (Boston: Beacon Press, 2014), 38.

15 Daniel K. Richter, *Before the Revolution: America's Ancient Pasts* (Cambridge, MA: Harvard University Press, 2011).

16 Tim Pat Coogan, *1916: The Easter Rising* (London: Orion Publishing Group, 2016); Miriam Nyhan Grey, *Ireland's Allies: America and the 1916 Easter Rising* (Dublin: University College Dublin Press, 2016); Christine Kinealy, *Repeal*

Native Americans, similarly, were familiar with the harsh suppression of their resistance movements and the execution of their leaders by settlers and the government. Throughout the nineteenth century, Indigenous peoples were forcefully removed from their lands, their treaties were violated, and they witnessed the deaths of tens of thousands of their people. In the Dakota War of 1862, the natives had the upper hand with settler casualties outnumbering Dakota losses at a rate of ten to one.[17] The Dakota gained support from the Ojibwe and Ho-Chunk, but they were eventually "overpowered and defeated" by the "power of the whites."[18] In response to their humiliation at the hands of the young Dakota warriors, President Lincoln ordered the hanging of thirty-eight Dakota simultaneously in Mankato, Minnesota, on December 26, 1862, after which the Dakota were forcefully relocated from Minnesota to South Dakota.[19] Four thousand Anglos celebrated this spectacle on the day after Christmas and reveled in its unspeakable cruelty.[20] One year later, during the New York Draft Riots, local newspapers compared Irish rioters to the "Minnesota savages."[21]

Along with outright violence and displacement, Anglo colonizers destroyed the lifestyle, language, and culture of both the Irish and Indigenous.[22] The Anglophone world sought to annihilate "sav-

---

and Revolution: 1848 in Ireland (Manchester, UK: Manchester University Press, 2013); Fearghal McGarry, The Rising: Easter 1916 (New York: Oxford University Press, 2010); Laurence Fenton, The Young Ireland Rebellion and Limerick (Cork: Mercier Press, 2010).

17   John A. Haymond, The Infamous Dakota War Trials of 1862: Revenge, Military Law, and the Judgment of History (Jefferson, NC: McFarland, 2016), 3.

18   Gary Clayton Anderson, Massacre in Minnesota: The Dakota War of 1862, the Most Violent Ethnic Conflict in American History (Norman, OK: University of Oklahoma Press, 2019), 80–90; Wambdi Tanka interview, found in James E. Seelye and Steven A. Littleton, Voices of the American Indian Experience (Santa Barbara, CA: Greenwood, 2013), 296–299.

19   Waziyatawin Angela Wilson, In the Footsteps of Our Ancestors: The Dakota Commemorative Marches of the 21st Century (St. Paul, MN: Living Justice Press, 2013), 100–104; Kenneth Carley, The Dakota War of 1862: Minnesota's Other Civil War (St. Paul, MN: Minnesota Historical Society Press, 2001).

20   Wilson, In the Footsteps of Our Ancestors, 78–82.

21   Emmons, Beyond the American Pale, 147.

22   Dunbar-Ortiz, An Indigenous Peoples' History of the United States, 30–45.

agery" to fulfill their pursuit of civilization and progress. According to one legend, the *London Times* declared that a Celt "will be as rare in Connemara as is the Red Indian on the shores of Manhattan."[23] Yet, Irish Catholics and Native Americans fought against the extermination of their identities. In 1894, the Dakota chief, Wambdi Tanka, suggested that white settlers would do the same if the positions were reversed, noting, "the whites were always trying to make the Indians give up their life and live like white men. . . . If the Indians had tried to make the whites live like them, the whites would have resisted, and it was the same way with many Indians."[24] The Irish at home also questioned how the British would feel if they were being colonized rather than acting as colonizers. Both criticized their Anglo foes' imperial aims and methods.

David Emmons notes that historians rarely found instances of Westerners speaking favorably about Native Americans, but he suggests that the Irish sympathized with North America's Indigenous nations because they related to their experiences.[25] Irishmen like Mici Mac Gabhann highlighted Native American victimization by Anglo-Americans.[26] After migrating to Montana, he witnessed the plight of the Salish, Kootenai, and Siksikaitsitapi peoples firsthand. In his memoir, Mac Gabhann argued that there was "no peace and comfort" for Indigenous nations because their way of life was constantly uprooted. He described how Native communities started "work on the rough ground around them until they would turn it into a fine rich field," but their labor was often undone by "some greedy white man" and the federal army.[27] He expressed anger and frustration at this displacement because "the same thing had happened to ourselves back home in Ireland." Mac Gabhann believed that the forceful removal of Native Americans from their lands mirrored both the British eviction of Irish Catholics from their ancestral homes and the

---

23   Kerby A. Miller, *Emigrants and Exiles: Ireland and the Irish Exodus to North America* (New York: Oxford University Press, 1988), 307.

24   Interview in Seelye and Littleton, *Voices of the American Indian Experience*, 296.

25   Emmons, *Beyond the American Pale*, 140–150.

26   Emmons, *Beyond the American Pale*, 133–135.

27   Michael MacGowan, *The Hard Road to Klondike* (Dublin: Gill and Macmillan, 2003), 60–68.

lands' concentration into the hands of a few absentee Anglo land-lords. The Trail of Tears and the American empire's continued brutality were a more barbaric version of the 1870s Irish Land War. Mac Gabhann argued that Native Americans, like the Irish, wanted to maintain their "attachment to the land of their ancestors" and "keep their customs and habits without interference from the white man."[28] While many Americans were unwilling to comprehend the damage they inflicted on Indigenous nations, Mac Gabhann contended that the Irish were more aware due to their own struggles.

Irish priests were among the most vocal critics of the conquerors' savagery. Father O'Reilly consistently informed his former mentor at All Hallows College about the Native Americans' struggles. He wrote, "The aborigines of the country" were once the "undisputed lords of the soil" until the "white man came and took possession of their territories." The Anglo-Saxon "treated them harshly, regarded them as ferocious animals not worthy of existence, and did all in his power to extirpate their race."[29] O'Reilly acknowledged that Indian attacks were brutal, but he saw them as acts of hearts "throbbing with grief at the destruction of their tribes."[30] The priest used such strong language to confront genocidal acts in the name of civilization and progress. A year after he met the Hupa, white settlers massacred the neighboring Wiyot people with axes, hatchets, knives, and guns.[31]

O'Reilly evidenced support for the anti-colonial cause, even failing to condemn Native Americans' use of violence. Though their chief eventually became convinced of their inability to overcome the Anglo-Americans' power, O'Reilly praised the warriors—men "as brave as ever bent a bow" who were "still waging war against the white inhabitants."[32] He acknowledged their unparalleled bravery in fighting against imperialism despite being heavily out-

28   Emmons, *Beyond the American Pale*, 133–135.

29   *Annals of All Hallows College for The Year 1863*.

30   *Annals of All Hallows College for The Year 1866* (Dublin: John F. Fowler, 1866).

31   Nelson and Bayer, *Our Home Forever*, 64–80.

32   *Annals of All Hallows College for The Year 1863*, 98; Nelson and Bayer, *Our Home Forever*, 64–80.

manned and outgunned. Thus, the Native Americans were portrayed as brave, intelligent, and only driven to violence by the aggression of a cruel, colonial power.

O'Reilly, like Mac Gabhann, lived in a world where Anglo-Saxonism claimed ownership of "civilization" and "modernity," but he condemned this imperialism as a barbaric ruse. Irish Catholics used anti-colonial discourse to turn the conventional language of civilization and savagery on its head. While Theodore Roosevelt and Frederick Jackson Turner celebrated the frontier's impact on American society and democracy, many Irish believed that Manifest Destiny was the offspring of Cromwellian plantation policies in Ireland.[33] Thus, Roosevelt's heroic Anglo-Saxon pioneers became the embodiment of savagery and brutality, not civilization and democracy.[34] The *Irish World,* a leading Irish American newspaper, explicitly made this point after the 1876 Battle of Little Bighorn.[35] Though many American newspapers waxed lyrically about the heroism of General Custer and demonized Sitting Bull, the *Irish World* was more complimentary of the Lakota leader. Patrick Ford, the newspaper's founder and a former Union soldier, declared, "Sitting Bull is said to be a savage, and the simple fact is that he stood between his people and extermination." Indeed, "John Bull," the embodiment of Albion, was "a hundred times a greater savage" than Sitting Bull and the Lakota.[36]

David Brundage argues that Patrick Ford was not just expressing sympathy for a downtrodden other but articulating a shared anti-colonial experience. Indeed, for many Irishmen, Sitting Bull more closely resembled Irish revolutionaries like Robert Emmett

---

33   Luke Gibbons, *Transformations in Irish Culture* (Cork: Cork University Press, 1996), 11–14.

34   For Roosevelt's views on Anglo-Saxons or the "English Speaking Race," see Clay Risen, *The Crowded Hour: Theodore Roosevelt, the Rough Riders, and the Dawn of the American Century* (New York: Simon and Schuster, 2019), 24; Thomas G. Dyer, *Theodore Roosevelt and the Idea of Race* (Baton Rouge: Louisiana State University Press, 1992), 68.

35   David Brundage, *Irish Nationalists in America: The Politics of Exile, 1798–1998* (New York: Oxford University Press, 2016), 120–123.

36   *Irish World* [New York], July 29, 1876.

and Wolfe Tone than the merciless savage that American newspapers portrayed. The Irish respected a leader willing to stand for his people against seemingly insurmountable odds. Sitting Bull's victory was a celebratory event for all who faced oppression under Albion's sons because his actions offered hope; the colonized could strike a decisive blow against the colonizer.[37]

Missionary Work and Catholicism's Spiritual Empire

Native-Irish solidarity was not just a rejection of Albion's sons; it helped form a broader Catholic offensive against Protestantism. The Anglophone world testified to the power of the British and American empires, but Anglo-Protestantism always feared a Catholic menace hidden in the shadows. While this threat could be exaggerated, many Catholics believed it was their purpose to overcome Protestantism. Some Irishmen argued, "God has so arranged the destiny of this kingdom that the faith of its children always accompanies the heresy of England, confronting its influence and unveiling its error."[38] This reading of Irish history suggests that being colonized by the British gave the Irish a unique ability to traverse the Anglophone world and undermine the sins of Protestantism from within. The Irish were exiled from their homeland by an oppressor and a famine of biblical proportion, but Irish priests believed that the diaspora was their special blessing from God to spread the gospel. They were a nation of prophets, and all prophets had to suffer trials as the British Empire became Ireland's Babylon. To this end, All Hallows sent roughly 1,000 Irish priests to the United States between 1840 and 1900.[39] In 1858 alone, the college had over 100 students, with more than twenty destined for the American Midwest and West. That year, their missionaries argued that God desired Irish clergy in the American West to fiercely battle an "army of evil" composed of American and English Protestants hoping to destroy Catholicism.[40]

---

37   Brundage, *Irish Nationalists in America*, 120–123.

38   *Annals of All Hallows College for The Year 1858* (Dublin: John F. Fowler, 1858).

39   William L. Smith, *Irish Priests in the United States: A Vanishing Subculture* (Lanham, MD: University Press of America, 2004), 33–35.

40   *Annals of All Hallows College for The Year 1863.*

Even though All Hallows sent legions of clergy to counter the heretical and money-driven imperialism of Anglo-Protestantism, anti-Catholicism was already steeped into the core of American national identity. Many middle-class Anglo-Americans saw the Catholic Church as backward, with the Irish bearing the brunt of ethnic-religious hatred and bigotry. Anglo-Americans took the same pride in their moral and intellectual superiority over the Celt as they did over the Indian.[41] In response, All Hallows College sent its most erudite alumni to serve as missionaries. Among them was Lawrence Scanlan, ordained in 1868, who spoke at least four languages, including German and French, and was quickly sent to California. His contemporaries compared him to John the Baptist, and his zealous construction of churches and hospitals made him a pillar of the Catholic West. His dedication to Catholicism's spread saw him appointed Vicar Apostolic of Utah and later the first bishop of Salt Lake City.[42] Scanlan and the hundreds of Irish priests like him were empire builders that maintained Irish Catholicism in America and spread their message to Indigenous nations.

In 1862, All Hallows celebrated the perceived success of their mission, boldly declaring, "What part of the world is there to which the sons of Ireland have not carried the Catholic faith, the true light of the world? . . . However, although dispersed over the whole globe, they are still united. From east and west, they turn to Ireland, and in the one, holy, catholic, and apostolic faith they had received from her, do they find a bond of union stronger than death!"[43] The seminary's missionaries sent to North America, South America, Africa, and Australia hoped to develop a spiritual empire that rivaled the worldly empire Britain and America had created.[44] Undoubtedly, Irish missionaries succeeded in evangelizing and undermining Anglo Protestantism,

---

41 Lawrence John McCaffrey, *The Irish Catholic Diaspora in America* (Washington, DC: Catholic University of America Press, 1997), 112.

42 William Richard Harris and Lawrence Scanlan, et al., *The Catholic Church in Utah: Including an Exposition of Catholic Faith by Bishop Scanlan* (Salt Lake City: Intermountain Catholic Press, 1909), 320–339.

43 *Annals of All Hallows College for The Year 1862.*

44 Hilary M. Carey, *God's Empire: Religion and Colonialism in the British World, c. 1801–1908* (New York: Cambridge University Press, 2011), 29–80.

but their spiritual empire could not compete with the worldly tools of American imperialism.

Irish Catholicism's message to Native Americans blamed the imperialist destruction of Indigenous communities firmly on Protestantism and pushed an alternate worldview based on Catholicism. Father Henry Ganss, speaking in 1903 at the American Federation of Catholic Societies, stated that American ideals were built on a "Pandora's box" of paradoxes. Americans, he claimed, inherited their policies toward Native peoples and a broad imperialist agenda from England.[45] He argued that "the Anglo-Saxon policy of dealing with dependent races was ever that of extermination. The Anglo-Saxon may have been a colonizer, and he was never a civilizer." Like many Irish Catholics, he believed that the seeds of Albion in Britain and the U.S. were not forces for advancement and morality; they were destructive powers that leeched resources from the nations they conquered. Ganss contrasted this Anglo imperial vision with the policies of the Latin (a "convertible term for Catholicity"). Highlighting what he saw as the Latin preference for amalgamation, he argued that the Catholic Church provided "life-giving currents" to those communities with which it came in contact. In short, Protestants were in the business of empire, while Catholics thought "the salvation of one soul is of infinitely more value than the conquest of an empire."[46]

Tellingly, he neglected to mention that Catholic empires such as Spain and France were known to be as violent towards Indigenous North Americans as Anglo-Saxons. Nor did he acknowledge that the Irish often benefited from the exploitation of Native Americans. Thomas C. Power and Martin Maginnis, two of the most powerful and wealthy men in Montana, built entrepreneurial empires by exploiting the "Indian trade." Maginnis, a former soldier, and Power, a savvy businessman, used their connections to Irishmen such as General William Sheridan and Thomas Francis Meagher to obtain wealth

---

45   H.G. Ganss, "The North American Indian and the Catholic Church," Address delivered before the American Federation of Catholic Societies, Atlantic City, New Jersey, August 4, 1903; printed in *The Messenger* 40, no. 3 (1903), 241–255, quote at 246.

46   Ganss, "The North American Indian and the Catholic Church," 246.

and political power. Despite this, contemporary historians and writers like Octavio Paz emphasize that although some Spanish and Irish Catholics were exploitative, they were willing to embrace Native nations' cultures while English Protestants sought to destroy them.[47]

Some Native Americans felt that Protestantism was designed to systemically destroy their culture, and they saw the Catholic Church's *sina sapa* (blackrobes/priests) as a better alternative. Ross Enochs argues that Catholic missionaries were considered distinct from Anglo-Saxon groups because they were celibates, they attempted to learn Indian languages, and their religious practices were more deeply steeped in ceremony and ritual than Protestant denominations.[48] Catholic missionaries often borrowed Indigenous theological vocabulary for their preaching, which had the dual function of making Catholicism more appealing and reinforcing the presuppositions of traditional Native religious beliefs. Harvey Markowitz demonstrates that the Jesuits' decision to use a native term to describe God had the unintended consequence of establishing Christian supernatural beings as similar to the Dakota gods.[49] Despite any similarities, there was still a distinct power imbalance between Catholics and Native Americans, the latter being forced to choose between two foreign ideological and cultural systems.[50] Those who converted might have chosen Catholicism because it allowed them to retain more of their traditions, but it was often a reluctant embrace.

Markowitz and Enochs offer convincing arguments, but they miss the ethnic distinctiveness of Catholicism. The Catholicism of Ireland was steeped in deeply rooted Celtic traditions and Brehon Law, an

---

47   Octavio Paz, "Mexico and the United States," trans. by R. P. Belash, *The Labyrinth of Solitude* (New York: Grove Press, 1994), 355–376.

48   Ross Enochs, "Native Americans on the Path to the Catholic Church: Cultural Crisis and Missionary Adaptation," *U.S. Catholic Historian* 27, no. 1 (2009), 71–88.

49   Harvey Markowitz, "Converting the Rosebud: Sicangu Lakota Catholicism in the Late Nineteenth and Early Twentieth Centuries," *Great Plains Quarterly* 32, no. 1 (Winter 2012), 27–55.

50   Vine Deloria, *Custer Died for Your Sins: An Indian Manifesto* (Norman, OK: University of Oklahoma Press, 1969), 101–107; David Treuer, *The Heartbeat of Wounded Knee: Native America from 1890 to the Present* (New York: Penguin, 2019), 94.

aboriginal Celtic legal system derived from the Irish word for "judge." David Emmons recognizes similarities between Celtic tradition and Native American practices.[51] Both cultures were nomadic and largely communal. Neither subscribed to Anglo standards of time or workplace discipline. In both cases, Anglo-Protestantism did not see them as capable cultivators of land.[52] The legal system of both reflects these cultural and social norms. For example, the Navajo built their legal system around the forces of *k'e* and *k' ei*, which can be understood as cooperation, friendliness, and compassion.[53] Similarly, Brehon Law was based on ideas of solidarity, community, and friendship. Both legal systems centered around a cattle or herd economy and principles of environmental sustainability and gender equality.[54]

These values of cooperation and community were the antithesis of the individualism and capitalism promoted by the Anglo-Protestant system.[55] The similarities in Irish and Native American cultures, beliefs, and legal codes confused Anglophone colonizers and were noted by many Anglo-Protestants. In fact, as far back as 1691, Sir William Petty demonstrated the colonial view of the Irish and Native Americans in the Anglo mind. He argued that Irish dwellings were "worse than those of the Savage *Americans.*"[56] Thus, members of nations such as the Lakota or Navajo could embrace Catholic understandings of spirituality and ritual because it was more tolerant of their views—especially in the Irish Catholic context, which had blended Catholic theology with Celtic traditions.[57]

---

51   Patrick James O'Farrell, *Ireland's English Question: Anglo-Irish Relations 1534–1970* (New York: Schocken Books, 1971), 25–27; Emmons, *Beyond the American Pale,* 143–147.

52   Emmons, *Beyond the American Pale,* 146.

53   Marianne O. Nielsen and James W. Zion, *Navajo Nation Peacemaking: Living Traditional Justice* (Tucson: University of Arizona Press, 2005), 157.

54   Sue-Ellen Jacobs, Wesley Thomas, and Sabine Lang, *Two-Spirit People: Native American Gender Identity, Sexuality, and Spirituality* (Chicago: University of Illinois Press, 1997); David Alderson, et al., *Ireland in Proximity: History, Gender and Space* (London: Routledge, 2002).

55   Emmons, *Beyond the American Pale,* 146.

56   Sir William Petty, *The Political Anatomy of Ireland* (London: D. Brown, and W. Rogers, 1691), 110–119.

57   Michael F. Steltenkamp, *Black Elk: Holy Man of the Oglala* (Norman, OK: University of Oklahoma Press, 1997), 48.

Native American converts to Catholicism confirm these compatibilities, viewing Catholicism as an alternative to Anglo-Protestantism and a faith that could be shared among Indigenous peoples. The most famous convert, Heȟáka Sápa (commonly known as Nicholas Black Elk), was a renowned Oglala Lakota warrior and holy man. As a young man at the Battle of Little Bighorn, he stood with the "bravest of the brave" on a battlefield that had the "smell of blood everywhere."[58] Later in 1881, he declared himself a holy man by performing the Horse Dance, but his work was forced underground when the government outlawed the Sun Dance and Native medicine. Black Elk converted to Catholicism in 1904 and soon became a catechist.[59] Zealous in his message, he acted as godfather for fifty-nine children between 1906 and 1910.[60] He played a vital part in the Catholic Sioux Indian Congress, an annual gathering of Indian Catholics from all Lakota Reservations, and he taught many young Lakota the importance of the rosary.[61] Black Elk's Catholicism supported his role as a critical Lakota leader and advocate for Indians. He found consistency in being both a shaman and a catechist for promoting the life of his people and the living cosmos.[62] Black Elk saw the Lakota way of life and Catholicism as compatible. He believed, for instance, that the suffering of the Sun Dance could be used to symbolize the suffering of Jesus.[63] An adaptive form of religious faith, Black Elk's Catholicism was anti-colonial, resisting the pressure to completely shed Lakota traditional beliefs and values.

Native American conversion could have been based on a strategy for survival. Many felt betrayed by the U.S. government and

---

58   Black Elk, John G. Neihardt, and Raymond J. DeMallie, *Black Elk Speaks: Being the Life Story of a Holy Man of the Oglala Sioux* (Albany, NY: State University of New York Press, 2008), 88–93.

59   Michael F. Steltenkamp, *Nicholas Black Elk* (Norman, OK: University of Oklahoma Press, 2012), 235.

60   William Powers, "When Black Elk Speaks, Everybody Listens," *Social Text* 24 (1990), 43–56.

61   Black Elk, Neihardt, and DeMallie, *Black Elk Speaks,* 300.

62   Philip P. Arnold, "Black Elk and Book Culture," *Journal of the American Academy of Religion* 67, no. 1 (March 1999), 85–111.

63   Clyde Holler, "Black Elk's Relationship to Christianity," *American Indian Quarterly* 8, no. 1 (Winter 1984), 37–49.

saw the Catholic Church's "blackrobes" as potential allies. The Church provided significant charitable aid and educational opportunities for Native American communities. Led and promoted by Irish-American priests and bishops, the Bureau of Catholic Indian Missions advocated for Catholic missions and schools in the American West.[64] The Sisters of the Blessed Sacrament for Indians and Colored People staffed schools, taught catechism, and provided healthcare to Native Americans, becoming cultural links to Catholicism. Between 1885 and 1928, the community's founder, Mother Katharine Drexel, donated millions of dollars from her own inheritance to evangelize and educate Indigenous peoples in the American West.[65]

Opportunities offered by Catholic schools made a positive impression on many Native communities. In 1877, Red Cloud and Spotted Tail, two Lakota leaders, petitioned President Rutherford Hayes to send Catholic priests to their territories. Their request was not entirely prompted by Catholic devotion but was a pragmatic appeal because Catholics were more successful than Protestants in teaching young Native Americans to read and write in English.[66] By the late 1890s, fearing the further conversion of Native Americans by Catholics, Protestant reformers and anti-Catholic groups urged the government to create public schools for Native Americans to limit the Catholic Church's influence.[67]

Political Solidarity Among Irish Nationalists and Native Americans

Irish-Indigenous relations in the United States led Native American nations, such as the Ojibwe, Siksikaitsitapi (Blackfeet), and

---

64   Allen Sinclair Will, *Life of James Cardinal Gibbons* (Baltimore: J. Murphy, 1911), 229–235.

65   Anne M. Butler, *Across God's Frontiers: Catholic Sisters in the American West, 1850–1920* (Chapel Hill: University of North Carolina Press, 2012), 220; Amanda Bresie, "Mother Katharine Drexel's Benevolent Empire: The Bureau of Catholic Indian Missions and the Education of Native Americans, 1885–1935," *U.S. Catholic Historian* 32, no. 3 (Summer 2014), 1–24.

66   Markowitz, "Converting the Rosebud," 27–55.

67   Bresie, "Mother Katharine Drexel's Benevolent Empire," 1–24.

Choctaw, into transatlantic solidarity. The British colonial policy forcing a single crop staple (potatoes) on Irish food culture led to the Great Famine, which resulted in the starvation of millions of Irish from 1845 to 1850. The Choctaw nation in Oklahoma related the famine to the misery and suffering they endured on the Trail of Tears when at least 13,000 died.[68] During the famine, their members in Skullyville sent $170 to the Memphis Irish Relief Committee.[69] The Choctaw in Doaksville raised $150, while the Cherokee nation raised over $200. Anglo-Americans believed these gifts demonstrated that Native Americans were becoming civilized and Christian, but, according to Anelise Hanson Shrout, these charitable acts were already rooted in Indigenous charitable practices. Moreover, Shrout convincingly argues that the Aniyvwiya (Cherokee) and Choctaw placed "themselves in the same imaginative and philanthropic frame" as the Irish to highlight the similarities between British imperial practices in Ireland and the United States' approach to the American West.[70] Thus, the gift was both an act of charity and a political statement against Anglo imperialism in America and Britain.

Father Philip Gordon, the first Ojibwe to be ordained a priest, embodied this transnational political solidarity and shared the anticolonial spirit between the Irish and Native Americans.[71] His strong faith and anti-colonialism made him a fierce critic of the government's Bureau of Indian Affairs and the Ku Klux Klan.[72] His biographer, Tadeusz Lewandowski, argues that Father Gordon's ideals were so upsetting to the Progressive Era's Anglo elite that the Commissioner of Indian Affairs labeled him "an agitator, Bolshevist, and

---

68   Anelise Hanson Shrout, "A 'Voice of Benevolence from the Western Wilderness': The Politics of Native Philanthropy in the Trans-Mississippi West," *Journal of the Early Republic* 35, no. 4 (2015): 553–578.

69   *Arkansas Intelligencer*, April 3, 1847; Kevin Z. Sweeney, *Prelude to the Dust Bowl: Drought in the Nineteenth-Century Southern Plains* (Norman, OK: University of Oklahoma Press, 2016), 93–104.

70   Shrout, "A 'Voice of Benevolence from the Western Wilderness,'" 553–578, quote at 577.

71   *The Catholic Advance* [Wichita, KS], December 27, 1913.

72   Tadeusz Lewandowski, *Ojibwe, Activist, Priest: The Life of Father Philip Bergin Gordon, Tibishkogijik* (Madison: University of Wisconsin Press, 2019), 118–120.

troublemaker."[73] This language would have been familiar to Irish nationalists who had been labeled troublemakers by British politicians like Lieutenant-Colonel Sir Frederick Hall, who later decried their "close association" with "the Russian Bolshevists."[74] Gordon's worldview expanded beyond the Native American struggle; he fought to combat Anglo-Protestantism throughout the world. This Catholic convert spoke to many Irishmen during his priestly and educational training, including Archbishop John Ireland and Cardinal James Gibbons. Both had been suspicious of Irish nationalism but eventually endorsed independence.[75]

Father Gordon was a driving force behind one of the most significant examples of anti-colonial and anti-Anglophone solidarity. In 1919, Éamon de Valera, Irish nationalist and leader of the 1916 Easter Rising, visited the Lac Courte Oreilles band of the Ojibwe in Wisconsin. At the time, de Valera was touring the United States as the newly-formed Irish Parliament's acting Prime Minister, though using the title of first President of the Irish Republic. When he visited the reservation, de Valera was thrilled to discover an ally in the anti-colonial struggle and became an honorary chieftain of the nation. He was named 'Dressing Feather' or Nay Nay Ong Abe, after a famous Ojibwe leader, before 3,000 Ojibwe during a ceremony filled with anti-colonial and anti-imperialist language. Joe Kingfisher welcomed de Valera to the nation: "I wish I were able to give you the prettiest blossom of the fairest flower on earth, for you come to us as a representative of one oppressed nation to another."[76] Kingfisher demonstrated a profound transatlantic, anti-

---

73   Lewandowski, *Life of Father Philip Bergin Gordon*, 3.

74   Sinn Fein and Bolshevism, House of Commons Debate, April 4, 1921, *Hansard,* Vol. 140, c13.

75   Timothy J. Meagher, *Inventing Irish America: Generation, Class, and Ethnic Identity in a New England City, 1880–1928* (Notre Dame, IN: University of Notre Dame Press, 2001), 361; Thomas J. Rowland, "Irish-American Catholics and the Quest for Respectability in the Coming of the Great War, 1900–1917," *Journal of American Ethnic History* 15, no. 2 (1996): 3–31; Anita Talsma Gaul, "John Ireland, St. Eloi Parish, and the Dream of an American Catholic Church," *American Catholic Studies* 124, no. 3 (2013): 21–43.

76   *Irish World and American Industrial Liberator* [New York], October 25, 1919.

colonial understanding of the Irish and Ojibwe as not just oppressed peoples, but as sovereigns of their own nations—nations that had been systematically eradicated by the same Anglo imperialist agenda. He highlighted the fact that both peoples were now fighting for the survival of their culture, tradition, and language.

After Kingfisher's introduction, de Valera addressed the mostly Irish and Indian crowd. In the heartland of the American West, he rejected the Anglophone world by speaking in Irish. During the ceremony, de Valera, commonly known as "The Chief" by his supporters, "accepted the headdress of a Chippewa chieftain with gravity," seemingly understanding the cultural significance of the honor. During his speech, he used bold, stirring, and passionate statements. He received thunderous applause when he proclaimed, "I want to show you that though I am white, I am not of the English race. We, like you, are a people who have suffered, and I feel for you with a sympathy that comes only from one who can understand as we Irishmen can." For both de Valera and the Ojibwe, it was the Anglo-Saxon that caused their suffering, and only these so-called savage twins had the emotional and spiritual capacity to understand their mutual suffering. Indeed, de Valera declared that the Native American was "the truest of all Americans" and asked them to share support in the Irish "struggle for freedom" because they were involved in "a similar fight."[77]

As the ceremony drew to an end, de Valera and Kingfisher exchanged gifts in solidarity. Kingfisher presented de Valera with moccasins, bows, a belt, and a headdress.[78] The Irish delegation complimented the Ojibwes on their hospitality, and de Valera provided Ma'iingan, the Lac Courte Oreilles village's hereditary civil chief, with personally engraved, first-class .38-55 caliber rifles that left him "immensely pleased."[79] These might have been ceremonial

---

77   *Irish World and American Industrial Liberator* [New York], October 25, 1919.

78   Dave Hannigan, *De Valera in America: The Rebel President's 1919 Campaign* (Dublin: O'Brien Press, 2012).

79   Letter from Father Philip Gordon to the Kennedy Brothers in Minneapolis, Minnesota, November 16, 1919, De Valera Papers P150/871, University College, Dublin, Ireland.

in nature, but it would have certainly been upsetting for the British and American governments to discover that their empires' rebellious "savages" were trading weapons.[80] The party left, noting that "the Indians venerate the Chief (de Valera), as a person holding the same ideals regarding Ireland as they do regarding their own rights."[81] Harry Boland of the Irish delegation wrote in his diary that the time with the Ojibwe was their "best day so far," while another de Valera associate, Liam Mellows, acknowledged that it was indicative of broader Indian support for Irish causes, already having support from the Sioux and Cree nations' chiefs.[82]

De Valera and his delegation never forgot the Ojibwe's kindness and solidarity. David Fitzpatrick argues that Boland envisioned using the diaspora for a global Irish revolution against the British, but the trip heightened the importance of the broader international anti-colonial struggle.[83] De Valera fondly regaled his children with tales of his trip to America, keeping the headdress as a prized possession. His children, Terry and Ruairi, often played "cowboys and Indians" with the headdress and "always insisted" on taking the "Indian's side."[84] De Valera maintained his friendship with Father Gordon throughout their lives. In 1932, the Irishman invited the priest to Dublin for the Eucharistic Congress, where the "Indian Priest" quickly became the main attraction among the city's thousands. Wearing his feathered headdress, Father Gordon upstaged the "cardinals and pope's legate," receiving a rapturous reception.[85] He headed a delegation from Minnesota to see de Valera and met with the city's Lord Mayor at the Mansion House.[86] The symbolic importance of Gordon visiting Dublin was not lost on American and

---

80   David Scott Bisonette of Lac Courte Oreilles Community College, email to the author, January 15, 2020.

81   David Fitzpatrick, *Harry Boland's Irish Revolution* (Cork: Cork University Press, 2004), 132–134.

82   Liam Mellows to Harry Boland on October 14, 1919, De Valera Papers 150/1163; Harry Boland Diary, October 18, 1919, De Valera Papers, University College, Dublin, Ireland.

83   Fitzpatrick, *Harry Boland's Irish Revolution*, 129–134.

84   Terry De Valera, *A Memoir* (Dublin: Currach Press, 2004), 16.

85   Lewandowski, *Life of Father Philip Bergin Gordon*, 123–124.

86   *The Irish Times* [Dublin, Ireland], June 23, 1932, and June 27, 1932.

Irish newspapers, who commented on the priest's role in de Valera being named an "honorary chieftain" in 1919.

Cultural Exchange and Intermarriage

The Irish seem to be the only European immigrant group accepted into both social and political positions within Native American nations. For instance, Thomas R. Roddy (1857–1924), the son of an Irish immigrant, succeeded Chief Black Hawk of the Ho-Chunk nation in 1899.[87] Since his father was a trader living among the tribe, Roddy grew up among the Ho-Chunk, becoming fluent in their language, and Ojibwe. Named Chief White Buffalo, he held a leadership role in the Ho-Chunk from Black River Falls, Wisconsin, for over twenty years.[88] Roddy promoted Native American education and created Ho-Chunk shows attended by white audiences.[89] David Emmons demonstrates that the Irish also held special status among the Cheyenne, being called *Ma-i-viho* (meaning "red white men"), whereas the Cheyenne word for African Americans was *Moqtai-viho* ("black white men"). The Cheyenne saw the Irish as closer to Native Americans while the black community was closer to whites.[90] These alliances were at times genuine and, at other times, opportunistic. Many Irishmen and Native Americans embraced each other's culture and values, but the more politically savvy Indigenous leaders saw Irishmen as a gateway to more significant political influence through the Irish lobby's strength and its connections to the Democratic Party.[91] Similarly, many Irishmen saw an opportunity to profit from Indigenous trade.

---

87   *Los Angeles Herald,* September 24, 1899.

88   *The Coffeyville* [KS] *Daily Journal,* May 4, 1911.

89   Grant P. Arndt, *Ho-Chunk Powwows and the Politics of Tradition* (Lincoln: University of Nebraska Press, 2016).

90   Emmons, *Beyond the American Pale,* 166.

91   For more on Indigenous interactions with the political system and parties of the United States, see George E. Frizzell, "The Politics of Cherokee Citizenship, 1898–1930," *The North Carolina Historical Review* 61, no. 2 (1984): 205–230; Jameson Sweet, "Native Suffrage: Race, Citizenship, and Dakota Indians in the Upper Midwest," *Journal of the Early Republic* 39, no. 1 (Spring 2019): 99–109.

Along with political alliances, intermarriage became increasingly common between Irish immigrants and a host of Native American nations, including the Choctaw, Sisseton, and Blackfeet. Anglo-American newspapers often condemned these marriages with outright prejudice. For example, the *Wilkes-Barre Times Leader* described a missionary's encounter with an Irishman and his wife, who was a member of the Blackfeet.[92] Sent to preach to the Native Americans, the missionary was shocked when an "Indian chief with painted face and feather headdress" approached him speaking fluent English. Astonished, the missionary asked where the man learned to speak English, to which the chief replied, "old Ireland." The newspaper reported that the man was an Irish Catholic who had moved to the American West to overcome alcoholism. There he met his wife, and they had five children. While the Irish who moved to Montana were more likely in search of gold than sobriety, they married into Native American nations at higher rates than most other Europeans. Importantly, it was suggested that the man became entirely "Indian," a common trope among Anglo-Protestant newspapers proposing that the Irish were susceptible to losing their "whiteness" and "going native."

Despite an obvious bias in written primary source materials, interviews with Native American communities support the existence of a high rate of intermarriage between Irish and Indigenous North Americans. During oral interviews conducted in 1969, Native Americans discussed their Irish ancestry. Joe Harlow was born to a "full blood Cherokee" woman and an "old Irishman" who "done a lot of talking."[93] Richard Shannan was an Irishman who married a Cherokee woman in Vinita, Oklahoma. Members of his Cherokee community, Frank and May Casto, remembered Shannan fondly for his ability to "talk Shawnee" and his raising of orphans in the area.[94] The high rate of intermarriage with the Irish was undoubt-

---

92   *Wilkes-Barre* [PA] *Times Leader, The Evening News*, August 28, 1907.

93   John Harlow interview, February 3, 1969, Doris Duke Collection, Western History Collections, Vol. 015, University of Oklahoma, Norman, Oklahoma.

94   Frank and May Casto interview, February 18, 1969, Doris Duke Collection, Western History Collections, Vol. 011, University of Oklahoma, Norman, Oklahoma.

edly a result of their willingness to adopt Native American customs and the Native American communities' view that the Irish were separate from whites.

The remarkable Zelma O'Riley was the product of Irish-Native intermarriage. Born in 1897 in Durant, Oklahoma, O'Riley became one of six children born to an Irish Catholic father and a Choctaw mother. Activism ran in her blood; her maternal grandfather, George W. Harkins, was a Choctaw chief in the Apukshunnubbee District. He wrote the widely circulated "Farewell Letter to the American People," which condemned the policy of Indian Removal and the Trail of Tears.[95] O'Riley devoted herself to Native rights and the cause of Catholicism. She moved to Austin, Texas, in the 1930s to obtain the education and credentials needed for an audacious plan: to abolish the Indian Bureau and establish a federal bank for Native Americans. In 1947, she campaigned for president under the slogan, "She is Irish, she is Indian, and she will care for you." O'Riley ran on a platform of returning land to the Indigenous population, supporting African American rights, and increasing social welfare for Native communities, boldly professing that it would "take a woman to save America."[96]

Conclusion

The ninety years between Father O'Reilly's visit to the Hupa and Zelma O'Riley's presidential bid provide ample evidence of Anglophone imperialism. The governments of America and Britain tried to eradicate the cultures of the "twin savages" to replace them with a Protestant branded "civilization" and "Christianity." Anglo-Saxonism waged a brutal imperial battle against the Irish and Native Americans, forcing them off their lands. This involved violently uprooting the culture, religion, and land of the Irish and Indigenous nations, as well as promoting ideas of individualism, private property, and capitalism. The war-finance nexus of Anglo-Protestantism proved to be a force of destruction as the American

---

95   Daniel F. Littlefield, *Native American Writing in the Southeast* (Jackson, MS: University Press of Mississippi, 1995), 220-225.

96   *Wilmington* [CA] *Daily Press Journal*, September 25, 1947.

and British empires spread.[97] By the time of O'Riley, the Native Americans who had dominated the West were militarily, politically, and economically subjugated.

The Irish nationalists fared better, declaring a republic in 1949, but this came at the expense of their language and loss of six northern counties to British rule. As foot soldiers of Anglo imperialism, the Irish fought for the same causes of "civilization" and "progress" in America that were forced upon their people in Ireland, eventually becoming an acceptable part of American society by the mid-twentieth century. In many cities, the Irish multiplied their representation in the professions, formed influential political lobbies, and found success in higher education. While the federal government disguised oppressive laws, such as the Dawes Act of 1887 and the Indian Citizenship Act of 1924, as overdue emancipation, the Irish had themselves become influencers of domestic and foreign policy.[98] Today, the thirty million Americans who claim Irish ancestry are solidly within the highest levels of education and economic achievement, but approximately one in four Native Americans live in poverty, endure a sub-rate educational system, and have fewer opportunities for economic advancement.[99]

Native Americans and the Irish found remarkable ways to form religious-cultural solidarity, a legacy that remains. Catholicism, in promoting a worldview drastically different from Anglo-Protestantism, maintains a strong presence in Native American nations. Of the 2.9 million Native Americans in the U.S., 580,000 identify as Catholic.[100] Native American activists and lawyers, such as James W. Zion, chief solicitor of the Navajo Nation, continue to

---

97   Karuka, *Empire's Tracks,* 135–154.

98   Alexandra Witkin, "To Silence a Drum: The Imposition of United States Citizenship on Native Peoples," *Historical Reflections/Réflexions Historiques* 21, no. 2 (1995): 353–383.

99   Michael B. Sauter, "Faces of Poverty: What Racial, Social Groups Are More Likely to Experience It?," *USA TODAY,* September 28, 2018, https://247 wallst.com/special-report/2018/09/28/faces-of-poverty.

100   United States Conference of Catholic Bishops, "Demographics," http://www.usccb.org/issues-and-action/cultural-diversity/native-american/demographics/index.cfm.

promote Brehon and Indigenous law as a common law alternative to aid "the recognition of aboriginal rights in international law."[101] As recent as 2018, the Irish Prime Minister, Leo Varadkar, visited the Choctaw Nation in Oklahoma, stating, "Your act of kindness has never been, and never will be, forgotten in Ireland." Echoing de Valera's visit to the Ojibwe in 1919, Varadkar spoke of the "sacred bond" between them before announcing a scholarship program for Choctaw students to study in Ireland.[102] Varadkar's act of solidarity from, and Zion's call for, alternative law should not be seen as merely symbolic: they serve as reminders of a different vision's endurance, a vision of retaining Indigenous traditions while developing political and economic self-sufficiency.

101   "Brehon, American Indian Laws 'relevant' Today," *The Irish Times*, January 14, 2002, https://www.irishtimes.com/news/brehon-american-indian-laws-relevant-today-1.1046512.

102   "Choctaw Students Invited to Ireland," *BBC News*, March 12, 2018, sec. Europe, https://www.bbc.com/news/world-europe-43375368.

Black Elk's Vision:
The Ghost Dance, Catholic Sacraments, and Lakota Ontology

DAMIAN COSTELLO*

WITH THE RENAMING of the highest point in the Black Hills to Black Elk Peak and the initiation for his cause for canonization in the Catholic Church, Nicholas Black Elk (ca. 1866–1950) has gained renewed attention. At the same time, scholars continue to debate his participation in Christianity and how it relates to Lakota tradition. Many consider Black Elk's Christian life to be outside of or even in direct opposition to his role as *wic'áša wak'ą* (holy man). A correct understand of Lakota ontology, however, demonstrates the opposite, as his pre- and post-conversion religious identity was rooted in complementary spiritual and ritual traditions.

After detailing the role of visions in Lakota tradition and the covenantal relationship they establish between the Spirit World and humans, this article will examine the roots of Black Elk's Christian life: his extended investigation of Christianity in Europe; his participation in the Ghost Dance, whose core teachings encouraged active participation in all facets of the reservation system; and the last major vision of his life, *Waníkiya*, who he called "The Son of God." Black Elk's vision, like all visions in Lakota tradition, was actualized in a *káğa* ceremony, which was similar to his baptism in the Catholic Church. In highlighting the congruency of Catholic sacramental theology and Lakota understandings of ritual, it will be argued that the Jesuit missionaries' use of the Lakota language allowed Lakota Catholics to read their traditional view of sacred

*An earlier version of this essay was published as "Black Elk's Vision of Waníkiya: The Ghost Dance, Catholic Sacraments, and Lakota Ontology," in *The Journal of NAIITS: An Indigenous Learning Community* 16 (2018): 40–56. It is reprinted here in revised form with permission.

power into the Catholic sacraments. As a result, Black Elk's Christian life emerges out of and in continuity with Lakota ontology.

Lakota Ontology, Visions, and Covenant Ceremonies

Lakota tradition is usually categorized as an animist tradition.[1] Unlike Western Christian traditions, there is no distinction between the natural and the supernatural, human and other lifeforms. Humans, animals, plants, and even what Western traditions consider to be "non-living," such as rocks, mountains, celestial objects, and rivers have the potential to be subjects and thus share a "common interiority." Each non-human group is considered to be an *oyáte*, or "nation," governed by a Spirit. As a result, the cosmos contains countless Spirits with unique spiritual power. The Bear Spirit, for example, possesses unique healing power in that it walks on four legs and stands on two, thus bridging the human and animal nations.[2]

Lakota religious activity does not focus on obtaining moral purity or escaping a corrupt physical world to a pure spiritual one, but in the acquisition and cultivation of spiritual power, or *wak'ą́*, that is exercised in pursuit of a full life, exemplified by the phrase, "that the people may live." *Wak'ą́* power is attained through forming relationships with the Spirit World.

The Spirits may initiate contact with humans at any point but usually supplication is required by the human through ceremony, where offerings of fasting, prayer, song, and sacred items are made. When a Spirit manifests itself in a vision (*hąblé*), it is inviting the individual into a covenant relationship that, according to Vine Deloria, "places responsibilities on both parties and provides a means of healing any breach in the relationship."[3] The manifesta-

---

1   The following summary is drawn from David C. Posthumus, *All My Relatives: Exploring Lakota Ontology, Belief, and Ritual* (Lincoln: University of Nebraska Press, 2018). Many thanks to Basil Brave Heart, Arthur Amiotte, and David Posthumus for conversations that contributed to this paper. Also, with gratitude to David for reading a draft and offering comments and corrections.

2   Basil Brave Heart, in discussion with the author, January 2019.

3   Vine Deloria, *Spirit and Reason: The Vine Deloria, Jr., Reader*, ed. by Barbara Deloria, Kristen Foehner, and Samual Scinta (Golden, CO: Fulcrum, 1999), 52.

tion includes a gift of power and a calling. The gift of power, *šicų́*, is the Spirit's very self, the spiritual power that makes the Spirit unique. Actualizing this gift is a multi-step process that begins with discernment. Callings from the Spirits are often avoided as they usually entail a difficult life of service. It is not uncommon for people to avoid their calling for years or even decades, but Spirits are persistent and will continue calling despite resistance.

When a person accepts his or her calling, the individual next performs the *hąblóglaka* and tells the vision to a medicine man. This usually occurs after a formal vision quest, or *hąbléc'eyapi*. Visions are not always straightforward in their meaning and the elder assists in their interpretation. This does not mean that the content of the vision is radically new but is read in light of "the accumulated knowledge of nonhuman persons that already existed in other contexts."[4]

The medicine man also guides the next step, the *ká̇ǧa*, a public ritual that reenacts the vision. Callings and gifts from the Spirits must always be embodied in a ceremonial response that establishes a covenant relationship with the Spirit and demonstrates to the people one's new role. Through the *ká̇ǧa*, it is acknowledged that the person is forever adopted into the Spirit's *oyáte* (nation) and will act, dress, and perform the ritual in that *oyáte*'s manner. This is not merely symbolic; the person literally becomes the Spirit who had manifested itself. In the words of anthropologist David Posthumus, "The human was considered to be in league with that particular nonhuman collective or *oyáte* for the rest of his life, even to the point of complete identification, as when a Bear dreamer was simply referred to as 'a bear,' for instance."[5]

A pattern exists in traditional Lakota religious life: a manifestation of Spirits that give gifts of their *šicų́* and issue a call, followed by private discernment and insight from the *hąblóglaka*, the establishment of a covenant relationship and activation of the gift of power in the *ká̇ǧa* ceremony, and finally, embodiment in a new life. This pattern is very clear in Black Elk's life, starting with his Great

---

4   Posthumus, *All My Relatives*, 140.
5   Posthumus, *All My Relatives*, 150.

Vision at the age of about nine until he accepted his call to be a healer at seventeen.

Most visions occurred in the context of ritual preparation. Black Elk's Great Vision came unexpectedly while unconscious during a childhood illness. Black Elk was taken up into the sky to see the Six Grandfathers, given the power to heal and the power to destroy, and called to be an intercessor for his people. He was confused by what the vision meant and afraid of the call. As a result, Black Elk told no one about the vision and tried to act as if nothing had happened.

Eight years after his great vision, the Spirits' call finally overwhelmed Black Elk. Through the help of his parents, Black Elk told his vision to a medicine man, thus fulfilling the *hąblóglaka*. The medicine man told Black Elk that it was time to do his duty on earth and enact the *káǧa*. The whole village performed an elaborate Horse Dance ceremony to recreate Black Elk's vision. Black Elk remembered his *káǧa* this way: "I was making just exactly what I saw in the cloud. This on earth was like a shadow of that in the cloud."[6] Through the *káǧa*, the gifts were activated and the people affirmed Black Elk's role as a medicine man.

Apart from the Spirits initiating contact without supplication, everything about Black Elk's Great Vision and response fits into the traditional Lakota pattern of forming relationships with the Spirit World: manifestation, gift and call, resistance and counsel, acceptance and ceremony, and a new way of life in service of the people. This pattern structured Lakota spirituality from time immemorial but it was not just for the pre-reservation period. This way of interacting with the Spirit World continued in new situations. Indeed, a key function of this pattern is to engage unprecedented situations and introduce new ideas and practices into Lakota tradition. The most famous Lakota ceremony, the Sun Dance, was given in a vision when the people were growing weak from their new life on the plains. Black Elk's Christian life followed the same pattern. His "conversion" grew out of the Lakota tradition as an analogous

---

6   Raymond J. DeMallie, ed., *The Sixth Grandfather: Black Elk's Teachings Given to John G. Neihardt* (Lincoln, NE: University of Nebraska Press), 220.

encounter with the Spirit World: accumulated knowledge culminated in a manifestation of the Spirit *Waníkiya* in the Ghost Dance which issued a call that Black Elk avoided for years before accepting it ceremonially.

Accumulating Knowledge and the Manifestation of *Waníkiya*

Black Elk's accumulated knowledge of Christianity came from personal experience as part of an intentional quest. A few years after accepting his call from the Spirits in his Great Vision, Black Elk joined Buffalo Bill's Wild West Show and spent almost three years on tour, traveling as far away as Europe. Black Elk joined the troupe for the same reasons as others—adventure, economic opportunity, to escape the reservation—but also explicitly to look for new power. "If the white man's ways were better," Black Elk explained, "why I would like to see my people live that way."[7]

While on tour, Black Elk and approximately 100 Lakota performers had ample opportunity to explore the white man's world from the inside. While not working, performers took organized trips or wandered the area in small groups. Christian churches became an important destination. For the Lakota, churches were not just another part of the cityscape but powerful parts of the landscape. Red Shirt, the ceremonial chief of Black Elk's group, captured the effect of the strange *wak'ą* mountain-lodges "whose pinnacles reach the sky, and which have stood for more seasons than the red man reckon," he described in an interview with a reporter. They all "strike me with a terrible wonder."[8]

The Lakota were not just passive observers but actively engaged their surroundings, particularly through song. On Black Elk's trip, forty Sioux visited the Congregational Chapel at West Kensington in London. They sang "Nearer My God to Thee" in Lakota. The minister thanked them for attending and "some in the party remarking through their translator that it made their hearts

---

7   DeMallie, *The Sixth Grandfather*, 245.
8   Sam A. Maddra, *Hostiles?: The Lakota Ghost Dance and Buffalo Bill's Wild West* (Norman, OK: University of Oklahoma Press, 2006), 144–146.

glad to be welcomed with considerable kindness and respect."[9] This was not merely performance but the beginnings of the incorporation of Christian song traditions into Lakota spirituality. A clearer example comes from a minister's wife, who remembered that the Lakota sought copies of Christian songs and that "they are very fond of singing either in English or Sioux: indeed, their demand for hymns is insatiable." Many told her that they "talk to God" and overall, they were "very anxious to hear about Jesus Christ."[10]

New religious ideas, whether songs, experiences in churches, or theological ideas they learned from conversations with Europeans, must have all been discussed and influenced life back home. Black Elk wrote a letter from England in 1888 after being away for about a year. He described the difficulties of city life and what he had learned of the white man's culture: "One custom is very good. Whoever believes in God will find good ways—that is what I mean."[11] The statement is undeveloped and at first glance may seem to be a random thought, but it is the first direct evidence of what became a systematic study of Christianity.

The spiritual ferment even culminated in encounters with the Spirit World. Black Elk's group visited Westminster Abbey while they were in London and Red Shirt reported having a vision. Amidst the prayer and song "a great cloud came down towards me, and when it nearly reached me, it opened up and I saw in a blaze of light the girls with wings and they beckoned me." The effect of the Spirits on Red Shirt was powerful: "And I was so certain that what I saw was true that I called out to my young men who were with me 'Come and see what this is.'"[12] Some were skeptical, but Red Shirt was convinced of the validity of his experience: "Our

---

9   L.G. Moses, *Wild West Shows and the Images of American Indians, 1883–1933* (Albuquerque: University of New Mexico Press, 1996), 46. Interestingly, those that attended the Black Elk's Rite of Committal at St. Agnes Cemetery in Manderson, South Dakota, in 1950 sang "Nearer My God to Thee." Arthur Ammiotte, in discussion with the author, March 2019.

10   Maddra, *Hostiles?: The Lakota Ghost Dance and Buffalo Bill's Wild West*, 146.

11   DeMallie, *The Sixth Grandfather*, 8–9.

12   Moses, *Wild West Shows and the Images of American Indians*, 48–49.

people will wonder at these things when we return to the Indian Reservation and tell them what we have seen."

Christian ideas were not just aspects of a different world across the Big Water but relevant in the new reservation system. Though Black Elk reported that his healing power returned when he arrived home, he continued to process his journey and experience of Christianity. He offered his conclusions in a letter from December 1889: "So thus all along, of the white man's many customs, only his faith, the white man's beliefs about God's will, and how they act according to it, I wanted to understand." Black Elk wrote, "I travelled to one city after another, and there were many customs around God's will." He then quoted 1 Corinthians 13, Paul's famous hymn on *caritas*, Christian love: "So Lakota people, trust in God! Now all along I trust in God. I work honestly and it is good; I hope the people will do likewise."

Lakota communal religious engagement in Europe reverses our usual stereotypes about how Natives encounter Christianity. This was not in a colonial system but an equal exchange between Lakota securely inhabiting traditional culture and foreign people genuinely interested in Lakota people and their way of life. More importantly, the Native performers' investigation of Christianity was in continuity with the open-ended character of Lakota spirituality: new sources of *wak'ą* power through manifestations of the Spirit World. This is a key difference with many popular understandings of Western Christianity, which understand religion to consist of a set of truths that one either accepts or does not. For the Lakota, new ideas and power would be expected due to the unprecedented reality of their European sojourn.

In Black Elk's case, Christian love and trust in God's providence were not random or superficial ideas but spiritual insights gained through complete immersion in European culture and a simultaneous existential crisis of lost power and confusion resulting from his people's insertion in this vast new chaotic world. Christian love and trust in God's providence were not entirely new concepts. Indeed, love and trust in the Spirit World had been core principles of Lakota spirituality for centuries. Rather, Christian traditions provided these profound spiritual truths a new texture that was able to engulf, absorb, and transform his existential crisis in Europe. For the Lakota, as with all acquisition of spiritual knowledge and power, it was not a process of switching traditions but a deep integration of new spiritual truths. Black Elk's understanding of Christianity is not merely a reflection of a spiritual vacuum when he was in Europe but something that remained with him even when his power returned. In hindsight, this process was not complete but a preparatory stage, the accumulation of new knowledge for his life's last major vision.

Black Elk wrote in his December 1889 letter that he wanted to visit the Holy Land "where they killed Jesus" to further investigate Christian ideas and "to be able to go over there to tell about it myself."[13] In another one of the many strange coincidences in Black Elk's life, his desire to investigate this new Spirit was accomplished by the Spirit coming to the newly-established Pine Ridge Indian Reservation and finding Black Elk. Shortly after writing the letter, news arrived in Pine Ridge of Wovoka, a Pauite Native religious leader from Nevada, who taught that Jesus was returning to bring back the dead and restore the earth to the way it was before Europeans arrived. In advocating for the Ghost Dance, he exhorted that there was no need to fight, only dance the new dance that was revealed to Wovoka. The dance spread among the Lakota, who called the Ghost Dance messiah *Waníkiya*, meaning "He Who Makes Live." After a period of skeptical investigation, Black Elk joined the Ghost Dance movement.

While dancing, Black Elk had a vision of *Waníkiya*, who, as argued here, he later connected with his call to Christian baptism. *Waníkiya* was colored red, his hair hung loose with an eagle feather on the left side, wounds in his hands, outstretched arms, and standing against the sacred tree. *Waníkiya* spoke to Black Elk: "My life is such that all earthly beings that grow belong to me. My father has said this. You must say this."[14]

In *Black Elk Speaks*, John Neihardt tells the story of the Ghost Dance up to the time of the massacre at Wounded Knee (1890), but

---

13   DeMallie, *The Sixth Grandfather*, 10.
14   DeMallie, *The Sixth Grandfather*, 263.

does not explore the significance of Black Elk's vision of *Waníkiya*.[15] Those who understand Lakota ontology recognize the significance of this vision. There is a clear manifestation of a Spirit—who Black Elk called "The son of the Great Spirit himself"[16]—and a call, "You must say this." But what was the gift and would Black Elk answer the call? As David Martinez rightly emphasizes, some visions are unclear and require a long period of discernment in the context of community.[17] This was Black Elk's experience.

As previously mentioned, Spirits manifest themselves to give gifts of themselves: not objects but their very essence, *šicú*, the spiritual power that makes them unique. Arthur Amiotte, the Lakota artist and scholar, describes this transferrable spiritual power:

> The Sicun is that mysterious spiritlike power which all things possess. For the plant it may be its life-giving fruits, seeds, leaves, or roots or their chemical results as medicines. For animals it may be their unique traits, or the knowledge they have of plants or of celestial and earthly phenomena or behavior, that man desires for himself to help him survive. In some animals, it is their possession of the eternal and unfettered wisdom of the gods which man desires to know."[18]

The *šicú* of a being is the being's most prominent characteristic. The *šicú* of sage, for example, is its fragrant purifying smell. When it is burned, the *šicú* is released, both purifying the surrounding area and making itself available to the person's spirit. It is the same for more powerful spiritual beings, but receiving their *šicú* occurs in a vision of the Spirit. Along with a portion of their *šicú*, the Spirit may give songs, prayers, and rituals appropriate to the Spirit's way of life. *Šicú* must be cared for and cultivated and the grantee must always use it in line with the calling for which it was given and for the greater good; in the words of Amiotte, it is given "for the ben-

---

15   John G. Neihardt, et al., ed., *Black Elk Speaks: Being the Life Story of a Holy Man of the Oglala Sioux* (Lincoln: University of Nebraska Press, 2014).

16   DeMallie, *The Sixth Grandfather*, 266.

17   David Martínez, "The Soul of the Indian: Lakota Philosophy and the Vision Quest," *Wicazo Sa* 19, no, 2 (Fall 2004), 96.

18   Arthur Amiotte, "Perspectives on Lakota World View" (M.I.S. thesis, University of Montana, 1983), 14–15, at https://scholarworks.umt.edu/etd/5921.

efit it can bring to the people so that the proper relationships of all life will be maintained."[19]

The spirit-power of *Waníkiya* is very clearly contained in the name itself, "He Who Makes Live." "To make live" is a significant aim of Lakota ritual, illustrated in the purpose of ritual: "that these people may live."[20] The Spirits, collectively "make live" in the broad sense of creating and continually sustaining all life. The savior *Waníkiya*, having died and risen, adds a regenerative principle to "make live," not so much in relation to the decay and death of the natural order but the unnatural chaos and destruction of the post-contact period. *Waníkiya* is not just an eternal Spirit but a historic event occurring in the midst of and as a direct antidote to the colonial system. Thus *Waníkiya* "makes live" in a unique way, restoring the unprecedented disharmony unleashed by white conquerors, the *wašíču*, both in creation and within the Lakota cultural world. *Waníkiya*'s teaching that "all earthly beings that grow belong to me" is thus an amplification of the traditional work of Lakota ceremony "to make live." The new ceremonial principle could be called "to make live again." The Creator makes live and *Waníkiya* has power over death and resurrects what has been destroyed.

Accepting the Call and Performing the *Káǧa*

Seen from the perspective of Lakota ontology, *Waníkiya* is a new anthropomorphic Spirit incorporated into the Lakota cosmos at a specific time in history to address unprecedented needs.[21] What did *Waníkiya*'s call to Black Elk—"You must say this"—mean? In other words, when one sees *Waníkiya* and thus becomes *Waníkiya*, what specifically does one do? Seen in light of the integrative nature of the Ghost Dance, this vague saying comes into focus. Though often portrayed as a separatist movement based on a

---

19 Amiotte, "Perspectives on Lakota World View," 15.

20 Posthumus, *All My Relatives*, 214.

21 This may seem unprecedented but should be seen in light of Ptesáwí (White Buffalo Calf Woman). Like *Waníkiya*, Ptesáwí was an anthropomorphic Spirit incorporated into the Lakota cosmos at a specific point of need: after obtaining horses and living year-round on the plains. Posthumus, *All My Relatives*, 133–134.

revival of old ways, the Ghost Dance was not a call to military action or a rejection of the white man's world. It was just the opposite; Wovoka preached active engagement in all aspects of the colonial order: the new economy (such as the wage labor that Black Elk was already fortunate enough to have obtained), the educational system, and—especially important for this article—religion (as seen in the Christian churches). Big Road, the head of the band in which Black Elk was raised, reported Wovoka's message in January 1891: "The Messiah told us to send our children to school, to work on our farms all the time and to do the best we could. He also told us not to drop our church." Paired together, Christianity and the Ghost Dance "would be like going to two churches," he explained.[22] Short Bull, who was part of the Lakota delegation that went to Nevada to investigate the new teaching, was as explicit. "When you get back," he remembered Wovoka saying, "go to church. All these churches are mine."[23]

The overall thrust of the Ghost Dance, then, was not to push adherents away from the new reservation systems but to be active agents within the new structure, especially in the churches. Black Elk would have been particularly well-disposed to this aspect of Wovoka's message due to his three-year investigation of Christianity. This is not insignificant: Black Elk gathered his knowledge of Christianity almost entirely outside of American ecclesial structures and colonial systems. From the perspective of Lakota ontology, Black Elk would read his vision in line with previous knowledge of the Spirit. Even if American military buildup and the resulting massacre at Wounded Knee had not artificially truncated the Ghost Dance on Pine Ridge, there is reason to look for Black Elk's final *hablóglaka* and *káǧa* occurring outside of the context of the Ghost Dance.

Black Elk was not yet part of a Christian church during his participation in the Ghost Dance, but in the aftermath his family began pulling him toward the Catholic Church. In 1892 he married Katie War Bonnet, a survivor of Wounded Knee. In 1895, his two

---

22   Louis S. Warren, *God's Red Son: The Ghost Dance Religion and the Making of Modern America* (New York: Basic Books, 2017), 190.
23   Warren, *God's Red Son*, 186.

boys, and probably his wife, were baptized. No records exist of Black Elk's perspective, but any attraction he had to joining them in baptism was probably countered by Jesuit opposition to his healing practice. The early Jesuits were open to much of Lakota tradition, but they considered the *yuwípi* and other healing ceremonies to be an inappropriate invocation of the Spirits and unacceptable for Catholics.[24]

Jesuit opposition to Lakota healing practices does not mean that Black Elk was distant from the Lakota Catholic community. Father Florentine Digmann, a Jesuit missionary to the Lakota, recorded an interaction with a different healer in 1928. Black Thunderbird had all his children baptized but refrained himself, telling Digmann, "I know that before you pour the water on me, you will forbid me my practice. I am not yet ready for that." Black Thunderbird continued healing for several more years until he ceased the practice and was baptized.[25] The Jesuits were influential on the reservation, but most—especially those who learned the Lakota language—understood how dependent they were on Lakota collaboration, especially in far-flung communities like Manderson, where Black Elk lived. A general respect probably characterized most of Black Elk's growing interaction with the Lakota Catholic community.

As with Black Elk's Great Vision, Lakota elders counseled him in the process of discernment. A leader of the Manderson community, Sam Kills Brave, was Catholic and continued the work of pulling Black Elk into mainstream Christianity: "Why don't you give up your *yuwipi* and join the Catholic church? You may think it's best, but the way I look at it, it isn't right for you to do the *yuwipi*.'" This was not a one-time event but an ongoing conversation that amounted to an informal *hqblóglaka*. "Kills Brave kept

---

24   This amounted to an artificial barrier that could be looked at a different way, illustrated by a Catholic version of the ceremony that was conducted for Black Elk later in his life. See Michael F. Steltenkamp, *Black Elk: Holy Man of the Oglala* (Norman, OK: University of Oklahoma Press, 1993), 124–125. It is also common practice today for Lakota Catholics to attend or even conduct healing ceremonies.

25   Ross Enochs, *The Jesuit Mission to the Lakota Sioux: A Study of Pastoral Ministry, 1886–1945* (Kansas City, MO: Sheed and Ward, 1996), 105.

talking to him that way," John Lone Goose remembered, "and I guess Nick got those words in his mind. He said that after Kills Brave spoke to him, he wanted to change."[26]

If Lone Goose's memory is accurate, Black Elk underwent an extended period of discernment around the turn of the century. Black Elk was on the edge of the Catholic world and discerning a call to become Christian. He approved of the general thrust of Christian teaching. Black Elk's family participated in the church. He had a vision in which *Waníkiya* manifested himself and called him. The Ghost Dance encouraged him to engage in mainstream churches. Significantly, Lakota Catholics and the Jesuits used the word *"Waníkiya"* for Christ. Yet Black Elk probably held back from being baptized because of what it would cost him: economically, in status, and, most importantly, giving up part of what he understood as his calling. In this Black Elk was repeating the pattern from his childhood: not wanting to accept the sacrifices of a calling but increasing pressure from the Spirits.

Black Elk's spiritual uncertainty coincided with some significant real-world suffering. His wife and one son died, leaving him alone with two young sons and his elderly mother. Black Elk's own health deteriorated as he suffered from severe ulcers and had difficulty eating. He, like the rest of the Lakota, wrestled with their increasing captivity and humiliation. It is unclear how Black Elk interpreted his difficulties, but it is likely that he did so traditionally. "Obligations conferred in dreams were binding, and disregarding such obligations was considered bad conduct (*wówaȟtani*), tantamount to disregarding and denigrating kinship and one's role in an ordered, living cosmos," Posthumus explains. "Such disregard flew in the face of Lakota social and cultural values and was sure to incur disaster, often in the form of a stroke of lightening or some other catastrophe."[27] Black Elk needed to solidify a relationship with *Waníkiya*, accept his call, and allow the *šicų́* to be activated so that he might play his role in restoring an ordered cosmos—before it was too late.

---

26 Steltenkamp, *Black Elk*, 32.
27 Posthumus, *All My Relatives*, 138.

It all came to a head in November of 1904. According to Black Elk's daughter, Lucy Looks Twice, a Jesuit stopped a healing ceremony that he was conducting for an already-baptized Catholic youth. What the Jesuit did was clearly wrong by the standards of the Lakota tradition, but this incident nudged Black Elk to a breaking point. In the aftermath, Black Elk returned with the Jesuit to Holy Rosary Mission and two weeks later was baptized. While it is easy to see this event as a break with Lakota ontology, there is enough continuity to interpret Black Elk's stay at Holy Rosary Mission as a continuation of the informal *hablóglaka* with elders like Sam Kills Brave and his baptism ceremony in line with the *káǧa*, which actualized Black Elk's Ghost Dance vision of *Waníkiya*.

The broad material continuity between the Lakota approach to ceremony and Catholic ritual is critical to understanding their commonality. Catholicism, particularly before the liturgical reforms of the Second Vatican Council, was well known for its lengthy, complex rituals. Incense, bells, candles, water, fragrant oil, bodily movements, symbolic gestures, long prayers, and songs were used to enact spiritual truths.[28] Jesuits recognized this ceremonial continuity, illustrated by the 1933 statement of Father Joseph Zimmerman, S.J., that the "age-old love of ceremony enables the [Lakotas] to fit into our Catholic practices."[29]

Along with a similar emphasis on ritual, Lakota and Catholic traditions express a deep theological congruence. For instance, the *káǧa* establishes a covenantal relationship with the Spirit, activates gifts, and displays one's new life to the people. Christian baptism is similar: baptism publicly recognizes a calling by *Waníkiya*, establishes an eternal relationship, and infuses the theological virtues of faith, hope, and charity (which Black Elk explained in his December

---

28 Posthumus's use of ritual framing to describe Lakota ritual applies equally to Catholic ritual: "Ritual framing . . . opens participants to the particular logics of transformation and transition that are integral to the teleological process that the frame describes." See Posthumus, *All My Relatives*, 90–91, quoting Bruce Kapferer, "Dynamics," in *Theorizing Rituals, Volume 1: Issues, Topics, Approaches, Concepts*, ed. by Jens Kreinath, J.A.M. Snoek, Michael Stausberg (Boston: Brill, 2006), 517.

29 Enochs, *The Jesuit Mission to the Lakota Sioux*, 119.

1889 letter). Jesuits and Lakota Catholics adopted the term *wak'ą* to express the holy or sacred. This cannot be underestimated, as it allowed Lakota Catholics to read their understanding of what occurs in Lakota ceremony into Catholic ritual.[30] Lakota Catholics would then not understand sacraments in terms of other-worldly dualism or moral purity but as a source of power aiding in the pursuit of a full life. This is seen in the Lakota translation for sacraments: *Wóečhuŋ wakhaŋ*, or "sacred doings."[31] Black Elk's *káǧa* baptismal ceremony was called *mniákaštaŋpi* (to pour water upon) with *mniyúwakhaŋpi* (water that had been made *wak'ą*).[32]

Lakota and Catholic traditions also have a similar understanding of the relationship between spiritual power and the officiant. The medicine person is not the source of power but its conduit. Recognizing this, Frank Fools Crow, Black Elk's nephew and famous Lakota ceremonial leader, called the medicine person a "hollow bone," through which the Spirit's power acts on the patient.[33] The ceremony is not invented by the person but given by the Spirit. In a similar manner, the sacraments are not created by the priest but instituted by *Waníkiya*. The Catholic priest does not confect the sacrament himself but does so *in persona Christi*, enabled by the long chain of laying of hands directly from *Waníkiya* himself, which passes on his *šicú*. That is to say, the Jesuit outwardly performed the ceremonies, but it was the power of *Waníkiya* acting through them that accomplished the effect. The Catholic *wic'áša wak'ą*, like the Lakota medicine person, is a "hollow bone."

The *káǧa* baptismal ceremony that established a covenant relationship with *Waníkiya* also allowed Black Elk to fulfill his

---

30   In the words of Harvey Markowitz, the use of the term *wak'ą* "transmitted the ontological assumptions underlying the ideas and experiences of sacred power as they existed in traditional Lakota individual and collective life." Harvey Markowitz, "Converting the Rosebud Sicangu: Lakota Catholicism in the Late Nineteenth Century and Early Twentieth Centuries," *Great Plains Quarterly* 32, no. 1 (Winter 2012), 6.

31   Markowitz, "Converting the Rosebud Sicangu," 6.

32   Markowitz, "Converting the Rosebud Sicangu," 6–8.

33   Thomas E. Mails, *Fools Crow: Wisdom and Power* (Broken Arrow, OK: Millichap Books, 1991), 36.

calling through a new way of life, as seen in the stories, prayers, songs, ritual, and even clothing of Christianity. Other Lakota may have scoffed at Black Elk's new Catholic life, but even this was in continuity with Lakota ontology. In the pre-reservation days, "Each one believes in the spirits his sect believes in," James R. Walker reported, "and laughs at the spirits that another sect believes in."[34]

It cannot be over-emphasized that Black Elk's *kaǧa* baptismal ceremony does not represent a replacement of Lakota ontology. Lakota language and spiritual teachings that developed over thousands of years—"that the people may live"—formed Black Elk. He lived a *Wolakota* way of life, according to Lakota elder Basil Brave Heart, one "that embraces all of the Lakota ethnosphere, way of relating and navigating and negotiating this whole paradigm of spirituality."[35] For Black Elk's generation, Christian-inflected spiritual truths—"to make live again"—are a small part of a continuing Indigenous spirituality.

It should be remembered that early-twentieth century Lakota Catholicism was very different from the normative Catholicism experienced elsewhere. Lakota Catholic life in remote communities like Manderson did not have the presence of resident clergy. A Lakota-speaking Jesuit visited once a month and Lakota elders— including former healers like Black Elk—ministered to the community the rest of the time. The Lakota and their Jesuit partners shaped Lakota Catholicism into something distinct, as represented by the regional summer conference of Catholic Sioux, a gathering of as many as 9,000 persons modeled in many ways after the Sun Dance.[36] This creative engagement that Wovoka encouraged amounted to a third way between the pre-reservation independence and the totalizing reach of the reservation system.

---

34   James R. Walker, *Lakota Belief and Ritual*, ed. by Raymond J. DeMallie and Elaine A. Jahner (Lincoln: University of Nebraska Press, 1991), 105.

35   Basil Brave Heart, "Black Elk and Catholicism Part One," *Magnificast*, Podcast audio (September 2018), https://soundcloud.com/themagnificast/ep-79-black-elk-catholocism-pt-1.

36   For details, see Markowitz, "Converting the Rosebud Sicangu," 14–20.

Where Black Elk and the Lakota Catholic community found itself in the early twentieth century was not a fixed, resting state. As always, new situations would require reinterpretation. When Black Elk became Catholic in 1904, the trajectory of reservation cultural persecution, what can be clearly seen over a century later, was perceived incompletely. It was not obvious to anyone that European-born priests who learned Lakota would gradually be replaced by American clergy more interested in absorbing the Lakota people into a generic American Catholicism. It was equally unclear how brutally efficient the Indian residential schools would be at eliminating Lakota language, culture, and spirituality or that early economic success on the reservations would bottom out in the Great Depression. Black Elk would realize that a communal return to traditional ceremony was needed and turned to this in the 1940s in collaboration with other elders. Revitalization, however, would not be seen by Black Elk as a rejection of a lifelong covenant with *Waníkiya* but a correction to missionary interpretations of Lakota tradition.

Conclusion

Black Elk made Indigenous use of the Indigenous Christ's message given in an Indigenous context speaking directly to an Indigenous reality. This may be difficult to accept, especially given the advantage of perspective and knowledge of the ways that Jesuit missionaries reinforced the colonial system. But it is in continuity with the dynamics of Lakota ontology and the creative integration of the Ghost Dance. Black Elk is part of a broad trajectory of Native peoples whose relationship with *Waníkiya* drew them into mainstream Christianity without abandoning a connection to traditional identity. In the process, Black Elk made sacrifices and false-starts requiring him to circle back later in life, but his creative engagement with Catholicism was an extension of what Lakota believe the Spirits do: aid in the life movement of the people. In the words of David Treuer, the Ojibway writer, "Black Elk was determined to live and to adapt. That doesn't make him less of an Indian, as I see it; it makes him more of one."[37]

---

37   David Treuer, "2020 Vision," *Harper's Magazine* (January 2019), https://harpers.org/archive/2019/01/the-heartbeat-of-wounded-knee-david-treuer-ojibwe/.

Selected Bibliography

The following bibliographical entries are divided between general and regional studies. The regional studies are further divided into East, Midwest, and West.

General

Andraos, Michel, ed. *The Church and Indigenous Peoples in the Americas: In Between Reconciliation and Decolonization.* Eugene, OR: Cascade Books, 2019.

Archambault, Marie Therese, Mark G. Thiel, and Christopher Vecsey, eds. *The Crossing of Two Roads: Being Catholic and Native in the United States.* Maryknoll, NY: Orbis Books, 2003.

Axtell, James. *The Invasion Within: The Contest of Cultures in Colonial North America.* New York: Oxford University Press, 1985.

Bowden, Henry Warner. *American Indians and Christian Missions: Studies in Cultural Conflict.* Chicago: University of Chicago Press, 1981.

Burns, Jeffrey M., and Timothy J. Johnson. *Franciscans and American Indians in Pan-Borderlands Perspective: Adaptation, Negotiation, and Resistance.* Oceanside, CA: Academy of American Franciscan History, 2018.

Bunson, Margaret, and Stephen Bunson. *Faith in the Wilderness: The Story of the Catholic Indian Missions.* Huntington, IN: Our Sunday Visitor, 2000.

Carroll, James T. "Americanization or Indoctrination: Catholic Indian Boarding Schools, 1874–1926." PhD diss., University of Notre Dame, 1997.

———. *Seeds of Faith: Catholic Indian Boarding Schools.* New York: Garland, 2000.

———. "The Smell of the White Man is Killing Us: Education and Assimilation among Indigenous Peoples." *U.S. Catholic Historian* 27, no. 1 (Winter 2009): 21–48.

Clatterbuck, Mark. *Crow Jesus: Personal Stories of Native Religious Belonging.* Norman, OK: University of Oklahoma Press, 2017.

———. *Demons, Saints, and Patriots: Catholic Visions of Native America through "The Indian Sentinel" (1902–1962).* Milwaukee: Marquette University Press, 2009.

———. "Post Vatican II Inculturation among Native North American Catholics: A Study in the Missiology of Father Carl Starkloff, S.J." *Missiology* 31, no. 2 (April 2003): 207–222.

Cushner, Nicholas P. *Why Have You Come Here? The Jesuits and the First Evangelization of Native America.* New York: Oxford University Press, 2006.

Deloria, Vine. *Custer Died for Your Sins: An Indian Manifesto.* New York: Avon Books, 1969.

Enochs, Ross. "The Catholic Missions to the Native Americans." In *American Indian Studies: An Interdisciplinary Approach to Contemporary Issues,* edited by Dane Morrison. New York: Peter Lang, 1997.

Galgano, Robert C. *Feast of Souls: Indians and Spaniards in the Seventeenth-Century Missions of Florida and New Mexico.* Albuquerque: University of New Mexico Press, 2005.

Gortner, Collin. "Reconciliation and Cultural Empowerment at American Indian Catholic Schools." *Journal of the West* 59, no. 3 (2020): 25–37.

Gram, John R. "An Unintended Alliance: Catholic and Indigenous Resistance to the Federal Indian Boarding Schools." *Journal of the West* 59, no. 3 (2020): 38–54.

Grant, John Webster. *Moon of Wintertime: Missionaries and the Indians of Canada in Encounter since 1534.* Toronto: University of Toronto Press, 1984.

Hall, Suzanne E. *The People: Reflections of Native Peoples on the Catholic Experience in North America.* Washington, DC: National Catholic Educational Association, 1992.

Hanley, Philip M. *History of the Catholic Ladder.* Fairfield, WA: Ye Galleon Press, 1993.

Jacob, Michelle M. *Indian Pilgrims: Indigenous Journeys of Activism and Healing with Saint Kateri Tekakwitha.* Tucson, AZ: University of Arizona Press, 2016.

Kidwell, Clara Sue, Homer Noley, and George E. Tinker, eds. *A Native American Theology*. Maryknoll, NY: Orbis Books, 2001.

Kozak, David. "Ecumenical Indianism: The Tekakwitha Movement as a Discursive Field of Faith and Power." In *The Message in the Missionary: Local Interpretations of Religious Ideology and Missionary Personality*, edited by Elizabeth E. Brusco and Laura F. Klein. 91–114. Williamsburg, VA: Department of Anthropology, College of William and Mary, 1994.

Leavelle, Tracy Neal. *The Catholic Calumet: Colonial Conversions in French and Indian North America*. Philadelphia: University of Pennsylvania Press, 2011.

Lonc, William, et al., trans. *Early Jesuit Missions in Canada*. 17 vols. Midland, ON: William Lonc, S.J., 2001–2008.

Martin, Joel W. *The Land Looks After Us: A History of Native American Religion*. New York: Oxford University Press, 1999, 2001.

Martin, Joel W., and Mark A. Nicholas, eds. *Native American Christianity, and the Reshaping of the American Religious Landscape*. Chapel Hill: The University of North Carolina Press, 2010.

Martin, Kathleen J., ed. *Indigenous Symbols and Practices in the Catholic Church: Visual Culture, Missionization and Appropriation*. Farnham, UK: Ashgate, 2010.

McCleave, Christine Diindiisi. "The Catholic Church and U.S. Indian Boarding Schools: What Colonial Empire Has to Do with God." *Journal of the West* 59, no. 3 (2020): 61–71.

Moore, James T. *Indian and Jesuit: A Seventeenth-Century Encounter*. Chicago: Loyola University Press, 1982.

Peelman, Achiel. *Christ is a Native American*. Maryknoll, NY: Orbis, 1995.

Pelotte, Donald E. *Native American Catholics at the Millennium: A Report on a Survey by the United States Conference of Catholic Bishops' Ad Hoc Committee on Native American Catholics*. Washington, DC: United States Conference of Catholic Bishops, 2003.

Prucha, F. Paul. *American Indian Policy in Crisis: Christian Reformers and the Indian, 1865–1900*. Norman, OK: University of Oklahoma Press, 1976.

————. *The Churches and the Indian Schools, 1888–1912*. Lincoln: University of Nebraska Press, 1979.

Pullapilly, Cyriac K., Bernard J. Donahoe, David Stefanic, and William Svelmoe, eds. *Christianity and Native Cultures: Perspectives from Different Regions of the World.* Notre Dame, IN: Cross Cultural Publications, 2004.

Rahill, Peter James. *The Catholic Indian Missions and Grant's Peace Policy, 1870–1884*. Washington, DC: Catholic University of America Press, 1953.

Rivera, Luis N. *A Violent Evangelism: The Political and Religious Conquest of the Americas*. Louisville: Westminster/John Knox Press, 1992.

Ronda, James P. and James Axtell. *Indian Missions: A Critical Bibliography*. Bloomington: Indiana University Press, 1978.

Rostkowski, Joëlle. *La Conversion Inachevée: Les Indiens et le Christianisme*. Paris: Éditions Albin Michel S. A., 1998.

Shea, John Gilmary. *History of the Catholic Missions among the Indian Tribes of the United States, 1529–1854*. New York: P.J. Kenedy, 1854.

Starkloff, Carl F., "Aboriginal Cultures and the Christ." *Theological Studies* 53, no. 2 (June 1992): 288–312.

————. "Mission Method and the American Indian." *Theological Studies* 38, no. 4 (December 1977): 621–653.

————. *The People of the Center: American Indian Religion and Christianity*. New York: Seabury, 1974.

————. "Theology and Aboriginal Religion: Continuing 'The Wider Ecumenism.'" *Theological Studies* 68, no. 2 (June 2007): 287–319.

Steltenkamp, Michael F. "American Indian Sainthood and the Catholic Church." *American Catholic Studies* 124, no. 1 (2013): 95–106.

————. "Native Americans and Religion, Colonial Era to the Civil War." In *American Religious History: Belief and Society through Time: Colonial Era to the Civil War*, edited by Gary Scott Smith, 54–61. Santa Barbara, CA: ABC-CLIO, 2021.

Steinmetz, Paul B. *The Sacred Pipe: An Archetypal Theology*. Syracuse, NY: Syracuse University Press, 1998.

Stogre, Michael. *That the World May Believe: The Development of Papal Social Thought on Aboriginal Rights.* Sherbrooke, QC: Éditions Paulines, 1992.

Taylor, Colin F. *Sitting Bull and the White Man's Religion: Early Missionaries in North America.* Wyk auf Foehr, Germany: Verlag für Amerikanistik, 2000.

Thiel, Mark G., and Christopher Vecsey, eds. *Native Footsteps along the Path of Saint Kateri Tekakwitha.* Milwaukee: Marquette University Press, 2012.

Tinker, George E. *American Indian Liberation: A Theology of Sovereignty.* Maryknoll, NY: Orbis Books, 2008.

———. *Missionary Conquest: The Gospel and Native American Cultural Genocide.* Minneapolis: Fortress Press, 1993.

Treat, James, ed. *Native and Christian: Indigenous Voices on Religious Identity in the United States and Canada.* New York: Routledge, 1996.

True, Micah. *Masters and Students: Jesuit Missionary Ethnography in Seventeenth-Century New France.* Montreal & Kingston: McGill-Queen's University Press, 2015.

Vecsey, Christopher. *On the Padres' Trail.* Notre Dame, IN: University of Notre Dame Press, 1996.

———. *The Path of Kateri's Kin.* Notre Dame, IN: University of Notre Dame Press, 1997.

———. *Where the Two Roads Meet.* Notre Dame, IN: University of Notre Dame Press, 1999.

Ward, Katie. "The Formation of Identity and Culture in Native American Catholic Schools." *Journal of the West* 59, no. 3 (2020): 55–60.

East

Anderson, Emma. *The Death and Afterlife of the North American Martyrs.* Cambridge, MA: Harvard University Press, 2013.

Blackburn, Carole. *Harvest of Souls: The Jesuit Missions and Colonialism in North America, 1632–1650.* Montreal and Kingston: McGill-Queen's University Press, 2000.

Bonaparte, Darren. *A Lily among Thorns: The Mohawk Repatriation of Káteri Tekahkwí:tha.* Ahkwesásne, QC: Wampum Chronicles, 2009.

Greer, Allan, ed. *The Jesuit Relations: Natives and Missionaries in Seventeenth-Century North America.* Boston: Bedford/St. Martin's, 2000.

———. *Mohawk Saint: Catherine Tekakwitha and the Jesuits.* New York: Oxford University Press, 2005.

Hann, John H. *A History of the Timucua Indians and Missions.* Gainesville: University Press of Florida, 1996.

———, ed. and trans. *Missions to the Calusa.* Gainesville: University of Florida Press, 1991.

Hann, John H., and Bonnie Gair MacEwan. *The Apalachee Indians and Mission San Luis.* Gainesville: University Press of Florida, 1998.

Hogue, Kellie Jean. "A Saint of Their Own: Native Petitions supporting the Canonization of Kateri Tekakwitha, 1884–1885." *U.S. Catholic Historian* 32, no. 3 (Summer 2014): 25–44.

Kidwell, Clara Sue. *Choctaws and Missionaries in Mississippi, 1818–1918.* Norman, OK: University of Oklahoma Press, 1995.

McEwan, Bonnie Gain. *The Spanish Missions of La Florida.* Gainesville: University Press of Florida, 1997.

Milanich, Jerald T. *Laboring in the Fields of the Lord: Spanish Missions and Southeastern Indians.* Washington, DC: Smithsonian Institution Press, 1999.

Morrison, Kenneth M. *The Solidarity of Kin: Ethnohistory, Religious Studies, and the Algonkian-French Religious Encounter.* Albany: State University of New York Press, 2002.

Thwaites, Reuben Gold, ed. *The Jesuit Relations and Allied Documents.* 73 vols. Cleveland: Burrows Brothers, 1896–1901.

Tooker, Elisabeth. *Native North American Spirituality of the Eastern Woodlands.* New York: Paulist Press, 1979.

Midwest

Agonito, Joseph. "Josephine Crowfeather, Catholic Nun." In *Brave Hearts: Indian Women of the Plains.* 136–145. Guildford, CT: Twodot Books, 2017.

Archambault, Marie Therese. *A Retreat with Black Elk: Living in the Sacred Hoop*. Cincinnati: St. Anthony Messenger Press, 1998.

Beck, David R.M. *The Struggle for Self Determination: History of the Menominee Indians Since 1854*. Lincoln: University of Nebraska Press, 2005.

Berg, Carol J. "Agents of Cultural Change: The Benedictines at White Earth." *Minnesota History* 48 (Winter 1982): 158–170.

———. "Climbing Learners Hill: Benedictines at White Earth, 1878–1945." PhD diss., University of Minnesota, 1981.

Black Elk, John G. Neihardt, Philip J. Deloria, and Raymond J. DeMallie. *Black Elk Speaks: Being the Life Story of a Holy Man of the Oglala Sioux*. Lincoln, NE: University of Nebraska Press, 2014.

Bucko, Raymond A. *The Lakota Ritual of the Sweat Lodge, History and Contemporary Practice*. Lincoln: University of Nebraska Press, 1998.

Carroll, James T. "Self-Direction, Activity, and Syncretism: Catholic Indian Boarding Schools on the Northern Great Plains in Contact." *U.S. Catholic Historian* 16, no. 2 (1998): 78–89.

Carson, Mary Eisenman. *Blackrobe for the Yankton Sioux: Fr. Sylvester Eisenman, O.S.B. (1891–1948)*. Chamberlain, SD: Tipi Press, 1989.

Clifton, James A. *The Pokagons, 1683–1983: Catholic Potawatomi Indians of St. Joseph River Valley*. Lanham, MD: University Press of America, 1984.

Costello, Damian. *Black Elk: Colonialism and Lakota Catholicism*. Maryknoll, NY: Orbis Books, 2005.

Delfeld, Paula. *The Indian Priest, Father Philip B. Gordon, 1885–1948*. Chicago: Franciscan Herald Press, 1977.

DeMallie, Raymond, ed. *The Sixth Grandfather: Black Elk's Teachings Given to John G. Neihardt*. Lincoln: University of Nebraska Press, 1984.

DeMallie, Raymond J., and Douglas R. Parks. *Sioux Indian Religion: Tradition and Innovation*. Norman, OK: University of Oklahoma Press, 1988.

Enochs, Ross. *The Jesuit Mission to the Lakota Sioux: Pastoral Theology and Ministry, 1886–1945.* Kansas City: Sheed & Ward, 1996.

Foley, Thomas W. *At Standing Rock and Wounded Knee: The Papers of Father Francis M. Craft, 1888–1890.* Norman, OK: University of Oklahoma Press, 2009.

———. *Faces of Faith: A History of the First Order of Indian Sisters.* Baltimore, MD: Cathedral Foundation Press, 2008.

———. "Father Francis M. Craft and the Indian Sisters." *U.S. Catholic Historian* 16, no. 2 (1998): 41–55.

———. *Father Francis M. Craft, Missionary to the Sioux.* Lincoln: University of Nebraska Press, 2002.

Galler, Jr., Robert W. "The Triad of Alliances: The Roots of Holy Rosary Indian Mission." *South Dakota History* 28, no. 3 (1998): 144–160.

Garner, Sandra L. *To Come to a Better Understanding: Medicine Men and Clergy Meetings on the Rosebud Reservation, 1973–1978.* Lincoln: University of Nebraska Press, 2016.

Gaumer, Matthew Alan. "The Catholic 'Apostle of the Sioux': Martin Marty and the Beginnings of the Catholic Church in Dakota Territory." *South Dakota History* 42, no. 3 (2012): 256–281.

Giago, Tim A. *The Aboriginal Sin: Reflections on the Holy Rosary Indian Mission School (Red Cloud Indian School).* San Francisco: Indian Historian Press, 1978.

Hamilton, Raphael N. *Marquette's Explorations: The Narratives Reexamined.* Madison: University of Wisconsin Press, 1970.

Harp, Maureen Anna. "Indian Missions, Immigrant Migrations, and Regional Catholic Culture: Slovene Missionaries in the Upper Great Lakes, 1830–1892." PhD diss., University of Chicago, 1996.

Holler, Clyde, ed. *The Black Elk Reader.* Syracuse, NY: Syracuse University Press, 2000.

———. *Black Elk's Religion: The Sun Dance and Lakota Catholicism.* Syracuse, NY: Syracuse University Press, 1995.

Jackson, Joe. *Black Elk: The Life of an American Visionary.* New York: Farrar, Straus and Giroux, 2016.

Karolevitz, Robert F. *Bishop Martin Marty, "The Black Robe Lean Chief."* Yankton, SD: Benedictine Sisters of Sacred Heart Convent, 1980.

Kreis, Karl Markus, ed. *Lakotas, Black Robes, and Holy Women: German Reports from the Indian Missions in South Dakota, 1886–1900.* Translated by Corinna Dally-Starna. Lincoln: University of Nebraska Press, 2000.

Lamb, Mary Beth. "First Contact: Swiss Benedictine Sisters at Standing Rock Missions in a Cross-Cultural Frame, 1881–1900." PhD diss., Graduate Theological Union, 1998.

Lawson, Kirstin. "Healing the Frontier: Catholic Sisters, Hospitals, and Medicine Men in the Wisconsin Big Woods, 1880–1920." PhD diss., University of Missouri, 2008.

LeBeau, Casimir L. *St. Benedict's Mission, Farm School, Kenel, S. Dak.* Eagle Butte, SD: Casimir L. LeBeau, 2005.

Lewandowski, Tadeusz. *Ojibwe Activist, Priest: The Life of Father Philip Bergin Gordon, Tibishkogijik.* Madison: University of Wisconsin Press, 2019.

Markowitz, Harvey. *Converting the Rosebud: Catholic Mission and the Lakotas, 1886–1916.* Norman, OK: University of Oklahoma Press, 2018.

Monson, Paul. "*Stabilitas in Congregatione:* The Benedictine Evangelization of America in the Life and Thought of Martin Marty, O.S.B." PhD diss., Marquette University, 2014.

Roeber, A. G., ed. *Ethnographies and Exchanges: Native Americans, Moravians, and Catholics in Early North America.* University Park: Pennsylvania State University Press, 2008.

Rufledt, Susan. "United States Indian Education Policy and Reform: The Survival of Catholic Indian Education on the Menominee Reservation, 1884–1912." PhD diss., University of Kansas, 2009.

Schmidt, Andrea. "Christian Missions and Indian Assimilation—Role and Effects upon the Lakota Sioux of Pine Ridge Indian Reservation and their Institutions." PhD diss., Karl-Franzens-Universitat, Austria, 2001.

Seelye, James. "'Come into the Habits of Civilized Life': Nineteenth Century Catholic and Protestant Missionaries in Upper Michigan." PhD diss., University of Toledo, 2010.

Shillinger, Sarah. *A Case Study of the American Indian Boarding School Movement: An Oral History of Saint Joseph's Indian Industrial School.* Lewiston, NY: Edwin Mellen Press, 2008.

———. "They Never Told Us They Wanted to Help Us: An Oral History of Saint Joseph's Indian Industrial School." PhD diss., University of Pennsylvania, 1995.

Steinmetz, Paul B. *Pipe, Bible, and Peyote Among the Oglala Lakota: A Study in Religious Identity.* Syracuse, NY: Syracuse University Press, 1998.

Steltenkamp, Michael F. *Black Elk: Holy Man of the Oglala.* Norman, OK: University of Oklahoma Press, 1993.

———. *Nicholas Black Elk: Medicine Man, Missionary, Mystic.* Norman, OK: University of Oklahoma Press, 2009.

Stolzman, William F., *The Pipe and Christ: A Christian-Sioux Dialogue.* 3rd ed. Chamberlain, SD: Tipi Press, 1991.

Sweeney, Jon M. *Nicholas Black Elk. Medicine Man, Catechist, Saint.* Collegeville, MN: Liturgical Press, 2021.

Thiel, Mark G. "Catholic Sodalities among the Sioux, 1882–1910." *U.S. Catholic Historian* 16, no. 2 (Spring 1998): 56–77.

Vecsey, Christopher. "A Century of Lakota Catholicism at Pine Ridge." In *Religious Diversity and American Religious History: Studies in Traditions and Cultures,* edited by Walter H. Conser, Jr. and Sumner B. Twiss, 262–295. Athens, GA: University of Georgia Press, 1997.

White, James D., ed. *Diary of a Frontier Bishop: The Journals of Theophile Meerschaert.* Tulsa, OK: Sarto Press, 1994.

———. *Getting Sense: The Osages and their Missionaries.* Tulsa, OK: Sarto Press, 1997.

West

Bahr, Howard M., ed. *The Navajo as Seen by the Franciscans, 1898-1921: A Sourcebook.* Lanham, MD: Scarecrow Press, 2004.

———. *The Navajo as Seen by the Franciscans, 1920–1950: A Sourcebook.* Lanham, MD: Scarecrow Press, 2012.

Beebe, Rose Marie, and Robert M. Senkewicz. *Junípero Serra: California, Indians, and the Transformation of a Missionary*. Norman, OK: University of Oklahoma Press, 2015.

―――. *"To Toil in That Vineyard of the Lord": Contemporary Scholarship on Junípero Serra*. Berkeley, CA: Academy of American Franciscan History, 2010.

Bodo, Murray, ed. *Tales of an Endishodi: Father Berard Haile and the Navajos, 1900–1961*. Albuquerque: University of New Mexico Press, 1998.

Bolton, Herbert Eugene. *Rim of Christendom: A Biography of Eusebio Francisco Kino, Pacific Coast Pioneer*. New York: Macmillan, 1936.

Brugge, David M. *Navajos in the Catholic Church Records of New Mexico, 1694–1875*. Tsaile, AZ: Navajo Community College Press, 1985.

Buckley, Cornelius M. *Nicolas Point, S.J.: His Life & Northwest Indian Chronicles*. Chicago: Loyola University Press, 1989.

Burns, Robert Ignatius. *The Jesuits and the Indian Wars of the Northwest*. New Haven, CT: Yale University Press, 1966.

Carriker, Robert C. *Father Peter John De Smet: Jesuit in the West*. Norman, OK: University of Oklahoma Press, 1995.

Castillo, Edward D. *Native American Perspectives on the Hispanic Colonization of Alta California*. New York: Garland, 1991.

Cave, Dorothy. *God's Warrior: Father Albert Braun, O.F.M., 1889–1983*. Santa Fe, NM: Sunstone Press, 2011.

Chittenden, Hiram Martin, and Alfred Talbot Richardson. *Life, Letters, and Travels of Father De Smet*. New York: Arno Press, 1969.

Clatterbuck, Mark S. "Sweet Grass Mass and Pow Wows for Jesus: Catholic and Pentecostal Missions on Rocky Boy's Reservation." *U.S. Catholic Historian* 27, no. 1 (Winter 2009): 89–112.

Collier, Brian S. "St. Catherine Indian School, Santa Fe, 1887-2006: Catholic Indian Education in New Mexico." PhD diss., Arizona State University, 2006.

Cook, Sherburne F. *The Conflict Between the California Indians and White Civilization*. Berkeley: University of California Press, 1976.

Costo, Jeannette Henry and Rupert Costo, eds. *The Missions of California. A Legacy of Genocide.* San Francisco: Indian Historian Press, 1987.

De Smet, Pierre-Jean. *Letters and Sketches with a Narrative of a Year's Residence Among the Indian Tribes of the Rocky Mountains.* Philadelphia: M. Fithian, 1843.

———. *New Indian Sketches.* New York: D. & J. Sadlier, 1863.

———. *Oregon Missions and Travels Over the Rocky Mountains, in 1845–46.* New York: E. Dunigan, 1847.

Dorel, Frédéric. "From Religions to Lifeways: Jesuits and Native Americans, 1965–2015." In *Crossings and Dwellings: Restored Jesuits, Women Religious, American Experience, 1814–2014*, edited by Kyle B. Roberts and Stephen Schloesser, 650–692. Boston: Brill, 2017.

Engelhardt, Zephyrin. *The Missions and Missionaries of California.* 4 vols. San Francisco: James H. Barry, 1908–15.

Enochs, Ross. "The Franciscan Mission to the Navajos: Mission Method and Indigenous Religion, 1898-1940." *Catholic Historical Review* 92, no. 1 (2006): 46–73.

Espinosa, J. Manuel, ed. and trans. *The Pueblo Indian Revolt of 1696 and the Franciscan Mission in New Mexico: Letters of the Missionaries and Related Documents.* Norman, OK: University of Oklahoma Press, 1988.

Ewens, Mary. "Icy Crossings and Dwellings: John Fox, S.J., and the Sisters of Our Lady of the Snows." In *Crossings and Dwellings: Restored Jesuits, Women Religious, American Experience, 1814–2014*, edited by Kyle B. Roberts and Stephen Schloesser, 496–530. Boston: Brill, 2017.

Flood, Reneé S. *Renegade Priest of the Northern Cheyenne, The Life and Work of Father Emmett Hoffmann, 1926–.* Billings, MT: Soaring Eagle, 2003.

Fortier, Ted. *Religion and Resistance in the Encounter Between the Coeur d'Alene Indians and Jesuit Missionaries.* Lewiston, NY: Edwin Mellen Press, 2002.

Fowler, Loretta. *Shared Symbols, Contested Meanings: Gros Ventre Culture and History, 1778–1984.* Ithaca, NY: Cornell University Press, 1987.

Geiger, Maynard and Clement W. Meighan. *As the Padres Saw Them: California Indian Life and Customs as Reported by the Franciscan Missionaries, 1813–1815*. Santa Barbara: Santa Barbara Mission Archive-Library, 1976.

Gómez, Arthur R. *Documentary Evidence for the Spanish Missions of Texas*. New York: Garland, 1991.

Griffith, James S. *Beliefs and Holy Places: A Spiritual Geography of the Pimería Alta*. Tucson: University of Arizona Press, 1992.

Guest, Francis F. "The Indian Policy under Fermín Francisco de Lasuén, California's Second Father President." *California Historical Society Quarterly* 45, no. 3 (1966): 195–224.

———. "An Inquiry into the Role of the Discipline in California Mission Life." *Southern California Quarterly* 71, no. 1 (1989): 1–68.

Gutiérrez, Ramón A. *When Jesus Came, the Corn Mothers Went Away. Marriage, Sexuality, and Power in New Mexico, 1500–1846*. Stanford, CA: Stanford University Press, 1991.

Hackel, Steven W. *Children of Coyote, Missionaries of Saint Francis: Indian-Spanish Relations in Colonial California, 1769–1850*. Chapel Hill: University of North Carolina Press, 2006.

———. *The Worlds of Junipero Serra: Historical Contexts and Cultural Representations*. Oakland: University of California Press, 2018.

Harley, R. Bruce. *Seek and Ye Shall Find: St. Boniface Indian Industrial School, 1888–1978*. San Bernardino, CA: Catholic Diocese of San Bernardino, 1994.

Harrod, Howard L. *Mission Among the Blackfeet: An Evaluation of Protestant and Catholic Missions Among the Blackfeet Indians*. Norman, OK: University of Oklahoma Press, 1971.

Jackson, Robert H. and Edward D. Castillo. *Indians, Franciscans, and Spanish Colonization: The Impact of the Mission System on California Indians*. Albuquerque: University of New Mexico Press, 1995.

Kessell, John L. *Friars, Soldiers, and Reformers: Hispanic Arizona and the Sonora Mission Frontier, 1767–1856*. Tucson, AZ: University of Arizona Press, 1976.

———. *Kiva, Cross, and Crown: The Pecos Indians and New Mexico, 1540–1840*. Washington, DC: National Park Service, 1979.

―――. *Mission of Sorrows; Jesuit Guevavi and the Pimas, 1691–1767.* Tucson, AZ: University of Arizona Press, 2016.

Kessell, John L., and Rick Hendricks. *The Spanish Missions of New Mexico.* New York: Garland, 1991.

Killoren, John J. *"Come, Blackrobe": De Smet and the Indian Tragedy.* Norman, OK: University of Oklahoma Press, 1994.

Knaut, Andrew L. *The Pueblo Revolt of 1680: Conquest and Resistance in Seventeenth-Century New Mexico.* Norman, OK: University of Oklahoma Press, 1995.

Kraman, Carlan. *A Portrait of Saint Labre Indian Mission through One Hundred Years, 1884–1984.* Great Falls, MT: 1984.

Kreis, Karl Markus. "Indians Playing, Indians Praying: Native Americans in Wild West Shows and Catholic Missions." In *Germans and Indians: Fantasies, Encounters, Projections*, edited by Colin G. Calloway, Gerd Gemunden, and Susanne Zantop. 195–212. Lincoln: University of Nebraska, 2002.

Lightfoot, Kent G. *Indians, Missionaries, and Merchants: The Legacy of Colonial Encounters on the California Frontiers.* Berkeley: University of California Press, 2004.

Llorente, Segundo. *Memoirs of a Yukon Priest.* Washington, DC: Georgetown University Press, 1990.

Mahoney, Irene. *Lady Blackrobes: Missionaries in the Heart of Indian Country.* Golden, CO: Fulcrum Publishers, 2006.

Markowitz, Harvey. "The Reformer, the Monsignor and the Pueblos of New Mexico: Catholic Missionary Responses to New Directions in Early Twentieth Century Indian Policy." *New Mexico Historical Review* 88, no. 4 (2013): 413–436.

McKevitt, Gerald. *Brokers of Culture: Italian Jesuits in the American West, 1848–1919.* Stanford, CA: Stanford University Press, 2007.

Milliken, Randall. *A Time of Little Choice: The Disintegration of Tribal Culture in the San Francisco Bay Area.* Menlo Park, CA: Ballena Press, 1995.

Newell, Quincy D. *Constructing Lives at Mission San Francisco: Native Californians and Hispanic Colonists, 1776–1821.* Albuquerque: University of New Mexico Press, 2009.

Orfalea, Gregory. *Journey to the Sun: Junípero Serra's Dream and the Founding of California*. New York: Scribner, 2014.

Peterson, Jacqueline. *Sacred Encounters: Father De Smet and the Indians of the Rocky Mountain West*. Norman, OK: University of Oklahoma Press, 1993.

Polzer, Charles W. *Kino, A Legacy: His Life, His Works, His Missions, His Monuments*. Tucson, AZ: Jesuit Fathers of Southern Arizona, 1998.

——. *Rules and Precepts of the Jesuit Missions of Northwestern New Spain*. Tucson, AZ: University of Arizona Press, 1976.

Riley, Carroll L. *Rio Del Norte: People of the Upper Rio Grande from Earliest Times to the Pueblo Revolt*. Salt Lake City: University of Utah Press, 1995.

Russell, Craig. *From Serra to Sancho: Music and Pageantry in the California Missions*. New York: Oxford University Press, 2009.

Sandos, James A. "Christianization among the Chumash: An Ethnohistoric Perspective." *American Indian Quarterly* 15, no. 1 (1991): 65–89.

——. *Converting California: Indians and Franciscans in the Missions*. New Haven, CT: Yale University Press, 2004.

Vecsey, Christopher, "Pueblo Indian Catholicism: The Isleta Case." *U.S. Catholic Historian* 16, no. 2 (Spring 1998): 1–19.

Weber, David J. *The Spanish Frontier in North America*. New Haven, CT: Yale University Press, 1992.

Weber, Francis J. *The California Missions as Others Saw Them: 1786–1842*. Los Angeles: Dawson's Book Shop, 1972.

Wilcox, Michael V. *The Pueblo Revolt and the Mythology of Conquest: An Indigenous Archaeology of Contact*. Berkeley: University of California Press, 2009.

Index